Footprint

Barcelona

Mary-Ann Gallagher

Contents

About the author

Mary-Ann Gallagher is the author of Footprint guides to Barcelona, Madrid and Valencia and the co-author of Footprint Spain. She has lived in various places, from New York to Japan, but has spent most of the last four years in Spain. Barcelona remains her favourite city in the world.

Acknowledgements

A huge thank you, as always, to Ajo and Raquel who have opened up Barcelona to me since I first arrived. Also to Pep, who told me fabulous stories, to Andreas, my early drinking pal and to Eduardo and Luís, who always invite me to their parties. Also to José, for all those coffees and long conversations at Pinotxo. *Besos* for my dear friend Ed and for Wendy, who showed me some of the bright lights. Thanks must go to the incredibly helpful staff at the tourist office and the Palau Robert and also to my patient, thorough and delightful editor, Julius Honnor.

Just for starters, there's the location: Barcelona dips its toes in the Mediterranean, lolls back against the Pyrenees and basks in year-round sunshine. Then there is the skyline, indelibly marked by Antoni Gaudí, one of the world's best-known architects, whose delirious buildings, resembling dragons, cliffs or gingerbread houses, seem to have magically erupted across the city. And at the heart of Barcelona lie the ancient passages, gargoyles and ghostly spires of the old Gothic city, apparently untouched by modernity. Add a fantastic and varied nightlife, a discerning cuisine, a nose for the latest and best in fashion and design and a population bent on having a good time and it's unsurprising that Barcelona has become the most popular city in Europe. But underneath the flirtation and glamour lies a city that had to work to get attention. Twenty years ago, the creamy stone of Gaudí's La Pedrera was black with bingo-parlour grime, parts of the city were too dangerous to walk through and the spectacular legacy of the Modernistas was slowly disintegrating through lack of interest or money.

The gold medal effect

The 1992 Olympics stopped the rot; with breathtaking and characteristic energy the city reinvented itself, demolishing and reconstructing across great swathes of land, unfurling itself along the long-ignored Mediterranean and turning the surrounding slopes into parkland. This dynamism is still blazing a trail: the Raval, once notorious for sex and drugs, has a new promenade and a gleaming new museum of contemporary art, while, down by the sea, the 2004 Universal Forum of Cultures is Barcelona's latest chance to preen and enjoy the world's attention.

Seny and rauxa

You won't find flamenco, paella or any of the other stock clichés about Spain in Barcelona – for the very good reason that it isn't properly part of Spain at all. Barcelona is the capital of Catalunya, an ancient empire which once straddled the Pyrenees and ruled the trading routes of the Mediterranean. It's a proud nation with its own language, customs and traditions and a fiercely democratic history. A thousand years ago the Catalans swore loyalty to their king with an oath that began 'We, who are as good as you, swear to you, who are no better than we, to accept you as our king and sovereign lord, provided you observe all our liberties and laws; but if not, not.' The Catalans are supremely proud of their *seny*, a deep-rooted natural wisdom which is treated with pious reverence. But *seny* is only half the Catalan story – the other half is *rauxa*, an outburst of uncontrollable emotion or just plain old craziness. *Rauxa* is what is going on when demons charge down narrow streets spitting flames, surrounded by leaping devils; when whipped ice-cream houses undulate wildly to the sky; or when thousands of sweating bodies converge on beaches for parties until dawn, or maybe next week. It is this combination of proud independence, intelligence and enthusiastic frenzy that makes the city so irresistibly vibrant. Barcelonans believe, with typical good sense, that a touch of madness will keep them sane.

At a glance

Finding your way around Barcelona isn't difficult; a glance at any map shows the Old City (Ciutat Vella) squeezed into a crooked oval shape at the heart of Barcelona. Spreading inland from the Old City is the elegant Modernista grid of the Eixample. Beyond this lies a ring of traditional towns like Gràcia which were once entirely independent of Barcelona. Further out are the Collserola hills with the lofty peak of Tibidabo at the centre. Hemming in the city at its western end is the hill of Montjuïc, while along the seafront are modern developments.

Las Ramblas

The best introduction to Barcelona is the Ramblas, the city's famous tree-lined promenade which meanders down to the port and divides the Ciutat Vella. Find a café, pull up a chair and watch the world go by: human statues and tourists by day, clubbers and partiers by night. Halfway down is La Boquería, Barcelona's loveliest market, overflowing with gleaming fruit and local specialities.

Barri Gòtic

The Ramblas, running roughly north–south, is the main artery of the Ciutat Vella. To the east is the shadowy, medieval maze of the Barri Gòtic, the Gothic Quarter, with the flamboyant cathedral at its centre. The heart of the city since Roman times, it still buzzes day and night with shoppers, party-goers and politicians.

La Ribera and Sant Pere

East of the Barri Gòtic is La Ribera, another medieval district, which has become the coolest neighbourhood in a city famed for its addiction to fashion. Packed with ultra-chic boutiques, designer stores and the trendiest restaurants, bars and clubs, it rubs shoulders with the dusty old area of Sant Pere, where the flamboyant Palau de la Música Catalana proudly displays her ceramic blooms.

El Raval

Back on the western side of the Ramblas, the Raval spreads south to the raffish old theatre district of the Paral.lel. Once the most talked-about red light district on the Mediterranean, it's been the focus of a massive clean-up and has got its own spanking new Rambla and a glossy museum of contemporary art. The hippest young artists have followed, bringing galleries, vintage fashion and record stores, bars, restaurants and clubs in their wake, soaking up what's left of the Raval's seductive bohemianism.

Eixample

When the city burst out of its medieval walls in the 19th century, the rich commissioned new mansions in the airy new grid of the Eixample (which means 'extension' in Catalan). Gaudí and his Modernista colleagues had a ball, leaving a spectacular legacy, which now comprises one of the greatest concentrations of art nouveau architecture in the world. Gaudí's most celebrated achievement is the enormous cathedral which he neither began nor completed, the Sagrada Família, an epic work which has caused controversy since the first stone was laid.

Montjuïc

The green, park-filled mountain of Montjuïc hems in the city on its southwestern side and overlooks the sea. The Olympics left their mark here with a string of excellent sports facilities. Close by is the Fundació Miró, a lovely light-filled museum dedicated to the Catalan artist, and at the bottom of the hill is the MNAC, with a mesmerising collection of Catalan art spanning several centuries. There's also plenty of enjoyable kitsch on Montjuïc, from the mini-Spain on show at the Poble Espanyol to the glorious Font Màgica, where the fountains leap colourfully to the sounds of ABBA.

Gràcia

Gràcia, beyond the Eixample district, was once independent from Barcelona and still feels that way. It's a relaxed neighbourhood with a reputation for liberalism and feistiness which has mellowed over the years. On the outskirts is Park Güell, Gaudí's fairytale park with its huge, sinuous, tile-covered bench which delivers magical views over the city below.

Seaside

The most dramatic change to Barcelona's skyline in the last few years has been down by the seaside. The long-neglected coastline was cleared for the construction of the glistening Olympic Village, a futuristic city of steel trees and glassy towers. The modern Port Olímpic is hugely popular, crammed with restaurants and bars and some excellent seafood restaurants and sandy beaches stretch for miles in both directions. Beyond it lies the site of the Universal Forum of Cultures 2004, a sleek business and entertainment complex built on reclaimed land. The traditional dock-workers' neighbourhood of Barceloneta is more atmospheric, with tiny tapas bars tucked away in its depths. The former warehouses of Port Vell have been handsomely restored to hold smart restaurants and museums and across the harbour is a gleaming entertainment complex with bars, clubs, an IMAX cinema and the aquarium.

Outskirts

The outskirts of Barcelona are home to parks, funfairs and museums: the best views in all the city can be had from Tibidabo, Barcelona's funfair mountain and highest peak, reached by a rickety tram and a funicular. Fans of FC Barça won't want to miss a tour of the celebrated stadium and museum and there is a cluster of elegant museums with everything from ceramics to old masters in the leafy, chi-chi suburb of Pedralbes.

Trip planner

Barcelona's mild Mediterranean climate means that there is never a bad time to visit. If it's sun you are after – this is Spain, after all – June and September are the best months to come. The beaches and hotels aren't too crowded and it's warm enough to swim. Winters are too chilly for sunbathing, but you could still go for some bracing beach walks. In July and August the city gets packed and accommodation, always tough to find in Barcelona, gets even scarcer. If you can, combine your visit with a festival (see p179).

24 hours

Get a feel for the city by strolling down the Ramblas then dive into the chaotic maze of the Barri Gòtic, where you'll find the Gothic cathedral (take the lift to the roof for fantastic views) and plenty of great shops, bars and restaurants. If you prefer something a bit edgier, take in the Raval (the neighbourhood on the other side of the Ramblas), which is home to the excellent museum of contemporary art (MACBA) and lots of vintage clothes stores and galleries. Spend the early afternoon exploring the elegant Passeig de Gràcia, home to some of the most emblematic Modernista buildings, including Gaudí's Casa Batlló and La Pedrera, and then relax for an hour or two on the beach if the sun is out. In the evening, check out the fashionable neighbourhood of La Ribera, where there are plenty of stylish bars, restaurants and clubs, as well as the sublime Gothic church of Santa María del Mar.

A long weekend

With a long weekend, you can afford to take things at a gentler pace and add to the suggestions outlined above. Arty types might like to spend a bit of time in the city's big cultural museums: check out MNAC on Montjuïc, where the highlight is the collection of Romanesque frescoes gathered from remote Pyrenean churches; or the Fundació Miró, a stunning modern museum dedicated to the spectacular Catalan artist; or the Museu Picasso, which houses a patchy collection of Picasso's work in five elegant Gothic palaces; or admire the old masters in the Thyssen collection in the Monestir de Pedralbes. Gaudí fans shouldn't miss Palau Güell in the Raval, Park Güell (try and visit in the evening as dusk settles across the city below) and the immense, unfinished masterpiece of the Sagrada Família cathedral (visit as early as possible to avoid the crowds). To see the Modernistas at their most flamboyant, visit the stunning Palau de la Música Catalana – for a concert if you can, or by guided visit if not. For fabulous views, head up to the top of the hills of Tibidabo or Montjuïc by funicular and cable car, or take a long stroll or bike ride along the beachfront from the cheerfully shabby *barri* of Barceloneta, past the glitzy modern Port Olímpic and out along quieter beaches to the dramatic site of the Universal Forum of Cultures 2004. Get off the beaten track a bit and spend an evening in laid-back, effortlessly cool Gràcia, with café-lined squares and great bars and restaurants.

A week

With a week, you can afford to explore some of Barcelona's more remote corners and offbeat sights and take a few day trips. Fans of the quirky might like odd museums like those dedicated to the shoe, chocolate or sex, and those looking for a break from the city hustle and bustle can lose themselves in the walking, biking and riding trails which criss-cross the Collserola hills above the city. Further afield, you can pay a visit to the monastery of Montserrat with its venerated statue of the Virgin and remote hiking paths; party hard or laze on the beach in the chic, gay-friendly seaside resort of Sitges; ponder on the extensive Roman ruins in the 'balcony of the Mediterranean' Tarragona; explore the old Jewish quarter of the beautiful city of Girona; or check out Dalí's surreal creations in his museum in Figueres.

★ Ten of the best

Best

1 Passeig de Gràcia A mesmerizing collection of Modernista monuments, including Gaudí's fairytale Casa Batlló and the undulating ice-cream swirls of La Pedrera, p64.

2 Las Ramblas The city's famous promenade has a magic fountain, cakes and the colourful market of La Boquería, p33.

3 Sagrada Família Magical or monstrous? Gaudí's enormous unfinished cathedral, the Sagrada Família has dizzying views across the whole city, p71.

4 MNAC Captivating Romanesque frescoes are gathered from remote Pyrenean churches in the Museu Nacional d'Art de Catalunya, housed in a vast palace built for the 1929 International Exhibition, p75.

5 Park Güell A spellbinding unfinished housing estate, now a leafy public park spilling colourfully down a hillside above the city, p82.

6 Fundació Miró A stunning collection of the work of the most sensuous, enigmatic and celebrated Catalan artist, p77.

7 Palau de la Música Catalana Valkyries charge massively across the stage, a choir of sculpted singers erupt from the facade and every inch is covered with rainbow-coloured mosaics in one of Modernisme's most flamboyant buildings, p56.

8 MACBA The latest in contemporary art at the gleaming Museu Nacional d'Art Contemporani, p58.

9 The Beaches Swim, sunbathe, chill out, picnic, take sailing lessons, listen to beachside DJs, tuck into seafood, hire a bike or rollerblades and explore the length of the boardwalk, p88.

10 Sitges Barcelona's fashion pack escape the city on summer weekends for great shopping, nightlife and restaurants, p101.

The ★ symbol is used throughout this guide to indicate recommended sights.

Contemporary Barcelona

Twentyfirst-century Barcelona is booming. The city's dazzling transformation from seedy port into one of the most glamorous destinations on the Mediterranean seems little short of miraculous. After years of repression under Francoism, Barcelona has exploded with pent-up energy: the cityscape has been remodelled, ancient monuments and Modernista mansions restored and repaired, grubby docks and red light areas flattened and rebuilt and shabby tenements torn down and replaced with airy boulevards. Museums and cultural foundations are thriving, the arts are flourishing and the humble chef is king of the city as the world wakes up to a revolution in Catalan cuisine. Barcelona is the style capital of the Mediterranean, with enough hip shops, bars, clubs and galleries to make many a bigger city envious.

The Universal Forum of Cultures 2004 is the city's latest success story: repeating the magic formula of the 1992 Olympics, Barcelona has hung a massive regeneration project on the hook of a glamorous international event. Cannily focussing on global buzzwords like 'cultural diversity' and a 'sustainable environment', the Universal Forum has attracted the world's attention. But the Forum's organizers are practising what they preach and the once-desolate northern end of the city has been utterly transformed in true 21st-century style: the swathe of reclaimed land is home to money-spinning state-of-the-art conference centres and entertainment complexes, but they are powered in part by wind and solar energy. The battered old sewerage works and waste incinerators that once blighted the mouth of the River Besos are being made sustainable and the riverside itself, once a gritty no-go area, is being transformed into a leafy park.

It isn't just architecture that has been galvanized through bold new projects in recent years. As the capital of the ancient kingdom of Catalunya, Barcelona (home to the Generalitat, the regional government) is at the forefront of the revival of Catalan culture.

The traditions, customs and language of Catalunya had been repressed by successive regimes for centuries, most recently by Franco, who sought to impose a single national identity on Spain. Under his dictatorship, speaking Catalan on the streets was punishable by imprisonment. Now, 30 years after his death, 75% of the population of Catalunya speak Catalan and that figure rises to 90% in the under 30s. New immigrants are offered free Catalan lessons (Spanish lessons are available for a fee) and Catalan pride and self-confidence is soaring. Independence is being asserted in more unlikely ways too: the Generalitat recently changed its website from gencat.es (denoting its origin in Spain) to gencat.net, which officials said made it sound 'more international'.

The much-loved former president of the Generalitat, Jordi Pujol, retired in 2003, after more than two decades in office. Recent elections have reflected a move away from his moderating influence. The new president is Pasqual Maragall, leader of a left-wing tripartite coalition which includes the pro-independence Esquerra Republicana de Catalunya (ERC, Catalan Republican Left). After years of caution, the political hot potato of Catalan independence has shot to the top of the agenda. Catalunya is the richest of Spain's 17 autonomous regions, providing around 20% of the country's gross national product. The Generalitat wants to take control of its own finances by creating a regional tax office independent of Madrid. It has also mooted plans for a new 'Euro-region', which would link the Catalan-speaking regions of Catalunya, Valencia, the Balearics and Aragón and Rousillon in France, into a loose economic unit. The issue of financial independence for Catalunya and the implications it might have on the possibility of future secession from the Spanish state, met with hostility under the national rule of the right-wing Partido Popular but may gain momentum under Prime Minister Zapatero and a socialist government in need of coalition support.

Catalan nationalism is nothing new. The Renaixença movement of the late 19th century kick-started a massive celebration of

Market forces
Pick up some fresh produce and mix with the locals at one of the city's street markets.

Catalan culture which spanned everything from literature to architecture. The Modernistas – Gaudí, Cadafalch and Muntaner among them – used their spectacular new buildings as showcases for traditional Catalan crafts, from ceramics to ironwork. Ancient traditions and popular customs were restored, from literature festivals, like the famous Jocs Florals, to the quaint custom of dancing hollow eggs on fountains.

Spoken and written Catalan was encouraged by poets like Verdaguer and some people, like Gaudí, refused to use anything else – even to the bemused king, who only spoke Castilian. During the grim years of Francoism, when anything that didn't conform to the state's notion of Spanish identity was crushed, only one outlet for Catalan nationalism was left: the football team, FC Barcelona. Waving the distinctive blue-and-burgundy colours of the team became a substitute for the banned red and gold standard of Catalunya and football matches with Real Madrid, formerly Franco's pet team, remain a tense and dramatically charged affair.

Rivalry with Madrid is fierce – and not just in footballing terms. Madrid may be the Spanish capital but *Barcelonins* won't play second fiddle to anyone. Madrid may have the national theatre, opera and orchestras but Barcelona has the edge when it comes to contemporary dance and drama. In fashion, too, Madrid is the historic home of Spanish haute couture but Barcelona's designers are quirkier and more creative. Its wealth of designer bars, restaurants, shops and clubs is virtually unrivalled in Europe.

Barcelona, like most major cities, faces some daunting challenges in the 21st century. One of the biggest is negotiating the tricky issue of multiculturalism, now that vast number of immigrants from other countries and cultures are settling in the city. This has been a source of tension in some areas, notably in the Raval, but, equally, Barcelona has benefited from the new cultural diversity, as celebrated in the Universal Forum 2004. Whatever the future holds for bold, confident Barcelona, one thing is clear: now that it's back on top, it doesn't intend to relinquish the limelight.

The easiest way of getting to Barcelona is by air: flights are remarkably cheap, particularly if you shop around on the internet. Book well in advance to get the best deals. The high season is Easter and from mid-May to mid-September and prices fall dramatically between November and February. Trains from Paris or other parts of Europe are scenic but take ages (although Barcelona is currently expanding its high-speed rail connections with France and Madrid). If you want to travel cheaply, the coach is an option, but the 36-hour journey from the UK is only for masochists with time to kill. If you drive, park the car and forget about it when you arrive in Barcelona. The city is engagingly walkable but, if you get footsore, the buses and the metro are clean, safe and easy to negotiate and you can swing up to Montjuïc in a cable car or take a vintage tram to Tibidabo. There are lots of discount travel passes on offer, including the useful T-10, which offers 10 journeys, including transfers, on the buses, metro and local trains and can be shared.

Getting there

Air

From Europe Flights to Barcelona can be remarkably cheap, especially if you book well in advance, can be flexible with dates and times and are prepared to shop around. A return ticket on a budget airline starts at £30 mid-week in the low season or about £60 in the high-season and national airlines like **British Airways** regularly offer deals to Barcelona for around £60. Weekend and high season flights are always considerably more expensive (a typical mid-summer flight at a weekend will cost around £100). There are plenty of airlines to choose from: the Spanish national airline **Iberia** has direct flights to Barcelona from most major European cities and **British Airways** offers direct flights from Heathrow, Gatwick and Manchester. Barcelona is also served by several 'no-frills' airlines, including **easyJet, bmi** and **MyTravelLite**. Note that some budget airlines, notably **Ryanair**, offer flights which terminate at Girona, a 90-minute journey from the centre of Barcelona.

From North America **Delta, United Airlines, American Airlines** and the Spanish national carrier **Iberia** all offer flights from most major US and Canadian cities via Madrid. There are no direct flights from the USA to Barcelona. Prices are in the range of around US$500-1000 from the east coast, US$700-1200 from the west coast and CAN$800-1100 from Toronto. Consider taking a cheap flight to London and getting a flight with one of the 'no-frills' airlines from there. If you travel via Madrid, there are regular shuttle flights to Barcelona with **Spanair** and **Iberia**.

Airport information **Barcelona's international airport** is in El Prat de Llobregat, 12 km to the south of the city. Airlines are allocated to one of the two main terminals – A and B – for arrivals and departures. (The smaller Terminal C is for national flights,

→ Airlines and travel agents

British Airways, **T** 0845 7733377 (phone numbers in the UK), www.britishairways.com
British Midland/bmi, **T** 0870 6070555, www.flybmi.com
easyJet, **T** 0870 600000, www.easyjet.com
Fly Globe Span, **T** 0870 5561522, www.flyglobespan.com
Iberia, **T** 0870 5341341, www.iberia.com
Jet2, **T** 0870 7378282, www.jet2.com
MyTravelLite, **T** 0870 1564564, www.mytravelite.com
Ryanair, **T** 0871 2460000, www.ryanair.com
Spanair, **T** 0870 1266710, www.spanair.es

www.cheapflights.co.uk
www.dialaflight.co.uk
www.e-bookers.com
www.expedia.com
www.flightseekers.co.uk
www.flynow.com
www.lastminute.com
www.openjet.com
www.opodo.co.uk

including the Madrid shuttle.) Both terminals have tourist information booths, car hire offices, ATMs, bureaux de change (0700-2300), cafés and a few shops. There are left luggage lockers in Terminal B (€4.50 for 24 hours). For flight information, call **T** 93 298 38 38, or visit www.aena.es The airport is conveniently connected to the city by train and bus. The airport trains (€2.25 one way) depart for Plaça de Catalunya and Sants train stations every 30 minutes from 0613 to 2340 (journey time about 25 minutes). The **A1 Aerobús** (€3.50 one way) departs from both terminals for Plaça de Catalunya, with stops at Sants train station and Plaça d'Espanya (daily 0600-0000 every 12 minutes). There are taxi ranks outside both terminals; count on paying €17-20 to the centre of town. Fares rise after 2200 and at weekends and there are supplements for luggage and pets. Use the taxi ranks outside the Terminals rather than the touts who will approach you in the arrival halls. Trains and buses from the airport stop at around 0000. After this, you'll have to get a taxi (see p27).

Girona airport (**T** 97 218 66 00, www.aena.es) is small and 12 km from Girona, 100 km from Barcelona. There are a couple of cafés, shops, ATMs, car hire facilities (Avis, Hertz and Europcar) and a seasonal tourist information point. A bus for the city centre meets flights (€1.65 one way, €3.25 return) and Ryanair runs a bus service to Barcelona (€15.80 return, journey time 90 minutes). A taxi into Girona costs around €12-15. There are regular train services to Barcelona from the city centre (see Around Barcelona).

Reus airport (**T** 977 779 832, www.aena.es) is 3 km from the city centre and 90 km from Barcelona. There is a café, a couple of shops, an ATM, car hire facilities (Avis, Hertz and Europcar, but you need to reserve in advance). Local bus 50 meets flights (€2 to city centre) and an inter-city bus service goes directly to Barcelona (€9 one way). There are regular trains from the city centre to Barcelona (roughly every 40 minutes, €5.10 one way on regional trains, up to €14.50 on express trains, which are more luxurious but don't go any faster, journey time 90 minutes).

Car
Barcelona is about 1500 km from London, or a good two days of steady driving. The main access road into Barcelona is the A-7 *autopista*, which crosses the eastern Pyrenees and runs down past Girona and Figueres. The tolls are high, which means that the other main access road, the N-II, is clogged with traffic most of the time.

Coach

The journey to Barcelona by coach is long and uncomfortable, but can be a cheap alternative in summer when flight prices soar. The main European long-distance coach company, **Eurolines**, **T** 08705 143219, www.gobycoach.com, offers several departures several times a week in the summer (once a week out of season) from London to Spain; the journey to Barcelona takes 24 hours. Single fares are about £80; return fares around £110. The main bus and coach station in Barcelona is the Estació d'Autobuses Barcelona-Nord (Carrer Ali Bei 80, **T** 93 265 65 08, **M** Arc de Triomf).

Ferry

There are regular ferries to the Balearics (Palma de Mallorca, Máhon and Ibiza) with **Trasmediterránea**, **T** 902 454 645 (Spain), **T** +34 93 295 91 00 (from abroad), www.trasmediterranea.es Regular ferries go to Genova with **Grandi Navi Veloci**, **T** 93 443 98 98, pasaje.bcn@amcondeminas.com **Umafisa Lines**, **T** 93 221 01 56, **T** 902 191 066, www.umafisa.com have services between Barcelona, Ibiza and Formentera.

Train

The main train station for international, regional and local trains is Estació-Sants, metro Sants. Many trains often stop at Passeig de Gràcia station, which is more convenient for the city centre. For **RENFE** information, call **T** 902 240 202, or visit www.renfe.es, which has timetable and price information in English.

Getting around

The Ciutat Vella (Old City) of Barcelona (which comprises the Ramblas, Barri Gòtic, Raval and La Ribera neighbourhoods) is very easy to get around on by foot, and strolling through the wide boulevards of the Eixample will throw up scores of exquisite Modernista details. Some major sights, like the Sagrada Família and the Park Güell, will mean a short bus or metro ride and others, like Montjuïc and Tibidabo, can be reached by cable car or funicular. The public transport network in Barcelona is excellent: clean, efficient, cheap, safe and easy to use.

Bus

The main hub for buses is Plaça de Catalunya. The bus stops display clear, user-friendly bus maps listing the stops made on each route, or you can pick up a map from the information office (see below). Single tickets cost €1.10. Buses usually run from Monday to Saturday 0600-2230, with a less frequent service on Sundays.

The night bus (*nit bus*) service runs daily, 2230-0400, and covers 16 routes (all route numbers are prefixed with N). Most pass through Plaça de Catalunya and arrive roughly every half hour. The discount passes like the T-Dia or the T-10 (see Metro, below) are not valid; you must buy a single ticket on the bus (€1.10). For maps and information in English, visit the TMB information office under Plaça Universitat, call **T** 93 443 08 59, or visit www.tmb.net

Car

Driving in Barcelona is not recommended: the streets are small and always clogged and parking is difficult to find. Cars with foreign plates or hire cars are prime targets for thieves so don't ever leave anything valuable in them and use monitored underground car parks when possible. The most central staffed underground car parks are in Plaça de Catalunya, Plaça Urquinaona, Avda Catedral, Passeig de Gràcia, Plaça dels Angels and Moll de la Fusta. The El Corte Inglés department stores throughout the city also have car parks, which offer discounts or free parking with a purchase from the store. Offices of the major car rental companies can be found at the airport and at Barcelona-Sants train station. The best deals are almost always available online and it is worth finding out in advance if the airline you fly with offers special car rental deals. For car hire firms, see p212.

Cycling

There are very few cycle lanes in Barcelona and cycling through the maze of narrow streets in the Old City isn't very practical. However, if you're happy to brave the kamikaze drivers on the roads in the Eixample, bikes can be a practical way of seeing some of the less central sights. Bikes are great if you want to do some off-road cycling in the wonderful Parc de Collserola (see p92) behind Tibidabo. Cycling along the seafront, from Barceloneta, along the Port Olímpic and out to the beaches of Mar Bella is a great way to spend an afternoon. For bike rental firms, see p212.

Metro

There are six metro lines (open Mon-Thu 0500-2300, Fri and Sat 0500-0200, Sun 0600-0000) in Barcelona, identified by number and colour. A single ticket costs €1.10, or you can get a T-Dia for €4.60 which allows unlimited transport on the bus, metro and FGC trains for one person during one day, or a T-10, which offers 10 trips on the bus, metro and FGC trains for €6 and can be shared.

For maps and information in English, visit the **TMB** information office under Plaça Universitat (**T** 93 443 08 59, www.tmb.net).

Train

Some city and suburban destinations are served by **FGC** trains (Ferrocarrils de Generalitat de Catalunya), which are run by the Catalan government. They are mainly useful for getting to the less central sights in neighbourhoods like Gràcia or Tibidabo. Stations are marked with a white interlocking symbol on a dark blue background. They have an information office at Plaça de Catalunya **FGC** station (**T** 93 205 15 15, www.fgc.catalunya.net).

The Spanish national rail company, **RENFE**, also runs local trains called *rodalies* (Catalan) or *cercanías* (Castilian,) which can be useful for crossing the city as well as for making day trips further afield. Stations are marked with a white circular symbol on a red background. The main central stations are Estació-Sants, Plaça de

→ Travel extras

Safety: Petty crime is a big problem in Barcelona. Keep your bag strapped across you and watch out for scams – particularly 'helpful' strangers who say you've dropped your keys, for example. Most areas are safe, but you should avoid going alone into parts of the Raval and there have been reports of muggings on Montjuïc. Don't leave valuables in the car and leave the glove compartment open to show there is nothing to take.

Tipping: Locals will round up the food or drink bill by a couple of euros, but visitors are generally expected to pay a bit more. Tip 10% in restaurants if the service was good and 5-10% in taxis if the driver has been helpful. In smart hotels, you could leave a few euros in the room for the cleaning staff but this is not expected.

Catalunya and the Passeig de Gràcia. For more information, call **T** 902 240 202, or check www.renfe.es

Tram/funicular/cable car
Barcelona's trams and funiculars are scenic and can be convenient, especially for the journeys to the top of Tibidabo and Montjuïc.

Taxi
City taxis are yellow and black and easily available. A green light on the roof means they are available for hire. There's a taxi stand on Plaça de Catalunya, just across the street from the main tourist information office. To call a taxi, try these numbers: **Barnataxi**, **T** 93 357 77 55; **Fono-Taxi**, **T** 93 300 11 00; **Ràdio Taxi**, **T** 93 225 00 00; **Taxi Ràdio Móbil**, **T** 93 358 11 11.

Walking
Barcelona is a delightful city to walk around and seeing it on foot is definitely the best way to appreciate its charms. The sights of the

Old City are all within easy walking distance, but those of Eixample are quite spread out. There are free maps provided by the big department store El Corte Inglés, but it's worth investing in the slightly better tourist office map (€1.50). There's also a great interactive Barcelona street map at www.bcn.es/guia

Tours

The tourist office has a full list of all sightseeing tours available.

Bike tours
Biciclot (Passeig Marítim 33, **T** 93 221 97 78. **M** Ciutadella-Vila Olímpica) organizes night-time tours around Barcelona from 2100 to 2300. They cost €18 and include bike hire and an aperitif.

   Mike's Bike Tours (**T** 93 301 36 12, www.mikesbiketours.com) offers English-speaking bike tours around the city, including a break on the beach (bring a bathing suit and a picnic or money for food). Tours take four to five hours and cost €24, €22 for students and backpackers. Tours begin at different times through the year and start at the Columbus Monument.

Un Cotxe Menys, (C Esparteria 3, **T** 93 268 21 05, www.bicicletabarcelona.com, **M** Barceloneta) conduct 2½-hour bike tours in English around the Old City and the seafront. €20, including bike hire.

Bus tours
The sightseeing **Bus Turístic** has two loops, a red/north one and a blue/south one, taking in the best-known sights of the city (ticket price includes both loops). Most are adapted for wheelchairs and all have multilingual guides. The hop-on hop-off buses run every 20 to 30 minutes and cost €16 for one day, €20 for two days, with discounts for children aged 4-12. You get a number of discount vouchers with the ticket, which need not be used the same day.

→ Discount tickets

The **Barcelona Card** offers unlimited public transport plus more than 100 discounts at shops, restaurants and museums. It costs between €17 for a one-day pass and €27 for a five-day pass. Discounts include 50% off the Museu d'Història de la Ciutat and the Museu Picasso, 30% off the Temple de Sagrada Família and 20% off La Pedrera, MNAC, MACBA, CCCB and Fundació Miró.

The **Ruta del Modernisme** ticket is available from the Centre del Modernisme (p65). For €3 it offers half-price admission at four Modernista attractions: Palau de la Música Catalana, Fundació Antoni Tàpies, Museu d'Art Modern and the Museu de Zoologia.

The **Art Ticket** offers free entrance to six of Barcelona's best art museums: MNAC, Fundació Joan Miró, Fundació Antoni Tàpies, CCCB, Centre Cultural Caixa Catalunya (La Pedrera) and MACBA. It costs €15 and is available from tourist offices and participating museums.

Boat tours

Golondrinas (T 93 442 31 06, www.lasgolondrinas.com, Oct-Mar, €5-10) offer tours of the harbour or longer trips around the coast leaving from Moll de la Fusta (in front of the Columbus monument).

Walking tours

The tourist office organizes two walking tours of the city, one of the Barri Gòtic (€7.50, €3 children 4-12) and the other of Picasso's Barcelona (€10, €5 children 4-12, including admission to the Museu Picasso). There is a discount on the tours on the first Sunday of the month. They are both very popular and you should book early. Barri Gòtic tours are held in English at 1000 on Saturdays and Sundays all year and also on Thursdays in summer at 1000. Picasso tours are on Saturdays and Sundays at 1030.

Tourist information

The main tourist information office in Barcelona at **Plaça de Catalunya** (daily 0900-2100) has a bureau de change, an accommodation-booking service and a gift shop. You can book tours here and buy the various discount cards . There are also branches at **Plaça Sant Jaume** (in the corner of the Ajuntament/ City Hall; Mon-Fri 1000-2000, Sat 1000-2000, Sun and holidays 1000-1400), **Estació Barcelona-Sants** (winter Mon-Fri 0800-2000, Sat, Sun and holidays 0800-1400, summer daily 0800-2000), **Palau de Congressos** (*Trade Fair office*, Avda Reina Maria Cristina, Montjuïc, during trade fairs only), **Airport** (terminals A and B, daily 0900-2100).

The office at **Palau Robert** (Passeig de Gràcia 107 , **T** 93 238 40 00, www.gencat.es/probert Mon-Fri 1000-1900, Sat 1000-1430) has information on all of Catalunya.

The information service for the Generalitat's culture department, the **Centre d'Informació de la Virreina**, has details of concerts, exhibitions and festivals throughout the city (Palau de la Virreina, Las Ramblas 99, **T** 93 301 77 75, Mon-Sat 1000-2000, Sun 1100-1500, ticket sales Tue-Sat 1100-2000, Sun 1100-1430).

For telephone information, call **T** 906 301 282 within Spain, or **T**+34 93 368 97 30 from abroad. There is plenty of information on the excellent www.barcelonaturisme.com and www.bcn.es

Outside Barcelona
Montserrat: Plaça de la Creu s/n, **T** 93 877 77 24, www.abadiamontserrat.net Information on accommodation, as well as plans and walking itineraries of the natural park.
Sitges: Carrer Sínia Morera (on the edge of town), **T** 93 894 42 51, www.sitges.org **Tarragona**: Carrer Mayor 39, **T** 97 724 50 64.
Girona: Rambla de la Libertat 1, **T** 97 222 66 12, www.ajuntament.gi, www.girona-net.com **Figueres**: Plaça del Sol s/n, Figueres, **T** 97 250 31 55, www.figueresciutat.com

Las Ramblas and Plaça Reial 33

Kiosks, flowers, canaries and street performers.

Barri Gòtic 39

Narrow passages, graceful palaces, the soaring Gothic cathedral, great shops, bars and restaurants.

La Ribera and Sant Pere 48

Medieval palaces, Picasso, the sublime church of Santa María and the gorgeous Palau de la Música.

El Raval 57

Contemporary art; hip, multicultural and edgy.

Eixample 64

Modernista masterpieces on an elegant grid.

Montjuïc 73

Dozens of leafy parks and a castle.

Gràcia and Park Güell 81

Independent, laid-back and bohemian; nightlife and Gaudí's magical Park Güell.

Seaside 85

Barceloneta, packed beaches, neon-lit Port Olímpic and the Universal Forum of Cultures 2004.

Outskirts 90

The Nou Camp, old masters, mountains, wilderness.

Las Ramblas and Plaça Reial

Almost inevitably, everyone's first glimpse of Barcelona will be Las Ramblas, the city's most famous promenade, which cuts through the Old City in a mile-long journey to the seafront. It may look like one street (and it's often referred to simply as La Rambla), but really it is made up of five separate ramblas, each with its own name and characteristics, all placed end-to-end in a seamless progress down to the harbour. Caught somewhere between banality and beauty, Las Ramblas presents a strange and oddly appealing mixture of the picturesque and the tacky. Almost lost among the hordes of 'human statues' are pretty turn-of-the-20th-century kiosks overflowing with flowers and songbirds; fast-food outlets are squeezed between crumbling theatres and mansions; banks pop up in whimsical Modernista houses. It's at its best early in the morning and especially on Sunday afternoons, when families stroll among the flower kiosks and couples amble towards the seaside.

▸▸ *See Sleeping p119, Eating and drinking p137, Bars and clubs p161*

◉ Sights

Plaça de Catalunya
M Plaça de Catalunya. Map 2, A5, p248

The mouth of Las Ramblas, and the best starting point for a stroll, is Plaça de Catalunya, a huge square which links the old city with the new, dotted with fountains and benches. This is where the Barcelonans once came to toast the death of Franco, unpopping every bottle of cava in the city in an ecstatic celebration; now it is blandly anonymous, overlooked by banks, shopping centres and department stores. It's also the main transport hub of the city centre, where buses and trains converge, disgorging endless crowds onto the Ramblas.

Floral Ramblas
Las Ramblas is a thronging mêlée of mime artists, tourists, birds, flowers and a magic fountain.

Rambla de las Canaletes
M Plaça de Catalunya. Bus 14, 38, 51, 59, 91. Map 6, A3, p254

The Rambla de las Canaletes is named after the **Font de las Canaletes**, a florid 19th-century fountain where fans of FC Barça come to celebrate their victories. Drink from this fountain, popular legend says, and you'll return to Barcelona.

Rambla dels Ocells
M Plaça de Catalunya. Bus 14, 38, 51, 59, 91. Map 6, A4, p254

Next to Rambla de las Canaletes is Rambla dels Ocells, the Rambla of the Birds, and it won't take long to work out why. The kiosks along this section sell cages full of parrots, canaries and even a few scraggy chickens and you can hear the clamour for miles.

Rambla de les Flors

M Plaça de Catalunya or Liceu. Bus 14, 38, 51, 59, 91.
Map 6, C3, p254

The Rambla de les Flors is the prettiest and sweetest-smelling section of the street, with dozens of kiosks spilling over with brightly coloured bouquets. Set back on the western side is the elegant **Palau de la Virreina**, which houses the city's cultural information offices and a temporary exhibition space (see p30).

● *Stop off for cakes in the pretty Modernista **Antigua Casa Figueres** (Rambla de les Flors 83, **T** 93 301 60 27, daily 0830-2100), now an outpost of the famous Escribà patisserie (p190).*

La Boquería

Rambla de les Flors   Market Mon-Sat 0800-1700, some stalls open until 2000.   M Plaça de Catalunya or Liceu. Bus 14, 38, 51, 59, 91.   Map 6, C2, p254

At the centre of the Rambla de les Flors is the colourful Mercat de Sant Josep, affectionately and more usually known as La Boquería, capped with a lacy wrought iron roof and a Modernista sign in bright jewel colours made in 1914. Inside are piles of gleaming produce and there's a liberal sprinkling of tiny bars for a coffee or some oysters and cava. Dive straight to the back of the market to avoid tourist prices and to better enjoy its buzzing atmosphere.

● *Back out on the Rambla, there's a large colourful pavement mosaic by Miró, overlooked by the delightful **Casa Bruno Quadros**. Formerly a Modernista umbrella shop, it is now a bank, with a huge Chinese dragon supporting a furled umbrella.*

Museu de l'Eròtica

Las Ramblas 96, **T** 93 318 98 65, www.erotica-museum.com
Jun-Sep daily 1000-0000, Oct-Mar daily 1000-2200. €7.50/€6.50.
M *Liceu. Bus 14, 38, 51, 59, 91. Map 6, D3, p254*

There are pleasures of a supposedly steamy kind to be had at the
Museum of Erotica, but it's all rather dull (Karma Sutra illustrations,
carvings, some mind-boggling modern art, slide shows) and
definitely overpriced.

Rambla de los Caputxins

M *Liceu. Bus 14, 38, 51, 59. Map 6, F2, p254*

The Rambla de los Caputxins is named after a Capuchin monastery
which was destroyed in 1835. A new opera house, the Liceu, was
built in its place and has become one of Barcelona's best-loved
institutions (making tickets very hard to come by). Beyond the
opera house, the grandeur fizzles out into shabby gentility pretty
quickly. Once-grand theatres and hotels struggle gamely to keep
up appearances despite their ageing facades.

Gran Teatre del Liceu

Las Ramblas 51-59, **T** 93 485 99 14, www.liceubarcelona.com *Visits
daily 1000-1300, guided visits at 1000.* **M** *Liceu. Bus 14, 38, 51,
59. Map 6, E2, p254 See also p176*

The Liceu opera house has had its share of disasters since it first
opened in 1847 and has burned down twice (rumours of a curse
persist). This latest incarnation dates from 1999 and, while faithful
to the original in terms of decoration, it's now equipped with
state-of-the-art technical improvements. There are tours around its
opulent interior, with marble staircases and nymphs floating across
the ceilings. Look out for the fresco in the main auditorium by one
of Catalunya's best-known contemporary artists Perejaume, which

has transformed the Liceu's trademark velvet chairs into a series of gentle mountain peaks, fading softly into the distance. Tickets for guided visits can be bought in the excellent new shop and café, called L'Espai de Liceu, in a modern annexe next door.

Plaça Reial
M Liceu. Bus 14, 38, 51, 59. Map 6, G3, p254

Leading off the Ramblas, a pair of tall arches open into Plaça Reial, a grand 19th-century square with neoclassical arcades and lofty palm trees. The fountain of the Three Graces is flanked by twin lamp posts designed by Gaudí for his first municipal commission. Until recently, the square was known for its squatters, prostitutes and drug-sellers. Some still linger in the corners, but it's now a tourist favourite, not least for the dozens of terrace cafes. It's best avoided at weekends, when it seems to fill up with stag parties, but if you explore the tiny passages which lead off the square, you'll discover some of the best nightlife in the city.

Rambla de Santa Mònica
M Drassanes. Bus 14, 38, 51, 59. Map 2, G3, p249

The last stretch of the Ramblas, called the Rambla de Santa Mònica after a long-demolished convent, is still the shabbiest despite ongoing restoration; for a long time it got the spillover from the surrounding red light districts, but only one sex shop has managed to hold out against the vigorous clean-up. Now, cafés sprawl across the pavements and there is a daily craft and souvenir market.

! In 1893, a fervent young revolutionary, Santiago Salvador, threw a bomb into the Liceu opera house, killing twenty people. Salvador was the first to be put to death in a specially designed execution chair which slowly garrotted its victims.

Museu de Cera

Passatge Banca 7, **T** 93 317 26 49. *Oct-Jun, Mon-Fri 1000-1330 and 1400-1930 , weekends and holidays 1100-1400 and 1600-1930; Jul-Sep daily 1000-2200. €6.65. **M** Liceu. Bus 14, 36, 38, 57, 59, 64 91. Map 2, G3, p249*

Tucked down an alley off the Ramblas, the city's waxwork museum was begun a hundred years ago by the city executioner, who enticed the prurient with wax effigies of famous criminals. It's pretty standard fare, with dummies of international criminals, Hollywood stars, royals and the 1992 Olympic mascot, Cobi.

Centre d'Art Santa Mònica (CSAM)

Rambla de Santa Mònica 7, **T** 93 316 28 10. *Tue-Sat 1100-2000, Sun 1100-1500. Free. **M** Liceu. Bus 14, 36, 38, 57, 59, 64, 91. Map 2, G3, p249*

It's worth a peek across the Ramblas at the Centre d'Art Santa Monica, a stark modern building which incorporates the ruins of the old convent and which has interesting temporary exhibitions.

● *The vast, medieval Drassanes Reials are just behind the Centre d'Art Santa Mònica. The largest surviving civil Gothic building in the world, it now houses the fascinating Museu Marítim (see p63).*

Monument a Colom

Plaça Portal de la Pau. *Oct-May Tue-Sat 1000-1330 and 1530-1830, Sun 1000-1900; Jun-Sep daily 0900-2030. €2 /€1.30. **M** Drassanes. Bus 14, 36, 38, 57, 59, 64, 91. Map 2, H3, p249*

Almost at the harbour, the Ramblas opens out into Plaça Portal de la Pau (Gate of Peace), where the world's largest statue of Christopher Columbus enjoys a bird's eye view of the city. The statue, erected in 1888, was immediately popular thanks to the addition of an interior lift which still swoops visitors up to a viewing platform.

Barri Gòtic

*The Ramblas mark the western boundary of the Barri Gòtic, the hub of
the city for more than two thousand years. It's one of the best
preserved Gothic quarters in Europe, a dizzy maze of palaces, squares
and churches piled on top of the remnants of the original Roman
settlement. But the Barri Gòtic is no picture-perfect tourist-museum;
the Barcelonans have always been too pragmatic to pickle their city
for posterity and the old city is grubby, noisy, chaotic and packed with
shops, bars and clubs which cater to every possible taste. The streets
are just as crowded at midnight as they are at midday.*

▸▸ *See Sleeping p122, Eating and drinking p139, Bars and clubs p161*

◉ Sights

Catedral de la Seu

Plaça de la Seu s/n, **T** 93 310 25 80. Cathedral *Mon-Fri 0800-1330
and 1600-1930, Sat-Sun 0800-1330 and 1700-1930. Free.* Lift and
choir, *daily 1000-1330 and 1600-1800, €2 each.* Museu de la
Catedral, **T** 93 310 25 80. *Daily 1000-1300 and 1600-1830 .*
€1. ***M*** *Jaume I. Bus 17, 19, 40, 45. Map 6, D7/8, p255*

It's impossible to miss the dramatic spires of the Gothic cathedral
of La Seu soaring above the old city. The main entrance overlooks
the wide Plaça Nova; from here, you'll get the full effect of the
fairytale facade, which was actually stuck on in the 19th century.
The main cathedral dates back to the 13th century and the interior
is magnificent, suitably dim and hushed, with soaring naves

! In 1992, the Columbus monument married New York's Statue
of Liberty. Antoni Miralda, a conceptual artist from Barcelona,
came up with the idea and outfitted the bride and groom in
fine style for the occasion. One of Columbus' outsized new
shoes can be seen at the Museu del Calçat (p41).

The Catalan crapper

During the Feria de Santa Llúcia, artisans display their collection of nativity scene figures (*santons*) in the streets around the cathedral. As well as the usual figures, the Catalans wouldn't consider a manger scene complete without the bizarre, squatting figure of the *Caganer*, the Crapper, usually wearing a cheerful red Catalan cap and an entranced expression, with his little pile of poo beneath him.

supported by heavily decorated Gothic cross vaults. Underneath the main altar lie the remains of the city's patron saint, Santa Eulàlia, in a 14th-century alabaster sarcophagus adorned with grisly depictions of her martyrdom. It's an operatic setting; to get the full effect, put a coin in the slot and watch the whole thing light up. Behind the altar, a lift just off the ambulatory will whip you to the roof for staggering views of gargoyles and ancient, huddled roofs. The delightful cloister has a lush palm-filled garden in the centre, home to a colony of white geese, which have lived here for so long that no one can remember why. The old tradition of dancing a hollow egg (known as the *l'ou com balla*) on the delicate 15th-century fountain of St George was recently revived and takes place on the feast of Corpus Christi in early June. Just off the cloister, a tiny museum in the Sala Capitular (Chapter House) displays a small collection of medieval paintings, including Bartolomé Bermejo's beautiful *retablo* of *La Pietat* (1490), one of the earliest Spanish oil paintings. Next door to the museum is the simple Romanesque chapel of Santa Llúcia, dedicated to the patron saint of seamstresses who queue up here for her blessing on the saint's day, 13th December. This date also officially marks the opening of the Feria de Santa Llúcia, a Christmas fair which is held outside the cathedral.

● *A short detour down Carrer de Montjüic de Bisbe will bring you to the enchanting Plaça de Sant Felip Neri, a little square with an old church still pocked with bullet holes from the Civil War, a tinkling fountain and a shoe museum: the **Museu del Calçat** (T 93 301 45 33, Tue-Sun 1100-1400, €2).*

Museu Diocesà

Avda de la Catedral 4 (entrance on Plaça Nova), **T** 93 315 22 13, *Tue-Sat 1000-1400 and 1700-2000, Sun 1100-1400. €2. **M** Jaume I. Bus 17, 19, 40, 45. Map 6, D8, p255*

To the left of the main cathedral entrance is the Pia Almoina, a Gothic almshouse which has been beautifully renovated to hold the Museu Diocesà (Diocese Museum), a goldmine of religious treasures from the Middle Ages onwards, including several shimmering *retablos* by Bernat Martorell.

● *The dull, concrete expanse of Plaça Nova is enlivened in the evenings by the odd flame-thrower or tango dancer. On Sundays from noon you can join in the traditional Catalan dance, the stately* sardana.

Museu Frederic Marés

Plaça Sant Iu (off C des Comtes), **T** 93 310 58 00, www.museumares.bcn.es *Tue-Sat 1000-1900, Sun and hols 1000-1500. €3. Note that the first floor is only open Wed, Fri and Sun; second and third floors are only open Tue, Thu and Sat. The basement and ground floors are always open. **M** Jaume I. Bus 17, 19, 40, 45. Map 6, D8, p255*

This large, peaceful museum is devoted to the obsessive collection of the eponymous sculptor and painter who had obviously never heard the phrase 'less is more'. On the lower floors are endless ranks of tiny Iberian ex-votos and a huge collection of sculpture spanning several centuries, including some exquisite Romanesque church architecture and early Christian tombs in the basement area. The upper floors contain the Museu Sentimental, with a mind-boggling collection of 18th- and 19th-century ephemera, including 108 snuffboxes, 1,295 books of cigarette papers and 158 pairs of opera glasses, which eloquently convey the hothouse atmosphere of a 19th-century bourgeois home.

● *The outdoor courtyard café in the Museu Marés is open to everyone. You can sit under the orange trees, surrounded by 16th-century stone arcades and tuck into delicious coffee and cakes. The busy modern city feels a world away. See p142.*

Plaça Sant Jaume
M St Jaume. Bus 16, 17, 19, 40, 45. Map 6, F7, p255

The solemn Plaça Sant Jaume would be even more impressive if a busy street (Carrer Ferran) didn't cut straight through it. Still, it's grand enough, thanks to the presence of the medieval palaces of the **Generalitat** (the Catalan parliament) and the **Ajuntament** (the city council), which have been struggling for control of the city for centuries and glower at each other across the square like two dowagers at a tea party.

Plaça Sant Jaume abandons its gravitas annually on 23 April – a kind of Catalan Valentine's Day, when couples exchange the traditional gifts of books and roses – and flower-sellers and book stalls fill the square in a flutter of petals.

● *Off Plaça Sant Jaume, Carrer de la Ciutat becomes Carrer Regomir, where you'll find the little 16th-century chapel of St Christòfol which sits under a 19th-century neo-Gothic facade. St Christopher is the patron saint of drivers and on his feast day, 10 July, cars squeeze down the narrow street to queue up for his blessing.*

! Stone faces leering above door lintels – such as those on Carrer d'Avinyó just off Plaça Sant Jaume – are from the days before mass literacy, when they marked brothels.

Palau de la Generalitat

Plaça Sant Jaume *(Entrance on C del Bisbe)*, **T** *93 402 46 00. Open for guided visits only, 2nd and 4th Sun of the month 1000-1400; arrive early to sign up for the English tour at 1100 and bring ID. Free.* **M** *Jaume I. Bus 16, 17, 19, 40, 45. Map 6, E7, p255*

The Palau de la Generalitat has housed the Catalan parliament since the early 15th century, when Mark Safont designed its graceful inner courtyard and the sumptuous Chapel (1432) on the first floor. The Pati dels Tarrongers (Courtyard of Orange Trees), with its pink marble columns, was begun a century later. The Golden Room, named for its 16th-century gilded ceiling, is purely ceremonial. The modern Sala Antoni Tàpies – where the assembly conduct business – is emblazoned with the eponymous artist's four-part series of medieval chronicles of Catalunya.

Casa de la Ciutat/Ajuntament

Plaça Sant Jaume, **T** *93 402 70 00. Sun 1000-1400, free.* **M** *Jaume I. Bus 16, 17, 19, 40, 45. Map 6, F7, p255*

Facing the Palau de la Generalitat is the late 14th-century Casa de la Ciutat, containing the offices of the Ajuntament (city council). The sumptuous staircase of honour leads up to the Saló de Cent, the core of the old Gothic palace. Designed by Pere Llobet, the hall was inaugurated in 1373, a masterpiece of monumental simplicity. On the other side is the Saló de les Cróniques, where Josep Maria Sert's sepia murals depict 14th-century Catalan victories in Greece and Asia Minor. There's a tourist office and exhibition space downstairs.

Plaça del Rei

M *Jaume I. Bus 16, 17, 19, 40, 45. Map 6, E8, p255*

Plaça del Rei (King's Square) is a tiny, exquisite square just off Plaça Sant Jaume. The rulers of Catalunya held court for centuries in the austerely beautiful **Palau Reial Major**, which closes off the square, and prayed in the adjoining **Capella Reial** (Royal Chapel) with its dainty belltower. These buildings can be visited as part of the Museu d'Història de la Ciutat (see below).

Museu d'Història de la Ciutat
Plaça del Rei s/n, **T** 93 315 11 11, www.museuhistoria.bcn.es *Oct-May Tue-Sat 1000-1400 and 1600-2000, Sun and holidays 1000-1400; Jun-Sep Tue-Sat 1000-2000, Sun and holidays 1000-1400; €4 (ticket includes audio-visual).* **M** *Jaume I. Bus 16, 17, 19, 40, 45. Map 6, E9, p255*

The fascinating Museu d'Història de la Ciutat reveals the history of the city layer by layer. The deepest layer contains the Roman city of Barcino, established here more than 2,000 years ago. Tacked on to it are Visigothic ruins, which were built during the 5th and 6th centuries, and on top of the whole are the palaces and churches of the middle ages, which still enclose Plaça del Rei.

A glass lift glides down a couple of millennia to the subterranean excavations of Roman Barcino. A vast swathe of the Roman city survives, an astonishing stretch of walls, watchtowers, baths, temples, homes and businesses, founded two thousand years ago and discovered by chance less than a century ago. Glass walkways lead over the ruins, where you can peer into the old wine vats or stroll along the top of a fortified wall. Still underground but heading steadily towards the site of the present cathedral, the Roman ruins become interspersed with the remnants of Visigothic churches which date back to around the 5th century. Stairs lead up to the Gothic Royal Palace and you enter the next layer of the city's history, the Golden Age of the medieval period.

The echoing throne room, the Saló de Tinell, was built in 1359 and is a masterpiece of Catalan Gothic. Seven solemn arches succeed each other in great broad arcs, creating an overwhelming impression of space and grandeur. Next to the throne room is the

► **Jewish Barcelona**

No one knows when the first Jews settled in Barcelona but by 694 they had established a large enough presence for the Visigoths to find them threatening and decree that all Jews become slaves. However, the community was thriving by the 11th century and many Jews worked for the king as advisors and translators, especially to the Arab courts, although they were taxed heavily and given no civil rights. In 1243, by decree of Jaume I, El Call became a ghetto, bounded by Carrer Banys Nous, Carrer el Call and the wall of the Generalitat building. Jews were forced to remain within its walls between dusk and dawn and identify themselves with capes and hats. Bitter jealousy of their influence at court erupted in sporadic attacks from the end of the 13th century. Hundreds were massacred in a vicious pogrom in 1391 and Jewish synagogues and cemeteries were suppressed throughout Catalunya a decade later. Finally, in 1424, Jews were expelled from the city, a harbinger of the expulsion of all Jews from Spain in 1492. Jews didn't return to the city until the early 20th century and, soon after, the triumph of Franco resulted in another exodus. It wasn't until 1948 that a Jewish synagogue opened again in the city.

Royal Chapel of Saint Agatha, with a single graceful nave and a dazzling polychrome ceiling supported by diaphragm arches. It was built at the beginning of the 14th century and topped with a whimsical octagonal belltower in the form of a crown. The glittering 15th-century *retablo* of the *Epiphany*, by Jaume Huguet, is considered one of the finest examples of Catalan Gothic painting. A stairway leads to the Mirador del Rei Martí, an old watchtower with fabulous views (currently closed for restoration).

Plaça del Pi

M *Jaume I. Bus 16, 17, 19, 40, 45. Map 6, D4, p254*

The pretty Plaça del Pi is named after a glade of pine trees which once stood here, their memory recalled now by a single pine. The hulking 15th-century Gothic church of **Santa María del Pi** is now remarkable solely for its enormous rose window, the biggest in Europe, as looters burnt the interior to a crisp during the Civil War. Plaça del Pi and the adjoining **Plaça Sant Josep Oriol** and miniature **Plaçeta del Pi** are now great spots for an evening *copa* out on the terrace, with plenty of wandering musicians for entertainment. On the first Friday and every Saturday of the month, a market selling local cheeses, honey and *embutits* (cured meats) sets up its stalls and on Thursdays there's a regular antiques market. Plaça Sant Josep Oriol has artists of dubious quality most weekends and an art market on the first weekend of each month.

Sinagoga Mayor

C Marlet, **T** *93 317 07 90. Tue-Sat 1100-1400 and 1600-1800, Sun 1100-1400. Free but donations gratefully accepted. A pamphlet, which includes a fascinating history of the Synagogue, is available for €5. Guided tours of the Call are available by prior arrangement, T 93 317 07 90, F 93 210 78 99, www.calldebarcelona.org* *M* *Jaume I. Bus 14, 17, 38, 40, 45, 59, 91, 90. Map 6, E6, p254*

Carrer Banys Nous, off Plaça Sant Josep Oriol, marks the boundary of the old Jewish Quarter, known as El Call from the Hebrew word *quahal*, meaning 'meeting place'. There is virtually no trace of what was once the most important Jewish population in medieval Spain and the quarter, a shadowy maze of twisting passages and overhanging buildings, is now mainly known for its antique shops. But recently, the local Jewish community have restored the remnants of the medieval synagogue, said to be the oldest in Europe, and opened it to the public.

Barri de Santa Ana

M Plaça de Catalunya. All buses to Plaça de Catalunya.
Map 6, p254/255

North of Plaça Nova is the unassuming district of Santa Ana, with few eye-catching monuments or museums, but plenty of shopping opportunities. The two main shopping streets of the Barri Gòtic meet here: **Carrer Portaferrissa**, with lots of young and trendy fashion stores, and **Avinguda del Portal de l'Àngel**, with several major chains and a branch of the El Corte Inglés department store. Avinguda del Portal de l'Àngel, the main artery of this neighbourhood, links Plaça Nova with Plaça de Catalunya. The area is known as Barri de Santa Ana after the simple, Romanesque monastery of **Santa Ana** (just off Carrer Santa Ana), which was founded by the Knights Templar in the early 12th century. East of Carrer Santa Ana is **Plaça Vila de Madrid**, a grassy little square with a transparent footbridge across a Roman sepulchral way, from where you can see a series of simple funerary monuments lined up beside one of the smaller Roman access roads into the city.

Els Quatre Gats

C Montsió 3, **T** 93 302 41 40. *Daily 0900-0200.* ***M*** *Plaça de Catalunya. All buses to Plaça de Catalunya. See also p49.*
Map 6, A7, p255

On the other side of Avinguda del Portal de l'Àngel, the famous Els Quatre Gats tavern has been faithfully recreated at number 3 Calle Montsió. Els Quatre Gats (*The Four Cats*) began life here in 1897, when the painters Ramon Casas and Santiago Rusiñol, along with Miquel Utrillo and Pere Romeu, nostalgic for their old stomping ground of Montmartre, opened the tavern in order to provide a meeting place for all their friends. It was partly inspired by the celebrated Parisian café Le Chat Noir, alluded to in the name which also means a 'handful of friends' in Catalan slang. The tavern survived just six years, but was a roaring success among its varied clientele of artists, intellectuals and bohemian hangers-on. It produced its own review, held concerts, poetry readings and art exhibitions and encouraged protegés, including Picasso who designed the menus and held his first exhibition here. It remains pretty but its bohemian atmosphere has inevitably succumbed to the temptations of expensive tourist attraction status.

La Ribera and Sant Pere

The old artisan's district of La Ribera is a funky, fashionable neighbourhood with some of the city's trendiest bars, restaurants and shopping, as well as its most popular museum (the Picasso Museum), its most beautiful church and a string of elegant palaces along Carrer Montcada. Just to the northwest, the neighbourhood of Sant Pere is divided from its fashionable neighbour by just one street but is a different world altogether: time seems to have stopped here and it's a quietly old-fashioned area of small shops, particularly along the engaging Carrer de Sant Pere mes Baix.

▸▸ *See Sleeping p123, Eating and drinking p144, Bars and clubs p162*

◉ Sights

Carrer Montcada
M Jaume I. Bus 14, 17, 19, 39, 40, 45, 51, 59. Map 6, F-H12, p255

Carrer Montcada was the swankiest address in the city during the 12th century, when merchants lined it with beautiful mansions set around elegant patios. Many have survived, some as private residences, others as museums or chic art galleries, and the street affords some tantalizing glimpses into graceful Gothic courtyards.

Picasso's Barcelona

In 1895, Picasso and his family moved from Málaga to Barcelona, where his father took up a post as professor of fine arts at the Academia Provincial de Bellas Artes.

In 1897, the famous tavern Els Quatre Gats (see p47) was inaugurated and became the heart of the city's avant garde; Picasso designed its menus and held exhibitions here.

In 1899, Picasso shared a studio just off Carrer Avinyó, a street famous for its brothels, which gave him the inspiration for his celebrated painting *Les Demoiselles d'Avignon* (it was also here that he contracted gonorrhea). The following year, one of his paintings was chosen to be exhibited at the Universal Exhibition in Paris and he travelled to France with Carlos Casegamas.

Casegamas, troubled and addicted to drink and drugs, killed himself the following year and Picasso returned to Barcelona. This time, he was able to afford a studio by himself at Carrer del Comerç 28, where he created many of the haunting works of his Blue Period, using the beggars, prostitutes and gypsies of the streets as his models.

In 1904, he moved permanently to Paris, although he regularly returned for visits.

His last extended stay in the city was in 1917, when he came to oversee a production of Parade, an avant garde ballet by Serge Diaghilev and his Ballets Russes for which Picasso designed costumes and sets.

He was adamant that he would not set foot on Spanish soil under the dictatorship of General Franco; his only concession was the series of sketches he sent in 1961 for the frieze which adorns the **Col.legi d'Arquitectes** (College of Architects) on Plaça Nova but which he refused to come and carry out himself.

Museu Picasso

C Montcada 15-23, **T** 93 319 63 10, www.museupicasso.bcn.es
Tue-Sat 1000-2000. €5, entrance to temporary exhibitions varies.
M *Jaume I. Bus 14, 17, 19, 39, 40, 45, 51, 59. Map 6, F12, p255*

The Museu Picasso draws more visitors than any other museum in the city except the FC Barça museum and it is well worth getting here early to avoid shuffling along behind the crowds. The collection includes few of Picasso's most famous paintings, instead focussing on the early works, particularly those created by the young artist in Barcelona and some of the chilly paintings of his Blue Period, like the stricken mother and child of *Desamperados* (The Despairing, 1904). Picasso was partly influenced by the grim studies of gypsies and beggars painted by Isidro Nonell, who also frequented the tavern of Els Quatre Gats (see p47) for which the young Picasso painted the menu (you can see it here). The works of his Rose Period are well represented but there is almost nothing from the Cubist years, just a small *Head* (1913), and a single *Harlequin* (1917) from the celebrated series. From 1917, there's another leap in time, this time to the extraordinary series of 44 paintings and drawings based on Velázquez's *Las Meninas*, which Picasso painted in a single concentrated burst over six months at the end of 1956 and in which every detail of the masterpiece has been picked out, pored over and fascinatingly reinterpreted.

Museu Tèxtil i d'Indumentària

C Montcada 12-14, **T** 93 319 76 03, www.museutextil.bcn.es
*Tue-Sat 1000-1800, Sun and holidays 1000-1500. €3.50. **M** Jaume I.*
Bus 14, 17, 19, 36, 39, 40, 45, 51. Map 6, G11, p255

The Textile Museum, in elegantly converted Gothic palaces, is a fashionista's dream, with a collection of historic fashions from the 16th to the 20th centuries. Check out the views across the rooftops from the top floor and relax in the delightful courtyard café.

Museu Barbier-Mueller d'Art Precolumbi

C Montcada 12-14, **T** 93 310 45 16, www.barbier-mueller.ch
Tue-Sat 1000-1800, Sun and holidays 1000-1500. €3. **M** *Jaume I.*
Bus 14, 17, 19, 36, 39, 40, 45, 51. *Map 6, G11, p255*

Next door to the Textile Museum, the Museu Barbier-Mueller d'Art
Precolumbi was established when the Swiss museum of the same
name offered to lend Barcelona 170 pieces from their collection on
a rotating basis. The city spent millions expensively converting
another of Carrer Montcada's palaces to exhibit them and now
three millennia of art treasures – powerful sculpture, jewellery and
ceramic ware from the ancient civilisations of Central and South
America – are theatrically arranged on spotlit plinths.

Santa María del Mar

Plaça de Santa María del Mar. *Daily 0900-1330 and 1630-2000.*
Free. **M** *Jaume I. Bus 14, 17,19, 36, 39, 40, 45, 51.*
Map 6, H11, p255

The loveliest church in all Catalunya sits at the bottom of Carrer
Montcada: the Església de Santa María del Mar. Construction
began in 1329 and was completed in just 54 years – record speed
for the era – which meant that other styles and forms couldn't
creep in as successive architects took over the job. As a result, the
church is considered one of the finest and purest examples of
Catalan Gothic. The hulking exterior, built to withstand wind and
storms, gives no hint of the spellbinding interior, a soaring central
nave flanked with supporting columns of ethereal slimness. The
ornate fittings accumulated over centuries were lost when the
church was gutted during the Civil War; only the stained-glass
windows, some dating back to the 15th century, were spared.
Regular concerts are held here; the Centre d'Informació de la
Virreina (p30) can provide details.

● *One of Barcelona's best tapas bars, La Vinya del Senyor, has a perfect location opposite Santa María del Mar. There's a great range of cavas and local wines and you can sit out on the terrace and admire the church's beautiful facade (see p146).*

Passeig del Born
M Jaume I/Barceloneta. Bus 14, 17. 19, 36, 39, 40, 45, 51. Map 6, H12, p255

Once a theatre for medieval jousting tournaments and carnivals, nowadays the fiesta continues at the string of ultra-trendy bars and clubs that line the street of Passeig del Born. Beginning at the side entrance to the church of Santa María del Mar, this is one of the hippest neighbourhoods in Barcelona, known simply as 'El Born', and the narrow streets which splinter off the Passeig are packed with slick tapas bars, restaurants and stylish interior design and fashion shops. Just off the Passeig is the **Fossar de les Morares** (Mulberry Cemetery), the burial place of the martyrs of 1714, who defended the besieged city against the Bourbon armies; they are remembered here annually on 11 September, Catalan National Day.

Museu de Xocolata
C Comerç 26, **T** 93 268 78 78, www.museudelxocolata.com
Mon and Wed-Sat 1000-1900, Sun and holidays 1000-1500. €3.60. M Jaume I. Bus 14, 16, 17, 19, 36, 39, 40, 45, 51, 57, 59, 69. Map 2, E8, p248

Just around the corner from Passeig del Born is one of the city's newest museums, the Museu de Xocolata (Chocolate Museum) tucked away in the old convent of San Agustín on Carrer Comerç. It describes the histories and legends behind chocolate and – best of all – does tastings.

Parc de la Ciutadella
M Ciutadella. Bus 14. Daily 0800-dusk. Map 5, p253

One of Barcelona's most popular parks is a quiet oasis in the heart of the city with a clutch of small museums, shady walkways and fountains and a cramped zoo (see below). The park was originally the site of an enormous star- shaped citadel, built after Barcelona fell to the Bourbon armies in 1714. It became the most hated building in the city and was finally torn down in 1869. The park was laid out in the late 19th century by a team that included the young Gaudí and expanded for the Universal Exhibition of 1888.

Zoo
Parc de la Ciutadella s/n, **T** 93 225 67 80. *Nov-Feb daily 1000-1700; Mar and Oct daily1000-1800; Apr and Sep daily1000-1900; Jun-Aug daily 0930-1930. €12.90. €8.30 for children aged 3-12.
M Ciutadella. Bus 14. Map 5, C2/3, p253*

The zoo takes up half of the park, but it's still not enough for the poor animals cramped into small concrete enclosures. The highlight for many years was *Copito de Nieve* (Snowflake), the only albino gorilla in captivity, who died in late 2003. Things will hopefully improve when the zoo moves to roomier quarters in the new complex being created in Diagonal Mar.

Museu de Zoologia
Parc de la Ciutadella s/n, **T** 93 319 69 12, www.museuzoologia.bcn.es *Tue, Wed, Fri-Sun 1000-1400, Thu 1000-1830. €3 (includes entrance to Museu de Geologia). M Arc de Triomf and Jaume I. Bus 14, 39, 40, 41, 42, 51, 141. Map 1, G8, p247*

Domènech i Montaner's **Castell dels Tres Dragons** sits in one corner of the park, the most daring of the new buildings created for the Universal Exhibition of 1888. One of the earliest Modernista edifices, it's now home to the comfortably old-fashioned Museu de Zoologia, with the usual ranks of bones, fossils and stuffed beasts.

Museu de Geologia

Parc de la Ciutadella s/n, **T** 93 319 69 12,
www.museugeologia.bcn.es   *Tue-Sat 1000-1400, until 1800 on Thu.*
€3 (includes Museu de Zoologia, see above). **M** *Arc de Triomf and Jaume I. Bus 14, 39, 40, 41, 42, 51, 141. Map 5, A1, p253*

Near the Castell dels Tres Dragons is the Museu de Geologia, the oldest museum in the city, opened in 1882. It hasn't changed much since and is only for dedicated fossil fans.

● *Next to the museum is the charming **Hivernacle** (winter greenhouse), a glassy pavilion with a great café (p146).*

Cascada

*Parc de la Ciutadella s/n. **M** Arc de Triomf. Bus 14, 39, 40, 41, 42, 51, 141. Map 5, A3, p253*

In the opposite corner of the park to the Museu de Geologia, the extravagant Cascada is a flamboyant fountain partly designed by Gaudí. It overlooks a small **boating pond**, a popular Sunday picnic spot for Barcelonan families.

Arc de Triomf

M *Arc de Triomf. Bus 14, 39, 40, 41, 42, 51, 141. Map 1, G8, p247*

The Passeig de Lluis Companys, a promenade which was designed as a spectacular entrance to the site of the Universal Exhibition (1888), heads northwest from the Parc de la Ciutadella. The main gateway is the huge red-brick neo-Moorish Arc de Triomf, topped with a gracious figure representing Barcelona handing out gifts.

Sant Pere
With a somewhat grizzled proletarian air, Sant Pere is full of old-Barcelona atmosphere.

Sant Pere
M Jaume I. Bus 45. Map 6, p255

The neglected neighbourhood of Sant Pere sits quietly across
Carrer Princessa, a wide road which divided Sant Pere from La
Ribera a century ago. These two *barris* may be neighbours but they
have nothing in common: fashionable La Ribera is a world away
from humble Sant Pere where life continues much as it has done
for decades. The main shopping street is the engaging Carrer de
Sant Pere mes Baix, where bakeries, tool shops and Modernista
pharmacies are nudged together in a comfortable huddle. The
Mercat Santa Caterina, currently in a temporary building in the
Passeig de Luis Companys, is about to return to its former location
in a brand-new home. Sant Pere boasts one important monument,
the opulent Modernista Palau de la Música Catalana (see below).

● *On Carrer de Sant Pere mes Baix, look out for Farmacía Fonoll
at number 52, one of the oldest pharmacies in the city. Founded in
1561, it was given a peppy Modernista makeover in 1890 including
some delicious stained glass by Joan Espinagosa and a crazy wrought
iron chandelier dripping with iron roses and coats of arms.*

★ Palau de la Música Catalana
C Sant Pere mes Alt s/n, **T** 93 295 72 00, www.palaumusica.org
*Daily 1000-1530, closed Aug. Visits by guided tour only, booking in
advance advisable. Tours depart every 30 mins in English, Castilian
and Catalan and last 50 mins including a 20-min video. €7.*
M Urquinona. Bus 17, 19, 40, 45. Map 6, A10, p255

The best way to see the Palau de la Música Catalana is to come for
a concert, but tickets are hard to procure. Otherwise you will have
to make do with the guided tour. The Palau was built between
1905 and 1908 as a new home to the Orfeò Català, the first and
biggest of the choral societies which sprang up during Catalunya's
Renaixença (cultural renaissance) a century ago. It was designed by

Domènech i Montaner, who collaborated with many of Catalunya's most celebrated craftsmen and artists. The extraordinary sculpted facade is a hymn to music and Catalanism and beneath it is a dense forest of floral columns, sprouting multi-coloured flowers of broken tiles. The main auditorium is spell-binding: rainbow-coloured light streams in through the vast stained-glass ceiling of flowers and musical angels. Galloping winged horses bearing Valkyries seem to erupt from the stage and shimmering three-dimensional 'spirits of music' flutter across its back wall. The palace won the Building of the Year award in 1908, but just two decades later it was being sneeringly referred to as 'the Palace of Catalan Junk' by architects who thought it old fashioned. And no one argued about the appalling acoustics. The glass walls may have allowed the sunlight to flood in but with it came all the street noise. Concerts were punctuated with church bells and warbling ladies catching up on their housework; it barely escaped demolition. After decades on the sidelines, interest in the building was revived: Oscar Tusquets extended and remodelled the building in the 1980s and made a largely unsuccessful attempt to improve the terrible acoustics. He's about to get another chance, as work is almost completed on a new 600-person choral hall.

El Raval

The Raval area is now one of the hippest neighbourhoods in the city, packed with slick clubs, bars, shops and restaurants, but just a century or so ago it was a miserable slum. The streets nearest the port formed the most notorious red light district on the Mediterranean, filled with whorehouses, seedy bars and music halls. Nicknamed the Barri Xinès after San Francisco's vice-ridden Chinatown, its heyday was in the 1920s and 30s. Tourists flooded in until Franco put an end to the party. By the 1970s, the arrival of heroin was causing serious problems and the city hall eventually stepped in to begin the latest regeneration project: rotting tenements have been replaced with new apartment blocks, bars and bordellos have been closed down and a new promenade, the Rambla de Raval, slices through its heart. It's still poor and shabby, but the construction of the glossy new Museu d'Art Contemporani has brought in trendy new galleries, fashion shops and arty bars and, with the arrival of immigrants particularly from north Africa and Pakistan, it's also becoming multicultural. Despite the improvements, you should watch out for your bags and don't walk the streets alone late at night, especially those nearest the port.

▸▸ *See Sleeping p125, Eating and drinking p147, Bars and clubs p163*

◉ Sights

★ Museu d'Art Contemporani de Barcelona (MACBA)

Plaça dels Angels, **T** 93 412 08 10, www.macba.es *26 Sep-24 Jun, Mon, Wed-Fri 1100-1930, Sat 1000-2000, Sun 1000-1500; 25 Jun-25 Sep Mon, Wed-Fri 1100-2000, Sat 1000-2000, Sun 1000-1500. €7, prices vary for temporary exhibitions.* **M** *Universitat. Bus 9, 14, 16, 17, 22, 24, 38 , 41, 55, 58, 59, 66, 91, 141.* *Map 2, B2, p248*

Richard Meiers' huge, glassy home for MACBA was built in 1995, a symbol of the city's dedication to urban renewal and a monument to its preoccupation with contemporary design. It overlooks a wide, modern square, which has become a favourite with skateboarders.

Although the museum's permanent collection officially begins after the Civil War, there are some earlier pieces by Alexander Calder, Paul Klee and Catalan artists like Leandre Cristófol, Joan Ponç and Àngel Ferrant. The collection is loosely structured around three periods; the first stretch, which roughly covers the 1940s to the 1960s, is represented by artists like Antoni Tàpies, Joan Brossa and Antoni Saura. These artists were members of the Dau al Set ('seven spot die' in Catalan) group, a loose collection of writers and artists influenced by the surrealists and particularly by Joan Miró. Their works marked an end to the torpor that had

Skateboarding meets modern art
Richard Meier's strikingly designed and shiny MACBA building is a favourite with the city's skateboarders.

settled on the cultural life of Spain after Franco's victory in the Civil War.

Popular and consumer culture had more of an impact on the art of the 1960s and 70s: there are several fun, kitsch pieces from Carlos Pazos, including the mocking *Voy a hacer de mí una estrella* (I'm going to make myself a star, 1975), a series of pouting, celebrity-style photographs.

The 1980s and early 90s are marked by a return to painting and its forms of expression; among Catalan artists, Miquel Barceló's paintings and Susana Solano's stark metal sculptures reflect this return to traditional forms. There are also several good photographic pieces from this period, including works by Anselm Keifer, Jeff Wall and Suzanne Lafont.

Many of the usually excellent temporary exhibitions focus on the latest digital and multimedia works. MACBA has a great bookshop and an attractive café-bar which shares a square with the CCCB (see below) around the corner.

Centre de Cultura Contemporània de Barcelona (CCCB)

C Montalegre 5, **T** 93 306 41 00. *9 Sep-May Tue, Thu and Fri 1100-1400 and 1600-2000, Wed and Sat 1100-2000, Sun and holidays 1100-1900; Jun-8 Sep Tue-Sun 1000-2000.* €5.50. **M** *Universitat. Bus 9, 14, 16, 17, 22, 24, 38, 41, 55, 58, 59, 66, 91, 141. Map 2, A2/3, p248*

The excellent Centre de Cultura Contemporània de Barcelona (CCCB) sits behind MACBA and is the second prong of the city's institution for contemporary culture. It's set in the former Casa de la Caritat, a hospice for pilgrims established in the 16th century which has undergone dramatic remodelling. The CCCB hosts wide-ranging and eclectic exhibitions on all aspects of contemporary culture not covered by MACBA, as well as running several community-based projects and dozens of other activities, including the Sónar music festival and an alternative film festival (see p182).

Antic Hospital de la Santa Creu

C Hospital s/n, no **T**. *Mon-Fri 0900-2000, Sat 0900-1400.*
M *Universitat. Bus 9, 14, 16, 17, 22, 24, 38, 41, 55, 58, 59, 66, 91, 141. Map 2, D3, p248*

An anachronistic leftover in the heart of this fashionably bohemian neighbourhood, this hulking stone complex, built in 1402, comprised an orphanage, leper hospital and wards for the city's sick and dying. The vaulted Gothic wards now contain the **Biblioteca Nacional de Catalunya** (National Library of Catalunya, entrance to members only but you can try begging for a peek), as the hospital was moved in 1926 to Domènech i Montaner's Modernista pavilions

! One of the last patients at the Antic Hospital de la Santa Creu before it moved to new premises was Gaudí. He was brought here after he fell under the wheels of a tram in 1926; he was so shabby that everyone mistook him for a tramp.

(see p73). The former chapel (**La Capella**, Tue-Sat 1200-1400 and 1600-2000, Sun 1100-1400) holds regular workshops, commissions pieces from local artists and has excellent shows of contemporary works from up-and-coming young Barcelonan artists.

● *Carrer Hospital is one of the main streets of the Raval. On 11 May, the Festival de Sant Ponç, patron saint of beekeepers and herbalists, is held here and the street is lined with stalls selling aromatic herbs and a dazzling array of honey.*

Palau Güell

C Nou de la Rambla 3, **T** 93 317 39 74. *Guided tours only. Mon-Sat 1000-1330 and 1600-1830. Tours fill up quickly – book in advance in summer. €2.50.* **M** *Liceu. Bus 14, 38, 51, 59. Map 6, G1, p254*

The Palau Güell on Carrer Nou de la Rambla was Gaudí's first major commission for the man who was to become his most important patron, Eusebi Güell. Both men were intensely Catalanist and intensely religious and these themes are replayed throughout the tall, narrow mansion. The small visiting room off the long glass vestibule (which Güell's horrified wife thought looked like a barber's shop) boasts a spectacularly ornate carved ceiling into which tiny spyholes were carved so that the Güells could overhear their guests' conversations. The main salon is overwhelming, a lofty hall topped with an arched cosmic dome covered with deep blue honeycombed tiles; thin shafts of light entering through tiny windows symbolize the stars circling the moon. This is the heart of the house, with all the rooms organized around the central hall in the Mediterranean fashion and surrounded by a series of galleries and miradors. Behind the salon is the family's dining room and private sitting room, with stained-glass windows featuring historical Catalan heroes. There's a small terrace which allows you to see the unusual shuttered tribunal, looking like a well-armoured armadillo, which juts out at the back. The tour continues upstairs through sober but elegant bedrooms and the pretty, ceramic-covered bathroom with all the period's latest mod cons. Despite the sumptuousness, this was never a comfortable palace and the Güells always preferred their main residence in Pedralbes (see p91). Dim lighting, heavy religious solemnity and the weight of historical references combine to make it a sombre experience (Antonioni used it as a setting for his unsettling thriller *The Passenger* in 1977). But the rooftop is its antithesis: a rippling terrace with a playful forest of swirling, *trencadí*-covered chimneys, surrounding a lofty central spire topped with a wrought-iron bat, a legendary guardian of Catalan heroes.

Rambla de Raval
M Liceu or Paral.lel. Bus 120. Map 2, D/E1/2, p248

In 2000, a great swathe of rundown tenement houses in the heart of the Raval were torn down and replaced with a new promenade, the palm-studded Rambla de Raval. Still too new and shiny to have much atmosphere, it does have a sprinkling of cafés and occasionally hosts outdoor concerts in summer. At weekends the Rambla hosts a hip market (see p191).

● *Chill out in one of the many nearby boho-chic cafés: El Café Que Pone Meubles Navarro (p163), a big airy café stuffed full of flea market furniture, is just a two-minute walk from the Rambla de Raval.*

Sant Pau del Camp
C Sant Pau s/n, no **T**. *Wed-Mon 1120-1300 and 1800-1930, Tue 1130-1230. Free.* **M** *Paral.lel. Bus 20, 36, 57, 64, 91, 120, 157. Map 2, E1, p248*

Just off the Rambla de Raval, Carrer de Sant Pau runs down to the tiny, delightful church of Sant Pau del Camp, the most important surviving Romanesque church in the city. The tranquil cloister has Moorish-inspired arches and simple columns carved with a menagerie of mythical creatures.

Drassanes Reials/Museu Marítim

Avda Drassanes s/n, **T** 93 342 99 20, www.diba.es/maritim *Daily 1000-1900. €5.40, temporary exhibitions €5.* **M** *Drassanes. Bus 14, 18, 36, 38, 57, 59, 64, 91. Map 2, H2, p249*

Almost at the harbour, in the southernmost tip of the Raval, are the magnificent Drassanes Reials, the vast medieval shipyards built at the height of the Catalan empire. Begun in 1243, the shipyards form the largest and most important surviving civil Gothic structure in the world. At their peak they could accommodate 40 galley ships. Now they contain the excellent Maritime Museum, where the star exhibit is a monstrous galley ship, a replica of the Royal Galley of John of Austria, which was built to lead the Holy Alliance against the Turks in the Battle of Lepant in 1571. There's also a fine series of ship figureheads and an absorbing collection of beautifully illuminated medieval maps. Down in Port Vell (see p85), the museum has recently renovated a graceful sailing ship from 1918, the Santa Eulàlia (Moll de la Fusta, Tue-Fri 1200-1700, Sat and Sun 1000-1700) and which is also part of the visit.

Barri Xinès

M *Drassanes. Bus 14, 18, 36, 38, 57, 59, 64, 91. Map 2, p249*

The dark, narrow web of streets in this southern section of the Raval are still the poorest (and most intimidating at night), but it's also here that a glimmer of the old Barri Xinès can still be found in a handful of old-fashioned bars – like the Kentucky and Bar Marsella (see Bars and clubs, p163) – which haven't changed in decades. A small square is named after Jean Genet, whose novel *Journal de Voleur* (Thief's Journal) describes how he scraped a living as a rent boy and thief in these streets in the 1920s and 30s.

Eixample

The Eixample (pronounced Ai-sham-play) is Barcelona's most upmarket neighbourhood, with its finest restaurants and designer boutiques and one of the greatest concentrations of art nouveau monuments in Europe. This elegant, bourgeois district was created by a utopian socialist, Ildefons Cerdà, who won the commission to create a new extension (which is what 'Eixample' means in Catalan) in the 19th century. Cerdà envisioned a modular city of regular blocks around airy central gardens in which people from all walks of life would live harmoniously side by side, but his design was rapidly undermined. The rich rushed out to the new district, commissioning the greatest Modernista architects to create trophy mansions that would dazzle their neighbours. This was Gaudí's playground and his delirious imprint is everywhere, from the creamy apartment building of La Pedrera to the looming, unfinished spires of the Sagrada Família.

▸▸ *See Sleeping p129, Eating and drinking p150, Bars and clubs p165*

◉ Sights

★ Passeig de Gràcia
M Passeig de Gràcia. Bus 7, 16, 17, 22, 24, 28. Map 3, p251

The Passeig de Gràcia is the heart of the Eixample, a glossy boulevard of chic boutiques lined with plane trees and twirling wrought-iron lamp-posts. It's overlooked by an eclectic mix of spiky neo-Gothic castles, pompous neoclassical insurance offices and fairy-tale Modernista mansions encrusted with stucco flowers.

Mansana de la Discòrdia
M Passeig de Gràcia. Bus 7, 16, 17, 22, 24, 28. Map 3, J5, p251

The most famous stretch of the Passeig de Gràcia is the 'block of discord' between Carrer Consell de Cent and Carrer d'Aragó, where flamboyant mansions designed by the three most famous Modernista architects nudge up against each other. The architects were independently invited by three of the city's most influential families to entirely remodel existing buildings, the 'discord' arising from their dramatically different styles.

The first, at the corner of Carrer Consell de Cent, is the **Casa Lleó i Morera**, built in 1864 and transformed by Domènech i Montaner in 1902. Sadly, much of the beautiful facade was destroyed by the luxury leather goods shop, Loewe, who ripped out the original ground-floor windows and stripped it of much of the original sculptural decoration. The surviving nymphs bearing symbols of the new age – electric light, photography, the telephone and the phonograph – flit across the facade, thickly clustered with garlands of flowers oozing like piped icing.

The **Casa Amatller**, three doors up at number 41, was the first of the three major remodellings. Antoni Amatller's fortune was built on chocolate and Puig i Cadafalch built him a fairy-tale castle, with a stepped gable covered with shimmering polychrome ceramics which almost look good enough to eat. The lobby of the Casa Amatller functions as the **Centre del Modernisme** where you can get information on the Ruta del Modernisme (p29) and which offers free guided tours of the three facades of the Mansana de la Discòrdia (the Casa Batlló is the only one with public access).

Barcelona

Casa Batlló

Passeig de Gràcia 43, **T** 93 216 03 06, www.casabatllo.es *Daily 0900-2000. €10, includes audio guide in English. Booking in advance recommended in high season.* **M** *Passeig de Gràcia. Bus 7, 16, 17, 22, 24, 28. Map 3, J5, p251*

Next door to Casa Amatller is the fantastical Casa Batlló (1904-06), unmistakably the work of Antoni Gaudí. Covered with shimmering, multicoloured *trencadis* (broken tiles) and culminating in an undulating scaly roof, it gleams like an underwater sea dragon. All kinds of theories abound about the symbolism of the facade, but the story of St George and the dragon seems to fit most neatly. The rippling waves of tiny ceramic tiles and the bone-white pillars which support the balconies evoke the curling dragon, his scaly back formed by the swaying roof ridge while St George is represented by the bulbous cross erupting from a thick column, or lance, spearing the dragon from on high. The interior opened to the public as part of the celebrations for Gaudí Year in 2002. Initially, it was expected to close at the end of the year, but it has proved so popular that it has remained open – although plans for its future remain uncertain, so go while you can. Gaudí was no fan of straight lines and the interior is as soft and undulating as whipped ice-cream (which is exactly what the ceilings in the main salon look like). He played with natural light, ingeniously tiling the interior patio with ceramics which pale as they descend in order to catch and reflect the light. There's a colourful, tile-covered terrace at the back, with playful multicoloured ponds and fountains.

La Pedrera (Centre Cultural Caixa Catalunya)

C Provença 261-265, **T** 902 400 973, www.caixacatalunya.es *Daily 1000-2000, last admission 1930. €7, free admission to temporary exhibitions.* **M** *Diagonal. Bus 7, 16, 17, 22, 24, 28. Map 3, G6, p251*

One of Gaudí's most famous buildings is a little further up the Passeig de Gràcia from the Mansana de la Discòrdia. The Casa Milà, better known as La Pedrera ('the stone quarry'), rises like a creamy cliff draped with sinuous wrought-iron balconies. The first occupants of the apartment building moved in around 1911 and there's a recreation of an apartment from that era on the top floor. There isn't a straight line anywhere, with the walls, ceilings, doorways and windows flowing around the interior patios. Many of the fittings in the apartment are original, including the elegant bedroom suite with its pretty polychrome floral motif, which was designed by the celebrated craftsman Gaspar Homar (whose work

Stone quarry views
*Gaudí's swirling chimneys on the roof of La Pedrera are much-
photographed frames for the city below.*

> ### Gaudí the Grump

Gaudí was undoubtedly an architectural genius, but his people skills were poor. Señora Batlló, who commissioned the Casa Batlló on the Passeig de Gràcia, was offended at his insistence on speaking Catalan (which she couldn't understand) and had him peremptorily dismissed. She was in exalted company – Gaudí also spoke exclusively in Catalan to the King of Spain, who was equally bemused. The Milàs, who commissioned the Casa Milà across the street (now better known as La Pedrera), were so shocked at the bill he submitted that they refused to pay it. The case went to court, Gaudí won and promptly donated the money to a convent. As the art historian Manuel Trens sighed, 'God is the only master with whom Gaudí finished on good terms'.

is also in the Museu d'Art Modern, see p75). The attic now houses **L'Espai Gaudí,** a slick museum providing a systematic overview of the architect's life and works in the city with models, photos, drawings and video installations. A spiral staircase leads up to the climax of the visit, the sinuous rooftop terrace which curls around the patios like a dreamscape studded with fantastical bulbous crosses and plump *trencadí*-covered towers, Gaudí's magical response to the building's prosaic need for chimneys, air vents and stairwells. On summer weekends, you can enjoy a drink and live music on the rooftop (see Bars and clubs, p165).

● *Near the Pedrera on Avenguda Diagonal, the fairytale castle at 416-420 was designed by Puig i Cadafalch in 1906. Conventionally known as the Casa Terrades, it's always referred to as the* **Casa de les Punxes** *(House of Spikes). It's a spectacular building, partly because of its tremendous size and partly because of its Baron Munchausen theatricality: ranks of pointy gables culminating in wrought-iron spikes with four slim corner towers topped with witches' hats.*

Museu Egipci de Barcelona (Fundació Arqeològica Clos)

C València 284, **T** 93 448 01 88, www.fundclos.com *Mon-Sat 1000-2000, Sun 1000-1400. €5.50.* **M** *Passeig de Gràcia. Bus 7, 16, 17, 20, 22, 24, 28, 45, 47. Map 3, l6, p251*

Just off the Passeig de Gràcia in Carrer Valencia is the Museu Egipci de Barcelona, with an excellent selection of artefacts spanning more than three millennia. Among the most interesting exhibits are the sarcophagi: the earliest are made of terracotta moulded vaguely into the form of the body within, but they grow steadily more elaborate. Burial scenes are dramatically recreated, with cult chapels, mummies – including bizarre x-rays of mummified animals – and tombs. There is also a rich collection of ceramics, some dating back to 3,500 BC and jewellery – gold and silver, glittering with lapis lazuli and cornelian for the rich, painted glass paste for the poor – revealing the astonishing level of craftsmanship that the early Egyptians attained.

Fundació Francisco Godia

C València 284, **T** 93 272 31 80, www.fundacionfgodia.org *Mon, Wed-Sun 1000-2000. €4.20.* **M** *Passeig de Gràcia. Bus 7, 16, 17, 20, 22, 24, 28, 45, 47. Map 3, l6, p251*

Francisco Godia (1921-90) was an odd combination: a successful racing driver for more than three decades, he also found time to acquire a dazzling collection of painting, medieval sculpture and ceramics. There's a mesmerizing gathering of gilded polychrome statues from the 12th century onwards and among the ceramics are lustrous 15th-century pieces from Manises. Godia also collected turn-of-the-20th-century art, including Ramon Casas' *At the Racecourse* (c.1905) and Isidre Nonell's haunting *Gypsy Woman* (1905). Godia's daughters are expanding the collection by adding works from the later 20th century and some contemporary art.

Barcelona

The Sagrada Família: a never-ending story

The Sagrada Família had a gloomy start. It was commissioned by a reactionary organization known as the Josephines, who wanted a temple where the faithful could go to beg forgiveness for the depravity of the modern age. The first architect quit after a year and Gaudí, aged just 31, was given the job in 1883. The project became an obsession and after 1914 he devoted himself solely to it, spending the last two years of his life living ascetically in a shack on the building site. In June 1926, he was crushed under a tram and died two days later. Ten thousand mourners followed his coffin to its burial place in the crypt of the Sagrada Família. By this time, Gaudí, his architecture and his ultra-conservative brand of Catholicism were thoroughly out of fashion. Work limped on for a few years but came to an abrupt halt with the start of the Civil War, when anarchists attacked the crypt, destroying every plan, model and sketch that they could find in an attempt to ensure that it would never be completed. The temple languished for decades until, in 1952, a group of architects decided to continue the work by raising money through public subscription. Japanese corporations are currently the highest contributors; Gaudí-mania was big in Japan long before it really took off Europe. In the absence of detailed plans, the architects are forced to conjecture what Gaudí might have envisioned, and this has inevitably caused controversy. The current team is directed by Jordi Bonet, the son of one of the temple's original architects. Gaudí, in the meantime, looks set to become a saint. The Vatican announced that it would consider the case for his beatification in 2000 and the Association for the Beatification of Antoni Gaudí are busy finding out the particulars of his miracles.

Fundació Antoni Tàpies

C Aragó 255, **T** 93 487 03 15, www.fundaciotapies.org *Tue-Sun 1000-2000. €4.20.* **M** *Passeig de Gràcia. Bus 7, 16, 17, 20, 22, 24, 28, 43, 44. Map 3, I5, p251*

On the other side of Passeig de Gràcia, down Carrer Aragó, you can't miss a red-brick building topped with what looks like a huge cloud of barbed wire, a vast sculpture entitled *Nuvol i Cadira* (Cloud and Chair) by Antoni Tàpies, probably Spain's best-known living artist. The building, known as the Editorial Montaner i Simon, was built in 1880 by Domènech i Montaner for the family publishing house and is one of the earliest Modernista monuments. It now houses one of the largest collections of Tàpies' works in the world. There are also interesting temporary exhibitions by contemporary artists.

In 1948, Tàpies became part of the Dau al Set ('seven-spot die') group, a gathering of writers and artists whose works were the first sign of cultural revival in Spain after the grim 'hunger years' that succeeded Franco's victory. He is most celebrated for his 'material paintings', adopting radically innovative techniques and media, particularly the use of found objects.

● *Around the corner on Carrer Mallorca, there's another extravagant Modernista mansion, the Casa Thomas. It's now one of Barcelona's sleekest shops, BD Edicions de Disseny (p188), selling contemporary and Modernista-style furniture and household goods.*

★ Sagrada Família

C Mallorca 401, **T** 93 208 04 14, www.sagradafamilia.org *Oct-Mar daily 0900-1800, Apr-Sept daily 0900-2000. €8.* **M** *Sagrada Familia. Bus 19, 33, 34, 43, 44, 50, 51. Map 1, E9, p247*

Gaudí's unfinished masterpiece, the Templo Expiatorio de la Sagrada Família (Expiatory Temple of the Holy Family), is undoubtedly the most emblematic and most controversial monument in Barcelona. Love it or hate it, it's impossible to ignore:

the completed towers stand at almost 100 m and the central spire, when finished, will soar 180 m into the sky. It's easily the biggest tourist attraction in Catalunya and the constant bustle of crowds and tour buses mean that it's hard to feel much sense of religious awe as you jostle your way through the iron gates at the entrance.

Gaudí designed three facades: Nativity and Passion on either side of the nave and Glory as the magnificent main entrance. Only one facade was completed by the time of his death in 1926: the craggy Nativity facade surmounted with a green cypress tree flecked with white doves of peace. Many of the thickly clustered statues were made from life casts – including, apparently, the donkey. Inside, you'll find a building site where work has begun on the construction of four huge columns which will eventually support the enormous domed roof. The Passion facade flanks the other side of the church: the antithesis of the joyful Nativity facade, this is supposed to represent death and sacrifice, but Josep Subirachs' grim, lifeless sculptures are entirely devoid of any emotion or vitality, veering in a mechanical sequence from the Last Supper at the bottom left, to Christ's burial in the top right. The temple is supposedly set for completion in 2026, the anniversary of Gaudí's death, but this seems increasingly unlikely in view of the technical problems surrounding the construction of the vast central tower which still need to be resolved.

Standing dwarfed by the forest of soaring unfinished columns and undulating vaults, it's impossible not to feel a sense of wonder at this extraordinary expression of faith in stone. Somehow the very fact that it remains unfinished makes its ambitious conception seem all the more spectacularly overblown.

There's a lift (with long queues) up the towers (1000-1745, €2) and the brave can climb even higher into the blobby spires for an uncanny sensation of stepping out into space, descending by the tight spirals of the vertiginous staircase. Underneath, the Crypt contains Gaudí's tomb and an interactive museum devoted to the history of the temple, with drawings, models and photographs.

Hospital de de la Sant Creu i Sant Pau

Avda Sant Antoni María Claret 167, **T** 93 291 91 01. **M** *Hospital de Sant Pau. Bus 15, 117.* *Map 1, D10, p247*

The pedestrian Avinguda Gaudí sweeps up to the city's second enormous Modernista project of this neighbourhood, Domènech i Montaner's Hospital de la Sant Creu i Sant Pau (1926-30), a fairy-tale assembly of delightful ceramic-encrusted pavilions ingeniously linked by underground passages and encrusted with mosaics. It's still a working hospital, but visitors are invited to wander freely around the grounds and admire the magical turrets and spires – it's particularly lovely, if ghostly, at dusk. Sadly, the squat pre-fab additions to the gardens are a sign of the lack of space which is forcing the hospital to consider new premises.

Montjuïc

The ancient promontory of Montjuïc rises up above the sea to the west of the city. A green, park-filled oasis, it's undergone dramatic face lifts in the last century or so. Palaces, museums and gardens were constructed for Barcelona's International Exhibition of 1929 and the upper reaches were entirely revamped to create the Olympic Ring, a string of dazzling sports complexes used for the 1992 Olympics. The latest phase of improvements, including more parks, a lake and a new information centre with a delightful café, has been completed in time for Barcelona's Universal Forum of Cultures 2004 (see p89). Despite all the development, in some ways nothing much has changed: it's still a popular weekend destination for locals, who come to wander through the parks and gaze down across the city from the hilltop castle.

▸▸ *See Bars and clubs p166*

Barcelona

Sights

Plaça d'Espanya and Font Màgica

Font Màgica, **T** 93 289 28 30. *May-Sep Thu-Sun and holidays fountain 2000-0000, music shows every 30 mins 2130-2330. Oct-Mar Fri and Sat fountain 1900-2100, music shows every 30 mins 1900- 2030. Free.* **M** *Espanya. Bus 9, 13, 30, 50, 55. Map 4, A4 and C3, p252*

This circular Plaça, now a big, busy thoroughfare, was built for the International Exhibition of 1929. Avinguda Maria Cristina, flanked by a pair of grim towers, leads to the Font Màgica, an over-the-top fountain best appreciated during the kitsch sound and light shows in which jets of fruit-coloured water leap and dance to music.

Pavelló Mies Van der Rohe

Avinguda Marquès de Comillas s/n, **T** 93 423 40 16, www.miesbcn.com *Daily Nov-Mar 1000-1830, Apr-Oct 1000-2000. €3.* **M** *Espanya. Bus 9, 13, 30, 50, 55. Map 4, C2, p252*

Close to Plaça d'Espanya is this sleek, glassy reconstruction of Ludwig Mies Van der Rohe's monument to rationalist architecture, built as the German pavilion during the 1929 International Exhibition. Misunderstood at the time, it was dismantled after the exhibition, but rebuilt on the same site in 1986. It is now home to the Mies Van der Rohe foundation, which hosts conferences and exhibitions.

ForumCaixa

Avda Marquès de Comillas 6-8, **T** 93 476 86 00, www.funcadion.lacaixa.es *Tue-Sun 1000-2000. Free.* **M** *Espanya. Bus 9, 13, 30, 50, 55. Map 4, B2, p252*

Just across from the Mies Van der Rohe pavilion is one of Barcelona's newest museums, the ForumCaixa, a vast Modernista textile mill which has been slickly redesigned to house an excellent permanent collection of contemporary art and several exhibition halls. Pick up a brochure for details of seasonal events, which include concerts, dance performances and other cultural events.

● *ForumCaixa has an excellent café-bar: good for a post-art rest.*

★ Museu Nacional d'Art de Catalunya (MNAC)

Palau Nacional, **T** 93 622 03 60, www.mnac.es *Tue-Sat 1000-1900, Sun and holidays 1000-1430. €4.80, exhibitions €4.20, combined entry €6.* **M** *Espanya. Bus 9, 13, 30, 50, 55. Map 4, E2, p252*

The dour Palau Nacional which looms from the hilltop houses the Museu Nacional d'Art de Catalunya. There's a spellbinding array of Romanesque murals gathered from the tiny churches of the Catalan hinterlands, hauntingly lit and displayed on reconstructed church interiors. The stars of the exhibition are the church murals from the Boí Valley in the Pyrenees, which was designated a World Heritage Site in 2000 for the richness of its Romanesque heritage. Some of the most important come from the Church of Sant Climent in Taüll, which features a huge resplendent Pantocrater (Christ depicted as a ruler) with a serene, hypnotic gaze. The paintings from the parish Church of Santa María (also in Taüll) are the most complete set in the museum, a blazing, richly coloured series which reaches its apotheosis in the splendid depiction of Mary as the Seat of Wisdom in the apse. The Gothic collection is less magical than the Romanesque, but equally magnificent. The 13th to the 15th centuries were Catalunya's glory years, when her ships ruled the seas and the arts flourished. Rooms 11 and 12 are devoted to one of the most brilliant periods in Catalan art and the three outstanding painters of the time: Bernat Martorell, Lluís Dalmau and Jaume Huguet. Tacked on at the end is a small collection of works from the 15th to the 18th centuries, including a couple of striking pieces from Zurbaran, a fleshy *Allegory of Love* by Goya and a swirling portrait of John the Baptist and St Francis of Assisi in the desert by El Greco. By the end of 2004, the holdings of

> ### ▶ Montjuïc Card
>
> This discount card costs €20, and offers free rides on the Montjuïc Tourist Train (a summer only service) and cable car, free bike rental and free entrance to many museums and attractions. It also includes entrance to the Bernat Picornell and Montjuïc swimming pools and a performance at the Teatre Lliure or the Mercat de les Flors theatres.

the Museu d'Art Modern, currently in the Parc de la Ciutadella, will join the rest of MNAC's collection in newly refurbished galleries, allowing visitors to see the best of Catalan art in one setting.

Poble Espanyol

Avda Marquès de Comillas s/n, **T** 93 508 63 00. *Sep-Jun, Mon 0900-2000, Tue-Sat 0900-0200, Sun 0900-0000; Jul-Aug Mon 0900-2000, Tue-Thu 0900-0200, Fri and Sat 0900-0400, Sun 0900-0000. €7 /€3.90. Hourly guided visits in Catalan, Castilian, English and French, €2.* **M** *Espanya. Bus 9, 13, 30, 50, 55. (Take a bus up the hill if you don't want to face a long walk from the metro.)* Map 4, B1, p252

After all the high art at MNAC, there's the pure kitsch of the Poble Espanyol to look forward to. The 'Spanish Village' was also built for the 1929 Exhibition, a gloriously tacky collection of traditional architectural styles from around the country. The entrance is marked by fake copies of the medieval towers in the Castilian town of Avila, which were turned into the most over-the-top designer bar in Barcelona by Alfredo Arribas and Javier Mariscal in the 1980s. Inside, there's an arcaded Plaça Mayor, a pretty little Barri Andaluz, a Catalan village and streets copied from villages all over Spain, from Extremadura to the Basque lands, all lined with scores of souvenir and craft shops, cafés, galleries and restaurants.

Annella Olímpica (Olympic Ring)

Galeria Olímpica: Estadi Olimpic, Passeig Olimpic s/n,
T 93 426 92 00, www.fundaciobarcelonaolimpica.es
Entrance by prior booking, Mon-Fri 1000-1300 and 1600-1800.
*€2.50. **M** Espanya, then bus 61. Map 4, G1, p252*

The new stadia and other buildings erected for the 1992 Olympics
are strung along the Avinguda de l'Estadi, halfway up the hill of
Montjuïc. The main stadium was originally built in 1929 (the
Catalans beat Bolton Wanderers in the inaugural football match),
but only the external structure of the stadium was retained during
the radical alterations necessitated by the 1992 Olympics. It
contains the **Galeria Olímpica**, a museum devoted to the Games,
where you can relive the highlights through videos and displays.

● *Take in a swim and a film at the Piscina Bernat Picornell, the
fabulous outdoor pool built for the Olympics, which regularly runs
classic films around the pool in summer.*

★ Fundació Miró

Parc de Montjuïc s/n, **T** 93 443 94 70 www.bcn.fjmiro.es *Oct-Jun,
Tue, Wed, Fri and Sat 1000-1900, Thu 1000-2130, Sun and holidays
1000-1430; Jul-Sep, Tue, Wed, Fri and Sat 1000-2000, Thu 1000-2130,
Sun and holidays 1000-1430. €7.20, temporary exhibitions €3.20.
M Espanya. Bus 50 or 55, or Montjuïc funicular from Paral.lel.
Map 4, G5, p252*

The fabulous Fundació Miró is set in a white, light-drenched
building designed by Josep Lluís Sert, further down the Avinguda
de l'Estadi from the Olympic Ring. Established in 1971, the
Foundation contains the most important and comprehensive
gathering of Miró's works in the world.

During the war years, a growing colony of exiled artists brought
new stimuli to local painters, including Miró, who began to
experiment; *Carrer de Pedralbes* (1917), a skewed, glowing street,

shows him dabbling with cubism and *Chapel of Sant Joan d'Horta* (1917), with its rich colouring and broad brushstrokes, is Fauvist in inspiration. Increasingly, objects float weightlessly in space – as in *The White Glove* (1925) and *The Music-hall Usher* (1925) – as Miró stripped away the unnecessary in pursuit of the essence. He never forgot his earthy Catalanism; *Man and Woman in front of a pile of excrement* (1935) has two figures, enormous feet planted firmly on Catalan soil, gesturing lewdly with their bulging genitalia in front of a turd raised up as though looking on with interest. He was fascinated by hair, which sprouts on snakes, in stars and on genitalia throughout his works.

In 1937, war broke out in Spain and Miró was devastated. He took his family to Normandy, where he claimed that his work began to reflect his 'profound desire to escape… night, music and the stars began to play an increasing role'. The poetic series of *Constellations*, of which the Foundation holds one, *Morning Star* (1940), date from this period. Delicate lines trace between floating symbols, suggesting interconnectedness between the earth and the sky, flooded with wheeling stars. The constant themes of the post-war years were woman, birds and stars – as in *Woman dreaming of escape* (1945) and *Woman and birds at daybreak* (1946). His sign language was being constantly refined and his paintings became increasingly gestural and impulsive – like the *Woman in a pretty hat* (1960), in which there are just two isolated spots of colour and the *Figure in front of the sun* (1968). This Zen-like urge to strip things to their essence is beautifully illustrated in the series of paintings he made after a visit to Japan, including the spare, luminous *The Day* (1974). There are some spectacular sculptures from this later period, including the soaring white *Solarbird* (1968), blazing against a brilliant blue background and more in a sculpture terrace on the roof.

● *A lovely, well-restored park called the* **Jardins Laribal** *next to the Fundació Miró contains the park information office in a prettily restored villa, with a delightful café and a summer terrace.*

Telefèric de Montjuïc

Cable car: *Jun-mid-Sep, daily 1115-2100; mid-Sep-mid-Nov daily 1100-1915; mid-Nov-mid-Mar weekends only 1100-1915; mid-Mar-mid-Jun daily 1100-1915. Daily over New Year and Easter holidays. €3.60 single, €5 return. Funicular: Metro tickets and passes are valid, or €1.10 single. Spring and summer daily 0900-2200, autumn and winter daily 0900-2200. Castle and museum:* **T** *93 329 86 13, Nov-mid-Mar 0930-1700, mid-Mar-Oct daily 0930-2000. €2.50, €1 for castleand ramparts only.   Map 4, H6, p252*

Just beyond the Fundació Miró is the funicular station which trundles down to the Paral.lel, and also the starting point for the cable car (telèfric) up to the **Castell de Montjuïc** at the top of Montjuïc. The castle (**T** *93 329 86 13, Nov-mid-Mar 0930-1700, mid-Mar-Oct 0930-2000*) houses a dull military museum but has stunning views across the harbour from the ramparts. Gardens will soon spread along this part of Montjuïc, and should be completed in time for the Universal Forum of Cultures in 2004.

Museu d'Arqueologia de Catalunya (MAC)

Passeig Santa Madrona 39-41, **T** 93 424 65 77, www.mac.es *Tue-Sat 0930-1900, Sun and holidays 1000-1430. €2.50.* **M** *Espanya. Bus 55. Map 4, D5, p252*

At the bottom of Montjuïc is a cluster of less visited museums in a crop of fanciful pavilions left over from the 1929 Exhibition. The best is the Museu d'Arqueologia de Catalunya, which contains finds from the Greco-Roman settlement of Empúries on the Costa Brava including mosaics and statuary, and some elaborate Visigothic jewellery and metalwork.

! Montjuïc has a bloody history. Thousands of Falangist prisoners were shot here during the Civil War; more were executed during Franco's vicious purge of Catalan resistance.

Ciutat del Teatre

Museu de les Arts Escèniques, Plaça Margarida Xirgù, **T** 93 227 39
00, www.diba.es/iteatre *Tue-Sat 1000-1300 and 1700-1930, Sun
and holidays 1000-1400. €3. **M** Espanya. Bus 55. Map 4, E5, p252
See also p177.*

Just across the road from MAC is another revamped pavilion from
the 1929 Exhibition. The former Palau de l'Agricultura is the new
home of the prestigious Teatre Lliure and forms part of the Ciutat del
Teatre (Theatre City). Behind it is the Mercat de les Flors, a former
flower market now transformed into a performance space (see
p178). These buildings look inward onto the circular Plaça Margarida
Xirgù, dominated by the spanking new, glassy building for the
Institut del Teatre and the **Museu de les Arts Escèniques**
(Museum of Performing Arts), which hosts interesting exhibitions.

Museu Etnolòlgic

Passeig Santa Madrona s/n, **T** 93 424 68 07.
www.museuetnologic.bcn.es *Tue and Thu 1000-1900,
Wed, Fri-Sun and holidays 1000-1400. €3. **M** Espanya. Bus 13, 55.
Map 4, E3, p252*

The Museu Etnolòlgic has extensive holdings from Africa, Oceania,
Asia, South America and Spain. They are shown on a rotating basis
– there is simply too much to show at one time – but the short,
temporary exhibitions are usually the most interesting. Below the
museum, steps lead down to the **Teatre Grec**, an amphitheatre
inspired by a model of Epidaurus and built over an old quarry for
the 1929 Exhibition. It's the main venue for the summer Grec
festival, the city's main performing arts festival (see p182).

Gràcia and Park Güell

Gràcia was an independent town until 1897, when it was dragged, under protest, into the burgeoning city of Barcelona. The 'Liberation for Gràcia' movement hasn't quite died out, with the occasional T-shirt and graffitied scrawl demanding freedom from big, bad Barcelona and most Graciencs are still fiercely protective of their distinct identity. In the 19th century, Gràcia was a hotbed of radicalism but now it has largely settled down to its role as a mildly bohemian, traditional neighbourhood of narrow streets and charming squares, far from the flashiness and pace of the Diagonal which divides it from the Eixample. Gràcia's unique identity is best expressed in the Festa Major (held in August), which turns the streets into a riot of streamers, stars and balloons, as everyone vies for the prize of best-decorated street. On the edge of Gràcia is Gaudí's magical Park Güell, a dreamy wonderland which looks over the whole city and out to sea.

▸▸ *See Sleeping p132, Eating and drinking p152, Bars and clubs p167*

 ## Sights

Squares, markets and Modernista mansions
M *Fontana. FGC Gràcia. Bus 22, 24, 28, 87. Map 3, p250*

The centre of Gràcia has no really big sights or monuments; its distinctive charm is best appreciated with a stroll, especially in the evening, when the names of streets and squares – Mercat de la Llibertat, Plaça de la Revolució – evoke its fiercely liberal past. **Plaça de Sol** is the hub of the area's nightlife, with dozens of bars and cafés. A couple of blocks away is **Plaça de la Virreina**, a quiet attractive square lined with a row of simple cottages and a pretty church. The oldest section of Gràcia is squeezed between the broad avenues of Carrer Gran de Gràcia and the Via Augusta; at the heart of the district stands the neighbourhood's oldest market, the pretty Modernista **Mercat de Libertat**. Two streets to the north is the delightful **Rambla de Prat**, with a cluster of Modernista buildings showing off their swirling facades. Dedicated Gaudí fans should make a pilgrimage to Carrer de Carolines, the site of Gaudí's first major architectural project in Barcelona, the neo-Mudéjar **Casa Vicens** (1883-88, no public access), designed for the ceramics manufacturer Manuel Vicens, whose business was advertized by the eye-popping proliferation of sea-green and white tiles.

★ Park Güell

*C Olot 7, **T** 93 413 24 00.   Nov-Feb, daily 1000-1800; Mar and Oct, 1000-1900; Apr and Sep, 1000-2000; May-Aug 1000-2100. Free.*
M *Lesseps, then a (signposted) 10-min walk, or take bus 24 right to the gate. Map 1, B8, p247*

The whimsical turrets, fabulous *trencadí*-covered creatures, floating balconies and sloping parklands of Park Güell are perhaps the most delightful and varied of Gaudí's visionary creations. It wasn't originally designed as a park: it was meant to be an aristocratic housing estate. Gaudí's benefactor and friend, Eusebi Güell, had visions of an exclusive garden city, modelled on the English fashion (which is why the Park is spelt with an English 'k' and not a Catalan 'c'), but it never took off and the empty grounds passed to the city for use as a public park in 1922.

Two fairy-tale pavilions, with their swirling roofs and shimmering coats of multicoloured *trencadis* guard the entrance to the park (one has been converted into an exhibition space, **T** 93 285 68 99, Mon-Fri 1100-1500, €2). From here, stairs sweep up past the multicoloured dragon which has become one of Barcelona's best-known and best-loved symbols (so beloved, in fact, that your chances of pushing past the coach parties of tourists and school kids having their pictures taken are pretty slim).

Trencadi seating
Gaudí's fantastical candy bench winds colourfully around Park Güell.

The steps culminate in the Sala Hipóstila, also known as the Hall of a Hundred Columns because of the forest of thick, Doric columns which support its undulating roof. Gaudí's talented collaborator, the architect and mosaicist Josep Maria Jujol, was given free reign to colour the vaulted ceiling with elaborate whimsy; look carefully and you'll see the designs are made of smashed china, ceramic dolls' heads, wine glasses and old bottles.

More steps lead up from the Hall to the main square which offers beautiful views of the city below. The endless bench which snakes around the square, is thickly encrusted with *trencadis*, which shimmer and change colour in the sunlight like the scales of a monstrous dragon. This, too, is the product of Gaudí's collaboration with Jujol, a dazzling collage of bizarre symbols, fragments of text, stars, butterflies, moons and flowers which presaged cubism and surrealism.

Surrounding the square are porticoes and viaducts, which hug the slopes and stretch for more than 3 km. The arches and columns are made from unworked stone quarried *in situ*, and they seem to erupt organically, swooping overhead like breaking waves.

Casa Museu Gaudí

Park Güell, **T** 93 219 38 11. *Oct-Mar daily 1000-1800, Apr-Sep daily 1000-1900. €4.* **M** *Lesseps. Bus 24. Map 1, B8, p247*

Just off the main esplanade of the Park Güell is the small, pink Torre Rosa, Gaudí's home for the last 20 years of his life. It's now the Casa Museu Gaudí, a delightful little cottage covered in creamy swirls and topped with a *trencadi*-covered spire surmounted with a cross. Inside, the modest rooms are filled with plans and drawings, examples of Gaudí's furniture designs for the grand mansions of the Eixample and a sparse collection of his few personal possessions. His bedroom, which has been conserved much as he left it, contains a narrow bed, a copy of his prayer book and his death mask.

Seaside

The seafront in Barcelona was the main focus for the frenzy of construction and redevelopment which heralded the 1992 Olympic Games. The brash, glistening development of the Port Olímpic was erected in all its towering, neon-lit splendour and the old port was utterly transformed: now, yachts and gin palaces bob in the harbour and smart restaurants have spread their awnings onto broad boulevards. Behind all the tourist gimmicks and laminated menus of the Port Vell sprawls the old fishermen's neighbourhood of Barceloneta, a shabby, old-fashioned district of narrow streets and traditional bars serving fresh seafood tapas. Beyond Barceloneta stretch the city's six beaches, not especially lovely, but buzzing and always packed in summer. They edge past the glitzy new Port Olímpic and culminate at the seafront of another quiet old workers' district, Poble Nou, where a vast new complex has been constructed to host the city's Universal Forum of Cultures 2004, Barcelona's latest excuse to dress itself up and show off.

▸▸ See Sleeping p134, Eating and drinking p154, Bars and clubs p167

◉ Sights

Port Vell

M Barceloneta. Bus 14, 17, 19, 36, 39, 40, 45, 57, 59, 64 and 157. *Map 2, p249*

The Port Vell ('old port'), once a grimy working port, was transformed beyond recognition for the 1992 Olympics. The port's activity was shunted down the coast to an industrial zone (the Zona Franca) and the docks and warehouses were demolished or restored to house elegant restaurants, shops, a marina and a string of glittering new tourist attractions. Designed with tourists in mind, authentic Barcelonans are usually in the minority. Now, the crowds sweep down from the Ramblas and across the undulating

Rambla de Mar, a floating wooden walkway which leads to the Maremagnum shopping centre, the IMAX cinema (see p209) and the aquarium. The glassy **Maremagnum** building is stuffed full of shops, bars and restaurants, many with terraces overlooking the yacht-filled harbour, as well as a couple of popular (touristy) clubs.

L'Aquàrium

Moll d'Espanya-Port Vell, **T** 93 221 74 74. *Jul and Aug daily 0930-2300, Jun and Sep daily 0930-2130; Oct-May Mon-Fri 0930-2100, Sat-Sun 0930-2130. €11. €7.70 for children. **M** Barceloneta. Bus 14, 17, 19, 36, 39, 40, 45, 57, 59, 64 and 157. Map 2, J5, p249*

This is one of the largest aquariums in Europe, with dozens of exhibits and special interactive centres for kids, but the highlight is the enormous central tank, which you can coast through gently on a conveyor belt to a shmaltzy soundtrack as sharks and glinting shoals of silvery fish wheel overhead.

Museu d'Història de Catalunya

Plaça Pau Vila 3, **T** 93 225 47 58, www.mac.es *Tue-Sat 0930-1900, Sun and holidays 1000-1430. €3. **M** Barceloneta. Bus 14, 17, 19, 36, 39, 40, 45, 57, 59, 64 and 157. Map 2, I7, p249*

The old dockside access road is now the Passeig Joan de Borbó, an elegant promenade overlooking the marina. A former warehouse complex has been carefully renovated to become the Palau del Mar, which houses a string of elegant restaurants as well as the engaging Museu d'Història de Catalunya, devoted to the story of Catalunya's fortunes from prehistory to the present with plenty of interactive toys and gimmicks. The rooftop café has fantastic harbour views.

Sun, sea and dominoes
Barcelona's beaches are a summer playground for the young and hip.

Telefèric de Barceloneta
Mid-Oct-Feb daily 1030-1730, Mar-mid-Jun and mid-Sep-mid-Oct daily 1030-1900, mid-Jun-mid-Sep daily 1030-2000. €9 return.
M Barceloneta. Map 2, L5, p249

The Passeig Joan de Borbó culminates in the scruffy Plaça del Mar, overlooked by the **Torre de Sant Sebastià**, where cable cars begin their terrifying journey over the harbour and up to Montjuïc with a stop at the World Trade Center. The tower now holds a very swish designer restaurant (see p154) with more fabulous views.

Barceloneta
M Barceloneta. Bus 14, 17, 19, 36, 39, 40, 45, 57, 59, 64 and 157. Map 2, p249

While tourists sit under canvas umbrellas and sip their cocktails in between visits to the beach, the shabby little neighbourhood of Barceloneta just behind goes about its business undisturbed. Pre-Olympic reforms only touched the fringes of the old neighbourhood, leaving its unassuming, down-to-earth heart intact. The best time to appreciate it is during the Festa Major de Barceloneta, when the lumbering figure of Bum Bum careers down the narrow streets – showering sweets onto the children – and fireworks fly in the evenings, watched from boats in the harbour. There are no sights or monuments, but it's a great place for an evening wander, when you'll discover scruffy little bars serving up wine from the barrel and freshly fried sardines.

★ Beaches
M Barceloneta/Ciutadella-Vila Olímpica/Bogatell. Bus 10, 36, 41, 45, 57, 59, 157.   Map 2, L7/8, p249 and Map 5, p253

Beaches extend for several kilometres from Platja Sant Sebastià at the end of Passeig Joan de Borbó in Barceloneta all the way to Platja Nova Mar Bella near the Besos River. They are not the most beautiful nor the cleanest on the Mediterranean, but they are fun, easy to get to and conveniently lined with cafés and snack bars. You can rent a sun-lounger for about €3 if you want to work on your tan for a while, but if you'd prefer something more active, stroll along to Mar Bella beach where you can get sailing and wind-surfing lessons, or hire snorkelling equipment (see p197). The crowds thin out slightly the further you walk.

Vila Olímpica
M Ciutadella-Vila Olímpica. Bus 10, 17, 45, 59, 92.   Map 5, p253

Until Barcelona was nominated to host the 1992 Olympic games, the city's seafront was a vast conglomeration of abandoned docks, warehouses and slums linked by a grimy railway track. This unglamorous stretch of land became the site of the city's biggest and most ambitious architectural project: the Vila Olímpica (Olympic Village). Although the city's finest architects were commissioned for the project, the result is a sterile mini-city of boxy, uninspired buildings. Do as everyone else does and head straight for the beach by the **Port Olímpic**. This neon-lit development is the undisputed success of the Olympic Village and encompasses a marina, sailing school and leisure complex stuffed with cafés, restaurants and shops. Above it flaps Frank Gehry's enormous shimmering copper fish.

Universal Forum of Cultures

www.barcelona2004.org *M* *El Maresme i Forum. Bus 7.*
Map 1, H12, p247

Barcelona's new project for getting the world's attention is the Universal Forum of Cultures 2004. The Exhibitions of 1888 and 1929 and the 1992 Olympics were all used as a means of underpinning grandiose regeneration schemes for the less salubrious sections of the city and the city's latest scheme for the rundown area of Poble Nou is no different. The Universal Forum of Cultures takes place between 9 May and 26 September 2004 and aims to promote cultural diversity, world peace and a sustainable urban environment with a dizzying array of activities from debates and lectures to concerts and circus acts. The glistening modern park that will host the Forum is partly constructed on reclaimed land and some of the buildings will use solar power, in order to press home the environmental theme. A Virtual Forum linked with points all over the world will celebrate the spirit of cultural diversity. The whole project is five times as a big as the Olympic Village – almost 3 km of coastline has been covered.

● *Poble Nou, just beyond the boundaries of the Universal Forum development, is an old-fashioned, sleepy neighbourhood with few tourist sights but plenty of eccentric charm. There's a pretty, leafy Rambla, lined with some attractive Modernista homes as well as one of the oldest orxaterias in Barcelona, El Tió Ché (see p155) where you can slurp up a refreshing orxata or granizado in surroundings which have survived virtually unchanged for decades.*

Outskirts

There are plenty of things to do around the edge of the city centre in Barcelona. Few attractions – besides the giddy peak of Tibidabo with its funfair and the huge Nou Camp stadium in Les Corts – are on the tourist trail but some lesser known sights, like the quiet monastery of Pedralbes, which holds part of the fabulous Thyssen-Bornemisza art collection, are worth the trek. Sloping up the hills which circle the city are some of its loveliest parks, including the delightful wilderness of Parc de Collserola.

➤➤ *See Sleeping p134, Bars and clubs p168*

 Sights

Museu FC Barcelona President Nuñez

C Aristides Maillol 7-9, **T** 93 496 36 08, www.fcbarcelona.es
Mon-Sat 1000-1830, Sun and holidays 1000-1400. €5, €9 with guided tour of stadium. **M** *Collblanc. Bus 15, 52, 54, 56, 57, 75. Map 1, C2, p246 See also p195.*

The Nou Camp stadium is one of the largest in Europe, built to accommodate 120,000 fans. And yet getting tickets for a match – particularly with arch-rivals Real Madrid – can be unbelievably tough. The club's unofficial slogan during the last years of the Franco regime, *Barça, mes que un club* ('more than a club'), signalled the extent to which it had become the embodiment of Catalan nationalism; waving the distinctive blue and burgundy colours of the team became a substitute for the banned red and gold standard of Catalunya. The club has more than 108,000 members – including, appropriately for a club which has assumed near-religious significance in the eyes of its fans, the Pope. Memberships pass down through generations and babies are signed up only hours after their birth. If you can't get into a game, a visit to the Museu FC Barcelona is a worthy substitute. It holds an evocative collection of mementoes, cups and footballing paraphernalia which recount the club's fortunes over the past century. The museum also runs guided tours of the legendary stadium itself. The highlight for many fans is the European Cup, won at Wembley in 1992.

Palau Reial de Pedralbes (Museu de les Arts Decoratives/ Museu de Ceràmica)

Avda Diagonal 686. Museu de les Arts Decoratives, **T** 93 280 50 24, www.museuartsdecoratives.bcn.es Museu de Ceràmica, **T** 93 280 16 21, www.museuceramica.bcn.es *Both museums Tue-Sat 1000-1800, Sun and holidays 1000-1500. €3.50 each.* **M** *Palau Reial. Bus 7, 63, 67, 68 , 74, 75, 78. Map 1, B2, p246*

North of the western end of Avinguda Diagonal is the plush, affluent suburb of Pedralbes, spilling down the once-wooded slopes of Collserola. Just off the Diagonal is the stately mid-19th century Palau Reial de Pedralbes, originally built for the Güell family, Gaudí's benefactors. It now houses two quiet museums in separate wings; on the right is the **Museu de les Arts Decoratives**, with an eclectic selection of furniture, tapestries, glasswork and jewellery dating back to the Middle Ages. The opposite wing of the Palace holds the charming **Museu de Ceràmica** with an exceptional collection of pieces from the most important Spanish ceramics manufacturers stretching back over the last millennium. There's a small gallery with works by Picasso, Miró and the Catalan sculptor Josep Llorens Artigas, who gave Miró his first ceramics lessons. The quiet, shady gardens contain a tiny recently discovered fountain in the shape of an alligator, which has been attributed to Gaudí.

Museu Monestir Pedralbes

Baixada Monestir 9, **T** 93 203 92 82, www.museuhistoria.bcn.es
Tue-Sun 1000-1400. €4. **M** *Maria Cristina. FGC Reina Elisenda. Bus
22, 63, 64, 75. Map 1, A3, p246*

At the top of Avinguda Pedralbes is the lovely 14th-century
Monestir de Santa Maria de Pedralbes. The convent still houses a
small community of Poor Clares, but a section of it is open to the
public as the Museu Monestir Pedralbes. The unusual three-tiered
Gothic cloister, one of the best preserved in Europe, is a still,
contemplative arcade of slender columns, surrounding groves of
cypress trees, rose gardens and a small pond.

Col.lecció Thyssen-Bornemisza

Baixada Monestir 9, **T** 93 280 14 34, www.museothyssen.org
Tue-Sun 1000-1400. €3.50. **M** *Maria Cristina. FGC Reina Elisenda.
Bus 22, 63, 64, 75. Map 1, A3, p246*

Within the monastery, the former nuns' dormitories have been
remodelled to hold the excellent Col.lecció Thyssen- Bornemisza, a
selection of works prised from the Thyssen bequest held in Madrid.
There's a shimmering collection of gilded medieval paintings and
sculpture, including Fra Angelico's lovely masterpiece, the
glowing, rosy-cheeked *Madonna of Humility*, works by Tintoretto,
Titian, Veronese, Rubens and Tiepolo. Among the Spanish artists
are portraits by Velázquez and Zurbarán.

Parc de Collserola

Centre d'Informació del Parc, **T** 93 280 3552, http://pmpc.amb.es
Daily 0930-1500. FGC Baixador de Vallvidrera. Off map 1, p246

The most unexpected delight in Barcelona is this beautiful natural
park, which stretches for more than 6,500 ha across the undulating
Serra de Collserola, the ring of hills which contains the sprawling

> ### Smog and the Devil

According to legend, Tibidabo is where the Devil is supposed to have shown Christ the world's treasures spread out at his feet and tempted him with the words 'haec omnia **tibi dabo** si cadens adoraberis me' (All this will I give you if you will fall down and worship me). Not even this vision of the city curled around the sea in one direction and the Collserolas undulating gently inland towards Montserrat and the Pyrenees, were enough to tempt Christ, but the name stuck and the views are usually tremendous – at least when a salty blast of sea air lifts the smoggy pall.

city. Despite being hemmed in with towns on all sides, it's possible to completely forget the bustling city and stroll, ride or mountain-bike through wooded paths, between old *masies* (farmhouses), ancient chapels and half-forgotten springs. For information on the various activities and for maps, visit the helpful park information office, a (signposted) 10-minute walk from the FGC station.

Tibidabo

Funfair *late Mar-Apr Fri-Sun 1200-1900; May Thu-Sun 1200-1900; Jun Wed-Sun 1200-1900; Jul and Aug Mon-Thu, Sun 1200-2200, Fri and Sat 1200-0100; early Sep Mon-Thu 1200-2000, Fri and Sat 1200-2200; late Sep Sat-Sun 1200-2000; entrance and 6 rides €8, free to children under 1m 10cm, or €15 for a day pass offering unlimited rides, €4.50 to children under 1m 10cm. FGC to Avinguda Tibidabo on Plaça John F. Kennedy where the Tram Blau leaves for Plaça Dr Andreu. From here, a funicular railway makes the final ascent. Off map 1, p246*

Tibidibo, the highest peak of the Collserola hills which surround Barcelona, is the city's mountain of fun. At the summit, reached by a rickety tram and a funicular railway, is a bizarre (but dull) church and a great old-fashioned funfair, **Tibidabo Parc d'Attraciones**, with a Ferris wheel, dodgems and plenty of rides for little kids. The views across the city can be breathtaking on a clear day.

Torre de Collserola-Mirador

Ctra Vallvidrera-Tibidabo, **T** 93 406 93 54, www.torredecollserola.com *Sep-May Wed-Fri 1100-1430 and 1530-1900, Sat and Sun 1100-1900; Jun-Aug Wed-Fri 1100-1430 and 1530-2000, Sat and Sun 1100-2000. €4.60.*

From Tibidabo you can't miss the needle-like Torre de Collserola which spikes the horizon. A glass lift will whoosh you up to the mirador, with panoramic views stretching for miles in all directions. A free mini-train runs between the funfair and the tower in summer; otherwise you can walk, or take the T2 or 211 bus from outside the main entrance to the funfair.

Museu de la Ciència

Avda Teodor Roviralta 55, **T** 93 212 60 50, www.newmuseumofscience.com *Tue-Sun and holidays 1000-2000. €5. FGC Avda Tibidabo. Bus 17, 22, 58, 60, 73. Map 1, A6, p246*

At the bottom of Tibidabo is a big touchy-feely museum and planetarium set in an old Modernista asylum which has just reopened after a major overhaul. Most of the descriptions are in Catalan or Castilian, but there are enough gadgets to keep kids occupied for hours; best is a wonderful exhibit called *Toca, toca*! (touch, touch!), which shows kids how to pick up all kinds of peculiar Mediterranean creatures, from sea anemones to starfish.

Listings ◉

Museums and galleries

- **Casa Museu Gaudí** Gaudí's home in the Park Güell, p84.
- **Centre d'Art Santa Mònica (CSAM)** Temporary modern art exhibitions in a converted convent, p38.
- **Centre de Cultura Contemporània de Barcelona (CCCB)** Contemporary culture exhibitions in a dramatic building, p60.
- **Col.lecció Thyssen-Bornemisza** A spectacular collection of Old Masters in a graceful medieval setting, p92.
- **ForumCaixa** Excellent collection of contemporary art, p74.
- **Fundació Antoni Tàpies** The biggest collection of works by Spain's best-known living artist, in a Modernista building, p71.
- **Fundació Francisco Godia** Gothic and contemporary art, p71.
- **Fundació Miró** A spectacular, light-filled Miró museum, p77.
- **Galeria Olímpica** Videos, costume displays and photos, p77.
- **La Pedrera** (Centre Cultural Caixa Catalunya) Rooftop and informative museum covering Gaudí's entire output, p66.
- **Museu Barbier-Mueller d'Art Precolumbi** Sculpture, art and jewellery from the ancient cultures of the Americas, p51.
- **Museu d'Arqueologia de Catalunya (MAC)** Artefacts from ancient settlements of Catalunya, p79.
- **Museu d'Art Contemporani de Barcelona (MACBA)** Glassy building with contemporary art, p58.
- **Museu d'Història de Catalunya** Catalan history, with lots of interactive gadgets and audio-visuals, p86.
- **Museu d'Història de la Ciutat** Roman ruins of Barcino and the medieval royal palace and chapel, p111.
- **Museu de Cera** Celebrity waxworks, p38.
- **Museu de Ceràmica** Ceramics from around Spain, p91.
- **Museu de Geologia** Dusty fossils and rocks museum, p54.
- **Museu de l'Eròtica** Overpriced erotica, p36.

Listings

Museums and galleries

- **Museu de la Catedral** Tiny museum with just a handful of works, including one of the earliest oil paintings, p39.
- **Museu de la Ciència** Well-designed science museum, p94.
- **Museu de la Sagrada Família** The history of Gaudí's vast, unfinished cathedral, set in its crypt, p71.
- **Museu de les Arts Decoratives** Furniture and decorations from the medieval period to the present day, p91.
- **Museu de les Arts Escèniques** Temporary exhibitions on the performing arts in the spanking new Theatre City, p80.
- **Museu de Xocolata** The history of chocolate, p52.
- **Museu de Zoologia** Old-fashioned natural history museum, set in one of the earliest Modernista buildings, p53.
- **Museu Diocesà** Religious art and other objects, p41.
- **Museu Egipci de Barcelona** (Fundació Arqeològica Clos) Egyptian artefacts in a sleek, modern museum, p69.
- **Museu Etnolòlgic** World cultures exhibitions, p80.
- **Museu FC Barcelona President Nuñez** History of the world's most famous football club, p90.
- **Museu Frederic Marés** A vast, eccentric collection, from Romanesque sculpture to 19th-century fans, p41.
- **Museu Marítim** Fascinating maritime museum, p63.
- **Museu Monestir Pedralbes** Peaceful, elegant medieval monastery with a beautiful chapel and cloister, p92.
- **Museu Nacional d'Art de Catalunya** Collection of Romanesque, Gothic and, soon, modern art, p75.
- **Museu Picasso** An erratic collection of Picasso's work, p50.
- **Museu Tèxtil i d'Indumentària** Fashion through the ages, p50.
- **Pavelló Mies Van der Rohe** A recreation of Mies Van der Rohe's glassy, Rationalist pavilion, p74.

Around Barcelona

Montserrat 99

Monastery and popular pilgrimage site set high in the jagged cliffs of Montserrat, surrounded by a natural park with hiking trails. Get there by cable car or rack-and-pinion railway.

Sitges 101

Trendy Barcelonans hang out in this pretty, whitewashed seaside town famous for its nightlife, great beaches, restaurants and a sprinkling of Modernista villas.

Tarragona 104

Busy, prosperous city overlooking the sea, with spectacular Roman ruins, an ancient cathedral, great beaches and a lively port.

Girona 110

Elegant, ancient city with a twisting medieval core, magnificent cathedral, fascinating museums and a lively studenty buzz.

Figueres 114

Down-to-earth provincial town: Salvador Dalí's birthplace and home to his spectacular museum, one of the most visited in Spain.

Montserrat

The Monastery of Montserrat, clamped high to a dramatic reddish massif (Montserrat means 'jagged mountain') and home to a miraculous statue of the Virgin known as La Moreneta ('the little brown one') is one of the most popular day trips from Barcelona. The Montserrat mountains erupt surreally from the surrounding plain about 40 km from the city, as unreal as a painted backdrop: their peculiar silhouette inspired Gaudí's designs for the Sagrada Família and Wagner envisioned Sir Parsifal discovering the Holy Grail in their secret hollows. The most dramatic way to arrive is by cable car which sways on a tiny thread across the valley. The area around the monastery itself gets unpleasantly crowded (try to visit on weekdays), but you can escape to the surrounding Natural Park, with fantastic hiking trails linking tiny half-forgotten hermitages.

▶▶ *See Eating and drinking p156, Tourist information p30, Map 7 p256*

The FGC train (line R5) runs from Plaça d'Espanya to Aeri de Montserrat, for connections with the thrilling cable car ride to the monastery. The same train continues to Monistrol de Montserrat, where the newly restored cremallera *(rack-and-pinion railway) is an alternative 15-minute climb up. There are several combined tickets available. Return train plus cable car is €11.80; return plus* cremallera *€12. There is a daily Juliá bus to Montserrat from outside Sants station.*

◉ Sights

Basílica de Montserrat
Plaça del Monestir, **T** 93 877 77 01. *Mon-Fri 0730-1930, Sat and Sun 0730-2030.* Chapel of the Virgin *daily 0830-1030 and 1200-1815 (also 1930-2030 in Jul, Aug and Sep).* Free.

Montserrat has long been an important pilgrimage site, thanks to the sacred statue of La Moreneta ('the brown one'), the miraculous polychrome wooden statue of the Black Virgin and Child which now presides over the altar of the basilica and is Catalunya's Holy of Holies. Floods of pilgrims, particularly newly-weds, pour in to touch the statue; Montserrat is one of the most popular names for a girl in Catalunya. The biggest annual pilgrimage takes place on 27 April and there's another on 8 September. A passage on the right of the gloomy 19th-century Basilica (with flashing neon-lights) leads to the statue of La Moreneta encased in glass above the altar and you can join the queue to touch it and pray for a miracle.

● *The Escolania, one of the oldest children's choirs in Europe, sings daily at 1300 (Sundays and bank holidays at noon) and 1910 (Monday to Saturday) except in July.*

Museu d'Art de Montserrat
Plaça del Monestir, **T** 93 835 02 51. *Mid-Sep-Jun, Mon-Fri 1000-1800, Sat and Sun 0900-1830; Jul-mid-Sep daily 1000-1900. €5.50, children 6-12 €3.50, seniors and students €4.50.*

The monastery's museum is divided into three sections: a good collection of paintings from the 19th and 20th centuries, including works by Picasso, Dalí and Monet; a substantial selection of Spanish, Flemish and Italian Old Masters; and a collection of archaeological treasures from Mesopotamia, Egypt and Palestine.

A separate audio-visual display (Espai de Montserrat, daily 1000-1800, until 1945 in summer, €2) offers a glimpse into the daily life of the community of monks who still live here.

Parc Natural de Montserrat

Funicular Sant Joan every 20 mins, 7-min journey; Dec-Feb
Mon-Fri 1100-1615, Sat and Sun 1000-1645; Mar and Nov Mon-Fri
1100-1645, Sat-Sun 1000-1645; Apr-Jun, Sep and Oct daily
1000-1800; Jul and Aug daily 1000-1915; single €3.80, return
€6.10. Funicular Santa Cova every 20 mins, 3-min journey,
Apr-Oct daily 1000-1745, Nov-Mar Mon-Fri 1100-1645,
Sat and Sun 1000-1645; single €1.60, return €2.50.

Bus-loads of tourists, jostling crowds, souvenir stalls and a 1960s
cafeteria have largely stripped the area around the monastery of
any sense of spirituality or contemplation, but if you head out into
the surrounding park, it doesn't take long to lose the crowds. There
are two funiculars: the funicular Sant Joan heads up to the top of
the massif for spectacular views and another drops down to the
tiny chapel of Santa Cova, built on the site where the statue of La
Moreneta was discovered. Trails of various lengths and difficulties
lead from both and wind across the park (get information and
maps from the tourist information office); one visits each of the
abandoned 13 hermitages and chapels which are scattered around
the mountain. Experienced rock climbers can tackle the sheer cliffs.

Sitges

The belle of the whole coastline south of Barcelona is undoubtedly
Sitges, a whitewashed town clustered around a rosy church out on a
promontory. Famously trendy, it gets packed with hip Barcelonans on
summer weekends and has become a mecca for gay visitors, who put
the kick into its famously over-the-top celebrations for Carnival in early
spring. The town's Festa Major, dedicated to Sant Bartomeu at the end
of August, is also a great party, with traditional parades featuring
Catalan folkloric characters like Giants, Fatheads and Dragons. It also
has some of the finest long sandy beaches on the coast.

▸▸ *See Eating and drinking p156, Tourist information p30, Map 7 p256*

Sitges is on the main coastal train line between Murcia and Barcelona, although not all the high-speed trains stop here. There are regular (every 15-20 mins, journey time 25-30 mins, €2.15 single) local trains between Barcelona-Sants (or Passeig de Gràcia) and Sitges. There are regular daily bus services from the main bus station (Mon-Bus, T 93 993 75 11, journey time 35-50 mins, €2.80) but the train is more reliable and the views are fantastic.

◉ Sights

Cau Ferrat

C Fonollar s/n, T 93 894 03 64. *15 Jun-15 Sep Tue-Sun 1000-1400 and 1700-2100; 16 Sep-14 Jun Tue-Sun 1000-1330 and 1500-1830. €3.50; combined entrance to Sitges' three museums €5.40, valid for one month.*

Sitges' big reputation for partying began when the Modernista painter Santiago Rusiñol (one of the founders of Els Quatre Gats in Barcelona, see p47) set up home here in the 1890s. Two little fishermen's cottages leaning over a sheer cliff in the heart of the old town were expensively and flamboyantly renovated, the walls painted a glowing azure blue and hung with paintings by Rusiñol's friends, including Picasso. The place was crammed with a hoard of fantastical Catalan ironwork – Rusiñol called it the Cau Ferrat ('Den of Iron') – and it is now a fascinating museum. Rusiñol made the top floor into one huge neo-Gothic hall, which looks like a cross between a cathedral and a junk shop: it's stuffed full of ironwork, bric-a-brac, paintings and bits of ancient pottery and glass which Rusiñol dug up himself. There are also two minor paintings by El Greco, which were the star attraction of the 1894 Festa Modernista (Festival of Modernism), when they were brought from Barcelona by train and then hoisted aloft by four artists and taken in a solemn procession to their new home in the Cau Ferrat – for years, the residents of Sitges thought Senyor El Greco was one of Rusiñol's relatives. Rusiñol's home was always filled with artists, musicians and writers and he organized five Modernist Festivals between 1892 and 1899 to celebrate the new ideas that were being expounded. The wild antics which accompanied these festivals gained the town a heady reputation for bad behaviour which it has been gleefully cultivating ever since.

Museu Maricel

C Fonallar s/n, **T** 93 894 03 64. *15 Jun-15 Sep Tue-Sun 1000-1400 and 1700-2100; 16 Sep-14 Jun Tue-Fri 1000-1330 and 1500-1830, Sat 1000-1900, Sun 1000-1500. €3.50; combined entrance to Sitges' three museums €5.40, valid for 1 month.*

Next door to the Cau Ferrat is the Museu Maricel with a collection of art from the medieval period to the early 20th century displayed in a light-filled old mansion hanging over the sea (the views are breathtaking). On the top floor there's a small naval museum with models and plans.

Museu Romàntic

C Sant Gaudenci 1, **T** 93 894 03 64. *15 Jun-15 Sep Tue-Sun 1000-1400 and 1700-2100; 16 Sep-14 Jun Tue-Fri 1000-1330 and 1500-1830, Sat and Sun 1000-1900. €3.50, combined entrance to Sitges' three museums €5.40, valid for 1 month.*

The third of Sitges' museums is tucked away in a small street in the centre of the old town. In an elegant townhouse the Museu Romàntic recreates the life of an affluent Sitges family at the end of the 19th century. Stuffed with knick-knacks, engravings and period furniture and carriages, it also has a large collection of working music-boxes and another of antique dolls.

Beaches

See also Gay and lesbian, p199.

Few come to Sitges for the museums; beaches, bars and the certainty of a good time are what draw the hordes of trendy Barcelonans on summer weekends. Since the 1960s, it's also become a hugely popular gay resort and the southernmost beaches are predominantly gay. The long sandy beaches are invariably crowded and right at the southern end are a couple of pretty wild nudist beaches, one of which is gay.

Tarragona

Tarragona, imposingly perched on a rocky outcrop overlooking the sea, is one of the oldest cities in Spain and one of the most significant in Catalunya. The Romans established a military base here at the end of the 3rd century BC which played an important role in the conquest of the Iberian peninsula. They liked it so much that they decided to make Tarraco the capital of Hispania Citerior and built temples, baths, an amphitheatre, a circus and a forum, bequeathing a spectacular series of Roman monuments which are among the most extensive in Spain and were declared a World Heritage Site by UNESCO in 2000. Nowadays, it's a brisk, industrious city with a shadowy, picturesque old quarter curled around the unusual Gothic cathedral and a busy working harbour lined with great seafood restaurants.

▸▸ *See Eating and drinking p157, Tourist information p30, Map 7 p256*

There are frequent local and express trains from Barcelona-Sants to Tarragona (local trains single €5.50, journey time 70 mins; express trains single €10.50, journey time 60 mins). Bacoma, T 93 231 38 01 and Hispania, T 93 231 27 56, run regular bus services from the Estació del Nord. Tickets are around €6 and journey times roughly 90 mins, depending on traffic.

Fishy delights
Tarragona has some of the area's finest seafood restaurants, p157.

Sights

Catedral

Plaça de la Seu, **T** 977 23 86 85. *16 Mar-May, Mon-Sat 1000-1300 and 1600-1900; Jun to 16 Nov, Mon-Sat 1000-1900; 17 Nov-15 Mar, Mon-Sat 1000-1400. Closed Sun and religious holidays. €2.50/€1.60.*

At the heart of the old city stands the austerely beautiful Cathedral. Construction began at the end of the 12th century and was completed in 1331 and the cathedral is a perfect example of the transition from Romanesque to Gothic.

A wide staircase sweeps up to the main facade with an imposing Romanesque portal surrounded with 13th-century sculptures of the Virgin and the Apostles surmounted by a vast rose window. The cloister has delicately carved pinkish columns featuring a world of fabulous creatures, including one which depicts the 'Procession de las Ratas' – the story of the clever cat who outwitted the mice by playing dead and leapt up from his own funeral to gobble them up. Hidden in the medieval gloom of the church is a magnificent 15th-century alabaster altarpiece by Pere Joan and the entrance ticket includes a visit to the small **Museu Diocesano**, with a dusty collection of ecclesiastical treasures (including a reliquary containing St John the Baptist's finger) and a 15th-century tapestry of medieval life, *La Bona Vida*.

Museu Casa Castellarnau

C Cavallers 14, **T** 977 24 27 52. *Jun-Sep, Tue-Sat 0900-2100, Sun 0900-1400; Oct-May, Tue-Sat 0900-1900, Sun 1000-1400. €2.*

The main street of the old city, Carrer Major, heads down from the cathedral; off to the right is Carrer de Cavallers, the city's most aristocratic address during the medieval period. Nowadays the sounds of pianos, opera singing and trumpets from the Conservatory of Music float across it. A former mansion, which dates back to the early 15th century, has been beautifully refurbished to hold the Museu Casa Castellarnau with a graceful Gothic courtyard and rather patchy exhibits outlining the city's history. The second floor has retained its opulent 18th-century fittings, with vast chandeliers dripping from frescoed ceilings and preserves the interior of a pretty 18th-century pharmacy, moved here when the original premises just down the street collapsed.

Passeig Arqueològic

Avda Catalunya s/n, **T** 977 24 57 96. *Oct-May Tue-Sat 1000-1330 and 1630-1830, Sun 1000-1500; Jun-Sep Tue-Sat 0900-2100, Sun 1000-1500. €2.*

The old walls which still ring much of the old city have been converted into an attractive walkway known as the Passeig Arqueològic. It winds along the Roman walls built in the 3rd century BC on top of hefty Iberian fortifications and a stretch of 18th-century walls built by the British during the War of the Spanish Succession. There are stunning views out across the plains and around to the sea.

Museu Nacional Arqueològic

Plaça del Rei 5, **T** 977 23 62 09. *Jun-Sep Tue-Sat 1000-2000, Sun and holidays 1000-1400; Oct-May Tue-Sat 1000-1330 and 1600-1900. €2.40.*

On the edge of the old town, just off Plaça del Rei, the huge, airy National Archeological Museum holds an excellent collection of artefacts gathered from archaeological sites. It provides a vivid picture of life in Imperial Tarraco.

Museu de la Romanitat

Rambla Vell s/n, entrances on Plaça del Rei, or via the Circus on Rambla Vell, **T** 977 24 19 52. *Jun-Sep Tue-Sun 1000-2100; Oct-May Tue-Sat 0900-1900, Sun 1000-1500. €2.*

Next to the Archeological Museum, the Museum of Roman Artefacts is housed in the Praetorium tower, once home to Augustus and Hadrian and later the Kings of Aragón who built a castle on top of the Roman ruins. Computer-generated images of the Roman city give a sense of its magnificence two millennia ago. A glass lift swoops to the roof for dizzying views across the rooftops of the old town and it is also linked by vaulted underground passages to the ruins of the **Circ Romans** (Roman Circus), built in the first century AD to hold chariot races.

Balcó del Mediterrani

Rambla Vell s/n.

To the south of the old city lies the Rambla Vell, a handsome promenade which culminates in the famous Balcó del Mediterrani (Balcony of the Mediterranean), a mirador with beautiful views over the amphitheatre, the town's main beach (Platja del Miracle) and out to sea.

Amphitheatre

Parc del Miracle, **T** 977 24 25 79. *Jun-Sep Tue-Sat 1000-2000, Sun 1000-1400; Oct-May Tue-Sat 1000-1300 and 1600-1700, Sun 1000-1400. €2.*

Take the path below the Balcó del Mediterrani to reach the ancient amphitheatre, where gladiators and wild animals fought to the death. Three Christian martyrs were tortured to death here in AD 259 and a basilica was erected to them in the sixth century on the site of their martyrdom.

Museu i Necròpolis Paleocristians

Avda Ramón y Cajal 80, **T** 977 21 11 75. *Jun-Sep Mon-Sat 1000-1300 and 1630-2000, Sun 1000-1400; Oct-May Mon-Sat 1000-1330 and 1500-1730, Sun 1000-1400. €2.40.*

Out on the edge of town, there's another fascinating collection of Roman remains at the Museu i Necròpolis Paleocristians. Roman law forbade burials within the city walls, so the necropolis, still scattered with amphorae, plinths and inscribed tablets, was established well outside the ancient city. It was used for pagan and Christian burials and the museum currently houses an extensive collection of sarcophagi and glimmering mosaics gathered from the site. It is being refurbished to house a new Early Christian Museum, in recognition of the importance of the city where St Paul is said to have preached.

The Port and Tarragona's beaches
See also Eating and drinking, p157.

A good 20-minute walk from the old city is Tarragona's port, **El Serrallo**, its busy harbour liberally sprinkled with fishing boats and densely packed with seafood restaurants. They are all good and crowded at weekends, but it's worth heading into the streets behind the seafront to get a better deal. Platja del Miracle, the city's main beach, falls short of its fancy name: it's a perfectly decent city beach but it can get very crowded. There are better, quieter beaches north of the city, such as Arrabassada (take bus 1 or 9 from the Rambla Vella), about 4 km from the centre, or Sabinosa (another kilometre beyond Arrabassada), which is for nudists at its northern end.

Girona

Girona, Catalunya's second city, is an unexpected charmer, sprawling languidly around the confluence of the Rivers Ter and Onyar. The expansive modern city, with its leafy avenues lined with galleries and a handful of Modernista mansions, lies on the west side of the Onyar; on its eastern bank is the shadowy huddle of the ancient city which grew up around an early Iberian settlement. A ribbon of yellow-, orange- and ochre-painted houses, once attached to the city walls, hang over the river and behind them lies a medieval web of crooked alleys and narrow passages built on top of the Roman colony. A long-established university town, the big student population means the city's nightlife is almost as buzzy as Barcelona's and the arcaded streets and placid squares of the old city are lined with trendy shops, bars and restaurants.

➤➤ *See Eating and drinking p157, Tourist information p30, Map 7 p256*

*Trains run every 30 mins from Barcelona-Sants and the Passeig de Gràcia (regional trains €5.85, journey time 90 mins; express trains €11.50, journey time 80 mins). Barcelona Bus, **T** 93 232 04 59, has several daily services from Estació del Nord. For information on flying to Girona airport, see p23.*

◉ Sights

Centra Bonastruc Ça Porta/Museo de los Judeos en Catalunya

C de la Força s/n, **T** 972 21 67 61. *15 May -14 Nov, Mon-Sat 1000-2100, Sun and holidays 1000-1400; 15 Nov-14 May, 1000-1800, Sun and holidays 1000-1400. €2.*

Carrer de la Força follows the line of the Via Augusta and was the main artery of the medieval Jewish quarter, called El Call, which remains astonishingly intact. Halfway up it, the Centra Bonastruc

Ça Porta is built around the old Synagogue of Girona which is being painstakingly restored. It houses an institute of Jewish learning, as well as the fascinating Museo de los Judeos en Catalunya, which describes the development of the Jewish community from the first mention of the Call in 898 and offers an interesting insight into the beliefs and practices of the Cabalistas.

Museu d'Història de la Ciutat

C de la Força 27, **T** 972 22 22 29, museu@ajgirona.org *Tue-Sat 1000-1400 and 1700-1900, Sun 1000-1400, closed Mon except holidays. €2.*

The most gruesome sight in the Museum of the History of the City is the Capuchin cemetery (just inside the entrance on the right): the Capuchins dissected the bodies of dead monks on perforated benches and buried them in vertical tombs. The museum is housed in a sturdy 18th-century mansion with well laid-out exhibits documenting the history of the city from prehistoric times to the introduction of electricity and the computer age.

Catedral

Plaça de la Catedral s/n, **T** 972 21 44 26, www.lacatedraldegirona.com *Jul-Sep daily 1000-2000, Oct-Feb daily 1000-1400 and 1600-1800, Mar-Jun daily 1000-1400; cathedral free, museum and cloisters €3.50.*

Just beyond the History museum, the street opens up into the lovely Plaça de la Catedral, flanked by the 18th-century Casa Pastors (law courts) and the imposing Gothic Pia Almoina (almshouse). A broad flight of steps sweep up to the Cathedral, one of the grandest in Catalunya, with an elaborate Baroque facade topped with a frilly belltower. The present cathedral was begun in 1312, but a century later Guillem Bofill added a single, daring nave in defiance of a committee of architects who swore it wouldn't work; it's the largest in Europe, with an audacious 23-m span. The delicate Romanesque cloister with its intricately carved capitals is a remnant of the previous cathedral which occupied the spot, as is the Romanesque belltower, the Torre de Carlemany, which was incorporated into the new construction as a buttress. The Museu Capitular holds a fine collection of religious art, including a powerful 12th-century tapestry of the Creation (the best preserved Romanesque tapestry in Europe) and the *Còdex del Beatus* exquisitely illuminated by Mozerabic miniaturists during the 10th century.

Museu d'Art

Pujada de la Catedral 12, **T** 972 20 95 36, www.ddgi.es/museu
Mar-Sep Tue-Sat 1000-1900, Sun 1000-1400; Oct-Feb Tue-Sat 1000-1800, Sun 1000-1400. €2 /€1.50.

The former Episcopal Palace tucked behind the cathedral houses Girona's excellent Museu d'Art. An eclectic collection of painting, sculpture, furniture, glass, gold- and silverware from the Visigothic period until the 19th century is displayed in cavernous vaulted halls. There is a particularly fine piece from Bernat Martorell and paintings from Joaquim Vayreda – of the Olot school – and the bohemian dandy, Santiago Rusiñol.

Banys Àrabs

C Ferran El Catòlic, **T** 972 21 32 62. *Apr-Sep Mon-Sat 1000-1900, Sun 1000-1400; Oct-Mar Tue-Sun 1000-1400. €1.50/€0.75.*

The Banys Àrabs, through the Portal de Sobreportes, were built on a Roman model, perhaps by Moorish craftsmen, in the 13th century, and they are among the most well preserved in Spain. The loveliest area is the frigidarium (cold water pool), which is subtly illuminated by a skylight supported by a ring of slim columns. The niches are filled with changing contemporary art exhibitions and there's a little walkway across the rooftop too.

Sant Pere de Galligants (MAC)

Plaça de Sant Llúcia, **T** 972 20 26 32, www.mac.es *Jun-Sep, Tue-Sat 1030-1330 and 1600-1900; Oct-May, Tue-Sat 1000-1400 and 1600- 1800. €2/€1.50.* Passeig Arqueòlogic, *daily 1000-2000. Free.*

Across the empty riverbed of the tiny Riu Galligans is Sant Pere de Galligants, a sober 12th-century monastery with an unusual octagonal belltower and a fine cloister, which now houses an outpost of the Museu d'Arqueologia de Catalunya (see p 79). The holdings date from the Paleolithic to the medieval period, attractively displayed in the former church and scattered around the overgrown cloister and include Roman monuments and everyday objects like lamps and vases, a lead plaque inscribed with Iberian writing and Iberian and Greek memorial stones. From here, you can climb up to the **Passeig Arqueòlogic** for a panoramic stroll across the top of the old city walls with sweeping views out across the rooftops and the valley Ter.

Museu del Cinema

C Sèquia 1, **T** 972 41 30 47, www.museudelcinema.es
Tue-Fri 1000-1800, Sat 1000-2000, Sun 1100-1500. €3/€1.50.

On the far side of the river, in the 19th-century extension to old Girona, the lively Museu del Cinema has an excellent collection of film memorabilia gathered by local film-maker Tomas Mallol: the 25,000 exhibits cover everything from 15th-century shadow puppets and magic lanterns to a rare piece of original film by the Lumière brothers.

Figueres

Figueres is a likeable, down-to-earth provincial town which would be entirely unremarkable but for its most famous son: Salvador Dalí, who was born here at 6 Calle Monturiol on 11 May 1906. Thanks to its links with the celebrated artist and the spectacular Teatre-Museu Dalí, which Dalí himself established in the centre of the city, it has become one of the most popular tourist destinations in Spain. The Teatre-Museu is as flamboyant and bizarre as one would expect from a master of the absurd, but, once you've seen it, there's little to make you linger in Figueres.

▸▸ *See Eating and drinking p158, Tourist information p30, Map 7 p256*

There are frequent (every 30 mins) trains to Figueres via Girona from Estació-Sants and Passeig de Gràcia in Barcelona (regional single €8.40, journey time 2 hrs 10 mins; express single €13.50, journey time 1 hr 35 mins). Barcelona Bus, T 93 593 12 16, runs daily services from Barcelona to Figueres via Girona.

◉ Sights

Teatre-Museu Dalí
Plaça Gala i Salvador Dalí, T 972 51 18 00, www.dali-estate.org
Jul-Sep daily 0900-1915; Oct-Jun daily 1030-1715. Night visits in Aug only. €9/€6.50.

Attracting almost as many visitors as the Prado in Madrid, Dalí's suitably surreal Teatre-Museu Dalí strikes a flamboyant pose in the centre of the city. Other Catalans have always suspected that the Tramontana wind which rages through the city has affected the Figuerans in the head, but Dalí was undoubtedly the battiest of them all. The Teatre-Museu is topped with a huge glass latticed dome like a fly's eyeball and surrounded with giant boiled eggs and leaping figures; the walls are covered in squidgy protuberances, which, from a man who had a special toilet installed in order to better inspect his excrement and then wrote a book about it, can only be turds. His scatological obsessions have their roots in the earthy Catalan culture which puts a *Caganer* ('Crapper', see p40) just downwind of the manger in the traditional Nativity scene that decorates good Catalan homes at Christmas. Inside, the museum twists around a central courtyard strewn with old bones and skulls, in which a naked singing diva sprouts out of a Cadillac with a snake and a thorny rose; rooms and passages lead off into unexpected dead ends and recesses hold classical statues with drawers for stomachs, or a velvet curtain providing a lush backdrop to an old fish skeleton. Surrealism demanded the participation of its viewers and Dalí delighted in optical tricks; in the Mae West room, a sofa and a fireplace suddenly melt into the features of the great screen actress when viewed through a special eye-piece (suspended over a ladder supported by a plastic camel). In the Palau del Vent, a vast ceiling fresco depicts the ascension of Dalí and Gala (his adored wife and muse) into heaven, their enormous feet flapping as their bodies disappear into clouds. Dalí retired to the Torre Galatea (attached to the museum) at the end of his life and died here in 1989; he is buried behind a granite slab, so plain and simple that it's impossible not to suspect some kind of trick. Dedicated Dalí fans will want to make the trip to the other two corners of the Dalí Triangle: his whitewashed house overlooking a beautiful little cove near Cadaqués and Gala's former home at the Castell de Púbol (now the Castell Gala Dalí 'museum-house'), near Peratallada (www.dali-estate.org).

Museu de l'Empordà

Ramblas 2, **T** 972 50 23 05, www.museuemporda.org *Tue-Sat 1100-1900, Sun 1100-1400. €2/€1.*

The Teatre-Museu Dalí may be the top crowd-puller, but there are a couple of other museums in Figueres which are worth a glance on a rainy day. The Museu de l'Empordà has a collection of Roman artefacts, ceramics from the monastery of Sant Pere de Rodes and a surprisingly good collection of 19th and 20th century art, including works by Sorolla, Nonell and Tàpies, as well as pieces by Dalí himself.

Museu del Joguet de Catalunya

C Sant Pere 1, **T** 972 50 45 85, www.mjc-figueres.net *Mon-Sat 100-1300 and 1600-1900, Sun and holidays 1100-1330 (also 1700-1930 Jun-Sep). €4.70/€3.80.*

The privately owned (and expensive) Museu del Joguet de Catalunya has more than 4,000 delightfully old-fashioned toys – including some owned by Dalí, Miró and Lorca – from train sets and Meccano, dolls and dolls' houses to balls and spinning tops.

Castell de Sant Ferran

Pujada al Castell, **T** 972 50 60 94. *Jun-mid-Sep daily 1030-2000; Nov-Feb daily 1030-1400; Mar-Apr and mid-Sep-Oct daily 1030-1400 and 1600-1800. Free.*

Although it is still owned by the military, you can walk around the star-shaped walls and bastions of the huge 18th-century Castell de Sant Ferran to the north of Figueres. It was the last stronghold of the Republicans during the Civil War and used as a barracks for new recruits to the International Brigade before they were sent to Barcelona.

Sleeping

Barcelona is one of the most popular weekend destinations in Europe and finding a place to stay can be a nerve-shattering experience. The number of beds has increased dramatically, thanks to the 2004 Forum, but securing a hotel room is still a test of endurance. Book as early as possible and never just turn up and hope to find something. Note that many of the really cheap places will only take reservations on the day you want to arrive, but call early. Check out the online deals and if all else fails, get an agent to find you a bed (see below). Most of the cheaper places can be found in the old neighbourhoods in the centre of the city (the Barri Gòtic, La Ribera and the Raval) which are also the noisiest places to stay. The smartest (and quietest) places are generally concentrated in the Eixample. There are relatively few places near the seaside, although that will undoubtedly change after 2004 and you might want to think about staying in Gràcia to get a feel for Barcelona without the tourists. The nearest campsite is 7 km away.

€

Price

Sleeping codes

AL	€250 and over	**D**	€60-90
A	€180-250	**E**	€40-60
B	€130-180	**F**	€20-40
C	€90-130	**G**	€20 and under

Prices are for a double room in high season. Breakfast is not included, unless otherwise stated.

Las Ramblas and Plaça Reial

AL Le Meridien Barcelona, Ramblas 111, **T** 93 318 62 00, **F** 93 301 77 76, www.lemeridien-barcelona.com *M Plaça de Catalunya. Bus 14, 38, 59, 91. Map 2, C4, p254* Before the Hotel Arts (see p133) stole its thunder, this was Barcelona's swankiest hotel. It's still a favourite with visiting opera stars thanks to its superb location right on the Ramblas and there's a fine restaurant and all the luxury trimmings. Four king-size rooms have been adapted for the disabled.

C Hotel Ramblas, Ramblas 33, **T** 93 301 57 00, **F** 93 412 25 07, www.ramblashoteles.com *M Liceu or Drassanes. Bus 14, 38, 59, 91. Map 6, H2, p254* This is a crisp, modern hotel set behind a graceful 19th-century exterior. There isn't a great deal of character, but it does have a great location at the bottom of the Ramblas, not far from the Port Vell and the rooms are pretty good value. Choose a balcony over the street theatre of the Ramblas itself, or take in views of the Palau Güell from some of the interior rooms. Take ear plugs: like most hotels in Barcelona, the double-glazing doesn't quite keep out the sound of the relentless partiers.

D Continental, Ramblas 138, **T** 93 301 25 70, **F** 93 302 73 60, www.hotelcontinental.com *M Plaça de Catalunya. Bus 14, 38, 59,*

91.   *Map 2, B4, p248*   George Orwell wrote some of the pages of*Homage to Catalonia* in this welcoming, century-old hotel. It's surprisingly good value for the location and outer rooms have balconies overlooking the Ramblas. Prices depend on the views. Family rooms are good value at €100.

D Hotel Monegal, C Pelai 62, **T** 93 302 65 66, **F** 93 412 24 88, www.hotelmonegal.com *M Plaça de Catalunya. Bus 9, 14, 16, 17, 24, 38, 41, 42, 55, 58, 59, 66, 91, 141. Map 2, A4, p248*   Just off Plaça de Catalunya, this is a very good mid-range choice, with spacious and comfortable rooms (the best have balconies looking out over the square) and en-suite bathrooms. Standard prices are high, but look out for great special deals on their website.

E Barcelona House, C Escudellers 19, **T** 93 301 82 95, **F** 93 412 41 29. *M Liceu. Bus 14, 38, 59, 91. Map 6, G3, p254*   This hostel is one of the best options in the Barri Gòtic – hip, colourful and fun, with individually decorated rooms. These run the gamut from the completely over-the-top (gold ceilings in some) to the more restrained but manage to always be stylish. Each floor has a different colour scheme and the whole place has been newly painted. Downstairs there's a cool little café which doubles as the breakfast room.

E Hostal Fernando, C Ferran 31, **T/F** 93 301 79 93. *M Liceu. Bus 14, 17, 45, 59. Map 6, F4, p254*   A simple hostel offering plainly furnished rooms with check bedspreads and TVs and some en- suite rooms (those without bathrooms are cheaper). In a great location on one of the main arteries of the Barri Gòtic, it's a reasonably quiet hostel which attracts a slightly older and calmer clientele. They also offer dorm accommodation from €14 per person.

E Hotel Mare Nostrum, Ramblas 67, **T** 93 318 53 40, **F** 93 412 30 69. *M Liceu. Bus 14, 38, 59, 91. Map 6, D2, p254*

A good two-star hotel right on the Ramblas (the entrance is around the corner on Carrer Sant Pau), with modest en-suite rooms all with TV and a/c. The best open out onto the Ramblas; dark interior rooms should be avoided.

E Hotel Roma Reial, Plaça Reial 11, **T** 93 302 03 66, **F** 93 301 18 39. *M Liceu. Bus 14, 38, 59, 91. Map 6, G3, p254* A bright, friendly hotel in the corner of the buzzy Plaça Reial, this offers decent rooms and a bar with terrace on the square. Like all the accommodation on the square, it's best for night owls who don't mind the noise.

F Pensión Ambos Mundos, 10 Plaça Reial, **T** 93 318 79 70, **F** 93 412 23 63. *M Liceu. Bus 14, 38, 59, 91. Map 6, G3, p254* This attractive little pensión is situated above the laid-back bar of the same name on the square; there are a dozen very basic, tiled rooms with bathrooms, some with balconies looking out over the square. But the downside of the central location is the fact that the square is always noisy, so bring ear plugs if you don't plan to party.

F Pensión Las Flores, Ramblas 79, **T** 93 317 16 34. *M Liceu. Bus 14, 38, 59, 91. Map 6, D2, p254* This tiny pensión is hidden up a narrow staircase off the Ramblas. Rooms are spotless, but can get very stuffy in summer. Some have bathrooms and those at the front have balconies overlooking the prettiest, flower-filled section of the Ramblas; interior rooms are darker and less attractive.

G Albergue Kabul, Plaça Reial 17, **T** 93 318 51 90, **F** 93 301 40 34, www.kabul-hostel.com *M Liceu. Bus 14, 38, 59, 91. Map 6, G3, p254* Right on Plaça Reial, the Kabul offers dorms and rooms sleeping from two to 12 people. It's noisy, but the rooms have recently been given a long overdue lick of paint and you can't get any closer to the action. Facilities include TV and video in the lounge area, coin-operated internet and laundry.

Barri Gòtic

AL Colón, Avinguda de la Catedral 7, **T** 93 301 14 04,
F 93 317 29 15, www.hotelcolon.es **M** Jaume I. Bus 17, 19, 40,
45. Map 6, C8, p255 A discreetly luxurious hotel in a fantastic
location facing the Gothic cathedral (you pay more for a view), the
aristocratic Colón has all amenities including a piano bar and
restaurant; the upper rooms have terraces and all are decorated
with classic elegance. There are less atmospheric but cheaper
rooms in a modern annexe called Regina Colón around the corner.

C Suizo, Plaça del Angel 12, **T** 93 310 61 08, **F** 93 310 40 81,
www.gargallo-hotels.com **M** Jaume I. Bus 17, 19, 40, 45. Map 6, F9,
p255 This is a dignified, traditional hotel handily placed for the
sights of the Barri Gòtic. It faces the noisy Via Laietana but the best
rooms overlook the narrow passage called Baixada Llibreteria.

E Hostal Jardí, Plaça de Sant Josep Oriol 1, **T** 93 301 59 00,
F 93 318 36 64, sgs110sa@retemail.es **M** Jaume I. Bus 14, 38, 59,
91. Map 6, D4, p254 Book well in advance if you want to get a
room at this extremely popular hostal; the nicest rooms overlook
the leafy Plaça del Pi, one of the main hubs of the Old City. The
simpler, less expensive rooms at the back look out onto a patio.

E Hostal Rembrandt, C Portaferrissa 23, **T/F** 93 318 10 11.
M Liceu. Bus 14, 38, 59, 91. Map 6, B5, p254 Spotless, good-sized
rooms decorated with 1970s wicker furniture and prints, many
with balconies overlooking the busy shopping street (which makes
it quiet by night – a real rarity among budget accommodation in
this city).

E-F Avinyó 42, C Avinyó 42, **T** 93 318 79 45, **F** 93 318 68 93,
www.hostelavinyo.com **M** Jaume I. Bus 14, 38, 59, 91. Map 6, G5,
p254 Very plain, very basic and very cheap, this is an excellent

budget choice close to the art school, right on a hip, narrow little street of fashion boutiques and bars. Rooms come with and without bathrooms.

G Itaca Hostel, C Ripoll 21, **T** 93 301 97 51, www.itacahostel.com *M Jaume I. Bus 17, 19, 40, 45. Map 6, B8, p255* A bright, friendly private youth hostel with colourful murals and laid-back owners. Dormitory accommodation is in large rooms with balconies, plus there's one twin room with en-suite bathroom. Facilities include a café-bar and internet.

La Ribera

✱**C Hotel Park**, Avda Marquès de l'Argentera 11, **T** 93 319 60 00, **F** 93 319 45 19, www.parkhotelbarcelona.com *M Barceloneta. Bus 14, 39, 51. Map 2, G8, p248* Built in the early 1950s by the celebrated architect Antoni de Moragas, the Hotel Park was renovated in 1990 by Moragas's son using the original plans. It's a narrow, slim hotel with good-sized balconies looking out towards Barceloneta, an exquisite interior wraparound staircase and comfortable, well-equipped rooms decorated with stylish simplicity. There's also a slick, expensive, Michelin-starred restaurant (www.restauranteabac.biz).

C Hotel Urquinaona, Ronda de Sant Pere 24, **T** 93 268 13 36, **F** 93 295 41 37, www.hotelurquinaona.com *M Urquinaona. Bus 14, 39, 40, 41, 42, 55, 141. Map 2, A7, p248* This is a friendly, well-equipped little hotel, offering unexpected extras like internet access. The rooms all have satellite TV and a/c, although recent price hikes mean it is not the bargain it used to be. Triple rooms are available.

✱**C Banys Orientals**, C Argentería 37, **T** 93 269 84 90, **F** 93 268 84 61, www.hotelbanysorientals.com *M Jaume I. Map 6, G10, p255* This is a chic little boutique-style hotel in a perfect location close to

★ Budget hotels

Best

- Gat Raval (El Raval), p126
- Hostal Jardí (Barri Gòtic), p122
- Peninsular (El Raval), p127
- Sea Point Hostel (Seaside), p134
- Hostal Windsor (Eixample), p132

the Picasso Museum. Rooms are a little small, but are furnished with sleek modern fabrics in bold prints.

E Hostel Levante, **T** 93 317 95 65, **F** 93 317 05 26, www.hostellevante.com **M** Liceu, Jaime I. Bus 14, 17, 59, 64. *Map 6, G5, p254* This hostel is set in a 19th-century building which apparently housed the brothel where Picasso got his inspiration for the *Demoiselles d'Avignon*. Nowadays, it's quiet and popular with long-term students, although it's still very convenient for the Barri Gòtic's hectic nightlife. The first-floor rooms have big windows but all the rooms are different so it would be best to take a look at them if you can. Some of the nicest have stone balconies.

F Hostal Fontanella, Via Laietana 71, **T/F** 93 317 59 43. **M** Urquinaona. *Map 2, A6, p248* This cosy little hostel is located very close to Plaça Urquinaona. The traffic can be a bit of a problem, but the owner is very welcoming and looks after her guests very well. Rooms are clean and simple and decorated with flowery prints. Rooms without bathrooms drop a price category.

G BCN Loft, C Mare de Deu del Pilar 7, no **T**, book online at www.bcnloft.com **M** Urqinaonoa. Bus 14, 39, 40, 41, 42, 55, 141. *Map 6, A11, p255* This is a really unusual place offering dormitory accommodation (two separate rooms for men and women) in a huge, light-filled loft space. It's furnished with the typical

Barcelona talent for design, with bright colours and funky modern fabrics. There is a shared kitchen and lounge area.

G Gothic Point Youth Hostel, C Vigatans 5, **T** 93 268 78 08, **F** 93 310 77 55, www.gothicpoint.com **M** *Jaume I. Bus 17, 19, 40, 45. Map 6, G10, p255* This hostel opened in 2001 and has neatly sussed out what budget travellers really want. The dormitories (all with heating and a/c) are split into 'modules', each with their own light and side table and the reasonable prices (from €21 per night) include breakfast . Facilities include bike hire, free internet access and a big terrace. They also run the Sea Point Hostel (see p134).

G Hostal Hedy Holiday, C Buenaventura Muñoz 4, **T** 93 300 57 85, **F** 93 300 94 44. **M** *Arc de Triomf. Bus 14, 40, 41, 42, 141. Map 1, G8, p247* Opened in 2000, the Hedy is close to the Parc de la Ciutadella and offers large, airy dorms which sleep between six and eight people, a bar-café and internet access.

El Raval

AL Hotel Ambassador, C del Pintor Fortuny 13, **T** 93 412 05 30, **F** 93 302 79 77. **M** *Plaça de Catalunya. Bus 14, 38, 59, 91. Map 2, C3, p248* A graceful, modern hotel just off the Ramblas with a piano bar and rooftop terrace with garden and swimming pool. The rooms are quietly elegant, although those on the upper floors are sunnier. However, it is surprisingly expensive, even by four-star hotel standards.

AL Principal, C Junta del Comerç 8, **T** 93 318 89 70, **F** 93 412 08 19, www.hotelprincipal.es **M** *Liceu. Bus 14, 38, 59, 91. Map 2, E3, p248* The nicest of several budget options along this street, the Principal is possibly the most eccentric, with florid rooms decorated with a mixture of antiques and knick-knacks. They are all equipped with TV, a/c, en-suite bathrooms and double-glazing which keeps the street noise out. The friendly owners also run the slightly cheaper Joventut (up the street at number 12 with the same email and website).

B Gaudí, C Nou de la Rambla 12, **T** 93 317 90 32, **F** 93 412 26 36, www.hotelgaudi.es *M Liceu. Bus 14, 38, 59, 91. Map 6, G1, p254*
This has a Gaudíesque fountain of broken tiles just inside the door, but you can get a glimpse of the real thing from the third-floor rooms which overlook the Palau Güell (see p61) opposite. Prices are fairly high for what's on offer and the smaller interior rooms lack views.

B Hosteria Grau, C Ramelleres 27, **T** 93 301 81 35, **F** 93 317 68 25. *M Liceu. Bus 14, 38, 59, 91, 120. Map 2, B3, p248*
Simple but warm and friendly, the Hosteria Grau offers very basic rooms furnished with floral fabrics with or without bathrooms plus five small apartments (from €70 per night) for self-catering. There's a cosy lounge area and the exceptionally helpful owners will happily give you tips on where to eat and what to do. Lack of a/c makes it pretty stuffy in summer.

B San Agustín, Plaça Sant Agustí 3, **T** 93 318 16 58, **F** 93 317 29 28, www.hotelsa.com *M Liceu. Bus 14, 38, 59, 91. Map 6, D1, p254* One of the city's oldest hotels, this graceful, apricot-coloured building overlooks the pretty Plaça Sant Agustí. Top-floor rooms have wooden beams and wonderful views, but are more expensive.

B-C Gat Raval, C Joaquin Costa 44, **T** 93 481 66 70, **F** 93 342 66 97, www.gataccommodation.com *M Universitat. Bus 64, 91, 141, 120. Map 2, A2, p248* A hip *hostal* painted in black, white and lime green on one of the Raval's funkiest streets. The modern rooms are bright, clean and well equipped, but their internet booking system doesn't work yet, so call to confirm.

C **Mesón de Castilla**, C de Valldonzella 5, **T** 93 318 21 82, **F** 93 412 40 20, www.husa.es *M Universitat. Bus 64, 91, 141, 120. Map 2, A3, p248* A chain hotel with a family feel. Breakfast is served out on the pretty interior patio garden and rooms are furnished in warm colourful fabrics and wicker. They also have some good-sized family rooms.

C **Universal**, Avda Paral.lel 76-80, **T** 93 567 74 47, **F** 93 567 74 40. *M Paral.lel. Bus 20, 36, 57, 64, 91, 120, 157. Map 1, G5, p246* A glassy, modern hotel, this is more stylish than most and there are often special deals which can cut prices considerably. Rooms have a vaguely Japanese, minimalist feel, with lots of wood, plain fabrics and elegant fittings. Facilities include a small pool, restaurant, solarium and tiny gym. Staff are unfailingly courteous and helpful.

D **España**, C Sant Pau 9-11, **T** 93 318 17 58, **F** 93 317 11 34 , www.hotelespanya.com *M Liceu. Bus 14, 38, 59, 91. Map 6, E1, p254* The España is marked on every tourist map thanks to Domènech i Montaner's stunning murals and swirling wooden fittings on the ground floor. Disappointingly, rooms are grimly functional; some at least open out onto a delightful interior terrace. Service can be surly.

D-E **Peninsular**, C de Sant Pau 34-36, **T** 93 302 31 38, **F** 93 412 36 99. *M Liceu. Bus 14, 38, 59, 91. Map 6, E1, p254* The Peninsular is a one of the best moderately priced options in the city and is set in an old convent almost opposite the Hotel España. There's an utterly charming interior patio crammed with trailing plants and greenery and lots of pretty Modernista detailing. The rooms are plain and basic, but they are still perfectly comfortable and offer exceptional value.

E **Hostal Morató**, C Sant Ramon 29, **T** 93 442 36 69, **F** 93 324 90 05, www.hostalmorato.com *M Liceu. Bus 14, 38, 59, 91,*

★ **Style hotels**

Best

- Actual (Eixample), p130
- Banys Orientals (La Ribera), p123
- Claris (Eixample), p129
- Hostal Palacios (Eixample), p130
- Park (La Ribera), p123

120. *Map 2, F2, p248* A basic, no-frills *pensión* in the heart of the Raval; all rooms are light, reasonably equipped and offer small balconies. Those without bathrooms offer better value than those with. There's a pleasant little café downstairs and it's well located for the Raval's buzzing nightlife.

F La Terassa, C Junta del Comerç 11, **T** 93 302 51 74, **F** 93 301 21 88. *M Liceu. Bus 14, 38, 59, 91. Map 2, E3, p248* This is a very popular pensión run by the same people as the Jardí (see p122); some rooms have balconies overlooking the street, or the pretty interior patio where breakfast is served in summer.

G Barcelona Mar Youth Hostel, C Sant Pau 80, **T** 93 324 85 30, **F** 93 324 85 31, www.youthhostel-barcelona.com *M Liceu. Bus 14, 38, 59, 91. Map 2, E2, p248* A big, new popular hostel which offers all kinds of activities including walking tours and pub crawls. It's not for quiet types, but it's a good bet if you are looking to make friends. There's a laundry, internet access and bike rental service. Accommodation is in dorms with six to 16 beds, but each have their own 'module' and there are also single, double and triple rooms available. Prices include breakfast.

G Ideal Youth Hostel. C Unió 12, **T** 93 342 61 77, **F** 93 412 38 48, www.idealhostel.com *M Liceu. Bus 14, 38, 59, 91. Map 6, F2, p254* Just off Las Ramblas, this is a good bet for backpackers. The interior of the historic building has been brightly decorated and it's popular with young travellers. It offers free internet access, a small café area and dorm-style rooms for four, six or eight people.

Eixample

AL Claris, C de Pau Claris 150, **T** 93 487 62 62, **F** 93 215 79 70, www.derbyhotels.es *M Passeig de Gràcia. Bus 7, 16, 17, 22, 24, 28. Map 3, H6, p251* In an old palace, this is one of the most fashionable and stylish hotels in the city and a favourite with pop stars and the fashion pack. Rooms and suites are individually decorated with luxurious fabrics, high-tech fittings and an elegant mix of sleek contemporary furniture and beautiful art and antiques. There's also a tranquil Japanese garden and rooftop pool to relax in.

AL Gallery Hotel, C Roselló 249, **T** 93 415 99 11, **F** 93 415 91 84, www.galleryhotel.com *M Diagonal. Bus 7, 16, 17, 22, 24, 28. Map 3, F4, p250* A chic, modern hotel with 110 sleek, spacious rooms elegantly decorated with state-of-the-art fittings, luxurious fabrics and large marble bathrooms. The facilities include a sauna, fitness centre, fine restaurant and bar, plus a business centre with complimentary facilities. Suites start at €300. Look out for special deals on their website which can halve standard prices.

AL Ritz, Gran Via des les Corts Catalanes 668, **T** 93 510 11 30, **F** 93 318 01 48, www.ritz-barcelona.com *M Tetuan. Bus 6, 7, 54, 56, 62. Map 3, L7, p251* Classic luxury, with all the Belle Epoque trimmings. The Ritz opened in 1919 and has hosted everyone from Ava Gardner to Salvador Dalí (who holed up in room 110). The rooms are still delightfully old fashioned with ornate fireplaces and plush drapes and fittings. The bathrooms in the deluxe rooms are magnificent, with marble, Roman-style baths and mosaic decoration. There's also a very fine restaurant, the Diana, which is open to non-residents, plus a health club and beauty centre.

✱ B Actual, C Rosselló 238, **T** 93 552 05 50, www.hotelactual.com *M Diagonal. Bus 7, 16, 17, 22, 24, 28. Map 3, G4, p251* Actual is a trendy new hotel , fashionably decorated in the slickest minimalist style, with plenty of white marble and dark wood. The location can't be beaten – it overlooks the Passeig de Grácia on the same block as La Pedrera. The rooms are small but impeccably furnished with crisp white fabrics and ultra-modern bathrooms and fittings. It also offers triple rooms, which are perfect for families and regularly posts special offers on its website.

B Prestige, Passeig de Gràcia 62, **T** 93 272 41 80, **F** 93 272 41 81, www.prestigepaseodegracia.com *M Passeig de Gràcia. Bus 7, 16, 17, 22, 24, 28. Map 3, I6, p251* This new (2002) and ultra-stylish hotel is in a perfect location on the beautiful Passeig de Gràcia. The building dates from the 1930s, but the interior is the epitome of chic, minimalist design. The rooms have high-quality fittings including Bang and Olufsen TVs and music systems, a free mini-bar and crisp white furnishings and drapes. Facilities include 24-hour room service and a gym and beauty centre. There's an oriental garden and in the futuristic Zeroom you'll find a small library on Barcelona full of the latest glossy coffee-table books.

✱ C Hostal Palacios, Rambla de Catalunya 27, **T** 93 301 30 79, **F** 93 301 37 92. www.hostalpalacios.com *M Passeig de Gràcia. Bus 7, 50, 54, 56, 67, 68. Map 3, K4, p251* A lovely *hostal* with just a handful of rooms in a magnificently restored Modernista building on the elegant Rambla de Catalunya. You'll find the original floor tiles, exquisitely carved wooden doors and a comfortable lounge area with internet access and even a piano. The delightful rooms have retained their swirling Modernista mouldings but the bathrooms are modern and pristine and the decor is a charming mix of crisp modern fabrics and antique furnishings.

D Hostal Plaza, C Fontanella 18, **T/F** *93 301 01 39,* www.plazahostal.com *M Passeig de Gràcia. Bus 7, 16, 17, 22, 24, 28. Map 2, B6, p248* Run by a very friendly and welcoming family, the Plaza offers simple rooms with showers and fans. Guests have use of a TV room, fridge and freezer and there's even a laundry service, but prices reflect the smart neighbourhood rather than the facilities.

D Hotel Paseo de Gràcia, Passeig de Gràcia 102, **T** *93 215 58 24,* **F** *93 215 06 03. M Passeig de Gràcia. Bus 7, 16, 17, 22, 24, 28. Map 3, F5, p250* A simple, friendly modern hotel in a superb location. The rooms are basic and the fittings are all pretty dated, but they all have phones and TVs and the staff are very helpful. It doesn't ooze charm, but prices are good value and the best rooms have wonderful views over the Passeig de Gràcia.

E Hostal Central Barcelona, C Diputació 346, Principal 2a, **T** *93 245 19 81,* **F** *93 231 83 07. M Tetuán. Bus 6, 19, 50, 51, 55. Map 3, K9, p251* A small, welcoming *hostal* in a creamy Modernista mansion with recently renovated rooms. These are all simple, although many have retained original features like pretty stained glass and plasterwork. Most have en-suite bathrooms. It's off the beaten track, but still handy for all the major sights. Triples are available.

E Hostal Edén, C Balmes 55, **T** *93 454 73 63,* **F** *93 350 27 02,* hostaleden@hotmail.com *M Passeig de Gràcia. Bus 7, 16, 17, 63, 67, 68. Map 3, J4, p251* A quirky and eccentric *pensión* in a rambling old Eixample building. The rooms are mixed – some have unexpected amenities like fridges, whirlpools and tiny terracotta patios, but others are small, dark, stuffy and, in some cases, windowless. Be sure you make it very clear when you book that you want one of the better rooms. Coin-operated internet access in the tiny lounge area.

E Hotel Ginebra, Rambla de Catalunya 1, 3º, **T** 93 317 10 63, **F** 93 317 55 65. *M Plaça de Catalunya. All buses to Plaça de Catalunya. Map 3, L5, p251* A friendly, cosy hotel in a graceful old building just off Plaça de Catalunya: rooms are double glazed, well equipped and some have balconies with views across the square. Excellent value.

E Hostal Windsor, Rambla de Catalunya 84, **T** 93 215 11 98. *M Diagonal. Bus 20, 43, 44. Map 3, H5, p251* A very popular place in a turn-of-the-century house, with good-sized rooms decked out in pure 1970s decor, this offers good value and a quiet location on the leafy Rambla de Catalunya. Interior rooms are darker and more cramped and none offer a/c which can be a problem in the sticky height of summer. The rooms with balconies and views are the ones to go for.

F Pensión Rondas, C Girona 4, **T/F** 93 232 51 02. *M Urquinaona. Bus 19, 39, 40, 41, 42, 55, 141. Map 2, B8, p248* This delightful little *pensión*, in a good quiet location, is run by a friendly brother and sister with a handful of spotless, if spartan, rooms (some with en-suite bathrooms). The wonderful wooden lift looks like a museum piece.

Gràcia and the Park Güell

E Pensión Abete, C Gran de Gràcia 67, **T** 93 218 55 24. *M Fontana. Bus 22, 24, 28, 87. Map 3, C6, p250* A simple, family-run *pensión* with basic, pleasant rooms, which is very friendly and well placed for the Gràcia nightlife.

Seaside

AL Arts Barcelona, C Marina 19-21, **T** 93 221 10 00,
F 93 221 10 70, www.ritzcarlton.com *M Ciutadella-Vila Olímpica.
Bus 10, 45, 59, 71, 92. Map 5, E4, p253* Easily the most glamorous
hotel in the city, the Hotel Arts is set in one of the enormous glassy
towers at the entrance to the Port Olímpic. It was inaugurated in
1992 and offers 33 floors of unbridled luxury, including an indoor
pool, an outdoor pool, a fine restaurant, a piano bar overlooking
the hotel gardens and the sea, a sauna, a gym and a beauty centre.

AL Grand Marina, Moll de Barcelona s/n, **T** 93 603 90 00,
F 93 603 90 00, www.grandmarinahotel.com *M Drassanes.
Bus 20. Map 2, K2, p249* This huge hotel in the World Trade Center
complex overlooks the port with stylish and spacious rooms with
large bathrooms and internet connection in all rooms. There's
also a gym, sauna, jacuzzi , outdoor swimming pool and a well-
regarded if expensive restaurant with panoramic views. It contains
an important collection of contemporary art. On the downside,
it feels rather corporate and anonymous. Suites start at €500.

B Hotel H10 Marina, Avda Bogatell, 64-68, **T** 93 309 79 17,
F 93 300 33 10, www.h10.es *M Ciutadella-Vila Olímpica. Bus 10, 71,
92. Map 5, A6, p253* A brand-new hotel (opened July 2003) right
by the Port Olímpic, with a restaurant, bars, outdoor swimming
pool and a Wellness Centre with heated pool, jacuzzi, gym and
treatment booths. It's huge (there are 250 rooms), all crisply
modern and the service makes up for the slightly sterile
atmosphere. There are often great deals on their website.

E Hostel Poble Nou, C Taulat 30, **T** 93 221 26 01,
www.hostalpoblenou.com *M Poblenou. Bus 6, 36, 92. Map 1, H10,
p247* This is a small and welcoming guest house with just five airy,
stylish rooms, in a charming and sensitively renovated building

dating back to 1930. It is set in the quiet and arty neighbourhood of Poble Nou, which means it is close to the beaches and the location of the Universal Forum of Cultures 2004. It's a 10-minute metro ride from the city centre, but there are plenty of shops, cafés and restaurants on the doorstep. Apartments are also available.

G Sea Point Hostel, Plaça del Mar 1-4, **T** 93 224 70 75, **F** 93 232 14 83, www.seapointhostel.com *M Barceloneta. Bus 17, 39, 64. Map 2, L6, p249* Right next to the San Sebastian beach in Barceloneta, this opened in summer 2002 and offers all kind of amenities including internet access and bike hire. Dorms sleep four, six or eight, all with heating and a/c. Unusually for Barcelona, breakfast is included in the price.

Outskirts

AL Relais de Orsà, C Mont d'Orsà 35, **T** 93 406 94 11, **F** 93 406 94 71, www.relaisdorsa.com *FGC to Peu del Funicular, then funicular to Vallvidrera.* With just nine elegant rooms in an luxurious Modernista *palau*, this is a delightful hotel in the hilltop town of Vallvidrera. Set in luxuriant gardens, it has a small pool but if you can tear yourself away, it's also close to the attractions of Tibidabo and is a perfect base for walking in the Parc de Collserola. Views from the top of the village are astounding.

B-C Turó de Vilana, C Vilana 7, **T** 93 434 03 63, **F** 93 418 89 03, www.turodevilana.com *FGC Sarrià Off map 1, p246* Gleaming attractive and modern, with stylish decor, this hotel is located in Tibidabo, not far from Norman Foster's telecommunications tower and the Parc de Collserola. There are only 20 rooms, all elegantly decorated and very well equipped. Prices drop at weekends.

Eating and drinking

The Catalans are renowned for their cuisine. The dishes are often simple and rely on the freshness of the local ingredients. The Catalan staple, for example, is *pa amb tomàquet*, bread rubbed with fresh tomatoes, drizzled with olive oil and salt. With extra toppings (like ham or cheese) it becomes a *torrade*. Meat and fish are often served simply grilled, or cooked slowly in the oven (*al horno*) in a tomato-based sauce. There are some delicious vegetable dishes – like the refreshing *escalivada*, a salad of roasted aubergine, peppers and onions, or *espinacas a la catalana*, spinach cooked with pine nuts and raisins. Rice is also popular, with variations on the famous Valencian dish *paella* like *arros nègre*, rice cooked with squid ink and shellfish, or *fideuà*, which is made with tiny noodles cooked in with meat and fish. The most popular Catalan dessert is *crema Catalana*, a local version of crème brûlée, or you could finish up with local curd cheese drizzled with honey, *mel i mató*. Wash it all down with Catalan wine (perhaps a sturdy red from Penedes or the delicious sparkling cava) or local Estrella beer.

Barcelonans eat breakfast on the run, usually a milky coffee (*café amb llet/café con leche*) and a pastry at around 0730 or 0800 in their local café-bar. Lunch is taken seriously and eaten late, usually around 1400, when many restaurants offer a special fixed-price menu with at least two courses plus a drink. Tapas is not as much of a tradition in Barcelona as in other parts of Spain, but a few evening drinks with some simple tapas is becoming increasingly common. There are plenty of old-fashioned bars near the harbour which offer fresh seafood tapas – like grilled sardines – but the most common Catalan tapas are *truita* (*tortilla*: thick omelettes), local cheeses or *embutits* (charcuterie). Dinner is rarely eaten before 2100 and tends to be lighter than the midday meal.

Las Ramblas and Plaça Reial

Restaurants

€€€ **Rúccula**, World Trade Centre, Moll de Barcelona, T 93 508 82 68. *Mon-Sat 1300-1600, 2030-2345, Sun 1300-1600. M Drassanes. Bus 20. Map 6, H2, p254* Fabulous views over the Mediterranean and adventurous, exquisite Catalan cuisine pull in the crowds at this glossy, minimalist and very chic restaurant in the World Trade Centre. A jazz singer and pianist regale the diners in the evenings.

€€ **Amaya**, Las Ramblas 24, **T** 93 302 10 37. *Daily 1300-1700, 2030-0000.* **M** *Drassanes. Bus 14, 38, 59, 91. Map 6, H2, p254* Despite its unprepossessing exterior, Amaya is an excellent Basque restaurant which is popular with everyone from local businessmen to opera stars from the Liceu. (Fans of Pepe Carvalho, Montalbán's laconic gourmet detective, will recognize the restaurant as a favourite.) Try the house speciality of *kokotxas a la vasca* (hake cheeks cooked in a delicate sauce) and there's a terrace on the Ramblas in summer.

€€ **Egipte**, Las Ramblas 79, **T** 93 317 95 45, www.garbi.com/egipte *Daily 1300-1600, 2000-0000.* **M** *Liceu. Bus 14, 38, 59, 91. Map 6, D2, p254* It can be hard to escape the endless fast-food joints on the Ramblas, but the Egipte, set in an elegant 18th-century building, is always a good bet. It offers a wide choice of popular Catalan dishes (including pigs' trotters stuffed with prawns for the gastronomically daring), all prepared with the freshest market produce from the nearby Boquería.

€ **Les Quinze Nits**, Plaça Reial 6, **T** 93 317 30 75. daily 1300-1545, 2030-2330. **M** *Liceu. Bus 14, 38, 59, 91. Map 6, F3, p254* Those long queues snaking across Plaça Reial are for this good-value restaurant, which serves up simple, fresh Catalan dishes in coolly modern surroundings. No bookings are taken, so be prepared to wait.

Tapas bars and cafés

Bar Pinotxo, Mercat de la Boquería 66-67, **T** 93 317 17 31. *Mon-Sat 0600-1700.* **M** *Liceu. Bus 14, 38, 59, 91. Map 6, D3, p254* The best-known and best-loved counter bar in the market, serving excellent, freshly prepared food; don't miss the tortilla with artichokes.

Café Zurich, Plaça de Catalunya 1, **T** 93 317 91 53. *Jun-Oct daily 0800-0200, until 2300 on Sun; Nov-May Mon-Thu and Sun 0800-2300, Fri and Sat 0800-0000. **M** Plaça de Catalunya. All buses to Plaça de Catalunya. Map 2, A4, p248* When the new El Triangle shopping mall was built, the infamous old Café Zurich was swept away. This new version doesn't have the same charm, but it's got a fine location at the top of the Ramblas.

El Café de l'Òpera, Las Ramblas 74, **T** 93 302 41 80. *Mon-Thu and Sun 0900-0215, Fri and Sat 0900-0300. **M** Liceu. Bus 14, 38, 59, 91. Map 6, E3, p254* Right on the Ramblas opposite the Liceu opera house, the perfect café for people-watching. Original Modernista fittings and an Old World ambience add to its charm.

Escribà, La Rambla de les Flors 83, **T** 93 301 60 27. *Daily 0830-2100. **M** Liceu. Bus 14, 38, 59, 91. Map 6, D3, p254* A delightful outpost of the wonderful patisserie set in a gilded Modernista shop very close to the Boquería market.

Barri Gòtic

Restaurants

€€€ **Agut d'Avignon**, C Trinitat 3, just off C de Avinyó, **T** 93 302 60 34. *Daily 1300-1530, 2100-2330. **M** Liceu. Bus 14, 38, 59, 91. Map 6, F5, p254* A very fine, traditional Catalan restaurant with comfortably old-fashioned decor reminiscent of an old farmhouse. Try the *farcellets de col* (stuffed cabbage leaves) or the succulent roast meats which include pheasant, duck (especially good with figs) and partridge.

€€ **Café de l'Acadèmia**, C Lledó 1, **T** 93 319 82 53. *Mon-Fri 0900-1200, 1330-1600, 2045-1130. **M** Jaume I. Bus 17, 19, 40 45.*

Map 6, F8, p255 An elegant and romantic restaurant just off the lovely Plaça Sant Just, with torch-lit tables out on the square in summer. Classic Catalan cuisine – try the *rossejat* (rice cooked in fish broth) or the unusual lasagne.

€€ **Can Culleretes**, C d'en Quintana 5, **T** 93 317 31 22. *Tue-Sat 1330-1600, 2100-2300, Sun 1330-1600.* **M** *Liceu. Bus 14, 38, 59, 91. Map 6, E3, p254* This is the city's oldest restaurant, founded in 1786, with a series of interconnected, wooden panelled and beamed rooms papered with pictures of celebrity visitors. Try the *canelones de brandada de bacalao* (pasta rolls stuffed with salted cod) but leave room for the great desserts.

€€ **Cometacinc**, C Cometa 5, **T** 93 310 15 58. *Mon, Wed-Sun 2000-0000.* **M** *Jaume I. Bus 17, 19, 40 45. Map 6, H7, p255* A very stylish restaurant set in an old 19th-century mansion tucked down a tiny alley, this is elegantly and simply furnished with white-washed walls and wooden tables and chairs. Relaxed jazz and excellent fusion cuisine accompanied by a very decent wine list.

€€ **Living**, C Capellans 9, **T** 93 412 13 70. *Mon-Fri 1230-1630, 2000-0000, Sat 2000-0000.* **M** *Urquinaona or Plaça de Catalunya. Bus 17, 19, 40 45. Map 6, B8, p255* This airy, loft-style restaurant with red walls and ancient columns is tucked away down a passage. Hip, arty but unpretentious, it serves deliciously fresh and creative Mediterranean dishes from a short list which changes regularly and there's always a good selection for vegetarians. It doubles as a café-bar and you can sink into a sofa and chill out for as long as you like, or sit out on the terrace. Staff are very friendly and helpful.

€€ **Pla**, C Bellafila 5, **T** 93 412 65 52. *Daily 2100-0000.* **M** *Jaume I. Bus 17, 19, 40 45. Map 6, G7, p255* An intimate, stylish restaurant on two levels, with brick walls, low lights and an

★ **Menú del día**

Best

• Hofmann (La Ribera), p144
• Elisabets (El Raval), p148
• La Bodegueta (Eixample), p152
• La Fonda (Barri Gòtic), p141
• S:Pic (La Ribera), p146

inventive menu which gives Mediterranean classics an unusual Asian twist. There is always a good choice of dishes for vegetarians and a thoughtful wine list. Friendly, laid-back but attentive service.

€€ **Slokai**, C Palau 5, **T** 93 317 90 94. *Mon-Fri 1330-1600, 2100-0000, Sat 2100-0000.* **M** *Jaume I. Bus 17, 19, 40 45. Map 6, G6, p254* A very fashionable, minimalist white restaurant with extraordinary sculptures and art and projections and screenings on Friday and Saturday evenings. There's a lunchtime salad buffet and the main menu leans towards fish – sea bass with a piquant sauce, for example. It is also a relaxed café and bar and the staff are happy to let you linger.

€ **Arc Café**, C Carabassa 19, **T** 93 302 52 04. *Daily 1000-0200, Fri and Sat until 0300 .* **M** *Drassanes. Bus 14, 36, 57, 59, 64, 157. Map 6, H5, p254* Small marble-topped tables, creamy walls, a blackboard with daily specials (the Thai curries are good) and lots of newspapers. Just the place to while away a lazy afternoon.

€ **La Fonda**, C Escudellers 10, **T** 93 301 75 15. *Daily 1300-1530, 2030-2330.* **M** *Liceu. Bus 14, 38, 59, 91. Map 6, H3, p254* Wooden floors, lots of plants and modern lighting are a perfect setting for simple Catalan cuisine at good prices. The lunchtime set menu is a very reasonable €6.60 and it's only €13.20 for the evening *menú del día*. No bookings are taken, so you'll have to queue.

Eating and drinking

€ **La Verónica**, C Avinyó 30, **T** 93 412 11 22. *Tue-Fri 1930-0130, Sat and Sun 1330-0130.* **M** *Jaume I. Bus 17, 19, 40 45. Map 6, G5, p254* A bright, sleekly contemporary space popular with hipsters from the nearby art school, with a spacious terrace out on Plaça George Orwell in summer. Bold red and white decor, great pizzas with imaginative toppings and an interesting range of starters.

€ **Zoo**, C Escudellers 33, **T** 93 302 77 28. *Daily 2030-0100, bar open until 0200, until 0230 Fri and Sat.* **M** *Liceu. Bus 14, 38, 59, 91. Map 6, H4, p254* This is a funky, very popular place decorated with toy animals and all kinds of kitsch. The dishes are simple, mostly variations on substantial toasted sandwiches, which arrive overflowing with fillings. Good salads plus a couscous of the day and a few daily specials.

Tapas bars and cafés

Bliss, Plaça Sants Just i Pastor, **T** 93 268 10 22. *Mon-Sat 1000-1530, 2030-2315, closed Aug.* **M** *Jaume I. Bus 17, 19, 40 45. Map 6, F8, p255* A small, cosy café specializing in teas (there's a great range), with a couple of leopard-print sofas to sink into. Delicious homemade quiches, salads and cakes. There are tables out on a pretty little square by the church in summer.

Bodega La Palmera, C Palma de St Just 7, **T** 93 315 06 56. *Mon-Sat 0800-1530, 1900-1000.* **M** *Jaume I. Bus 17, 19, 40 45. Map 6, G8, p255* Old-fashioned, neighbourhood bar with hanging hams, wine by the jar from barrels and a selection of simple tapas – tortilla, cheese, bread with tomato, cured meats.

Café d'Estiu, Plaça Sant Iu 5, **T** 93 310 30 14. *Easter-Sep Tue-Sun 1000-2200.* **M** *Jaume I. Bus 17, 19, 40, 45. Map 6, E8, p255* Prettily set among the orange trees in the courtyard outside the Museu Frederic Marés, simple snacks, pastries and cakes are on offer.

★ **Restaurants for a splurge**

ਕ **Best**
- Agut d'Avignon (Barri Gòtic), p139
- Hofmann (La Ribera) , p144
- Beltxenea (Eixample), p150
- Jaume de Provença (Gràcia), p152
- Botafumeiro (Gràcia), p152

Juicy Jones, C Cardenal Casañas 7, **T** 93 302 43 30. *Daily 1330-2330.* **M** *Liceu. Bus 14, 38, 59, 91. Map 6, D3, p254* A brightly lit juice counter with a small vegetarian restaurant downstairs, painted with big bold flowers. Good-value set *menú* (from the lentil school of cookery) and organic beers and wines, as well as delicious, freshly made juices and smoothies.

La Pallaresa, C Petritxol 11, **T** 93 302 20 36, www.lapallaresa.com *Mon-Fri 0900-2100, Sat and Sun 0900-2200.* **M** *Liceu. Bus 14, 38, 59, 91. Map 6, B4, p254* This is where to get your *chocolate con churros* (thick hot chocolate with fried dough rings) in the morning – locals swear it's the best *xocolatería* in the city. It's still got the lino, Formica tables and waiters in dicky bows.

Venus, C Avinyó 25, **T** 93 301 15 85. *Daily 1200-0000 in theory, fluid in practice.* **M** *Liceu. Bus 14, 38, 59, 91. Map 6, G5, p254* A deli-style café serving sandwiches, salads and quiches on a very fashionable street, Venus manages to be cool without being pretentious. Wooden tables, mellow music and lots of newspapers and magazines make it a very welcoming spot.

La Vinateria del Call, C de Sant Domènec del Call 9, **T** 93 302 60 92. *Daily 1900-0100. Two evening sittings at weekends, 2100-2300 and 2300-0100.* **M** *Liceu. Bus 14, 38, 59, 91. Map 6, E6, p254* Down a tiny side street, this is a dark, wooden-panelled bar

Eating and drinking

with very friendly and knowledgeable staff. Excellent, very fresh tapas (choose from the menu) – platters of cheese or cured meats, *pa amb tomaquet* – and a fine wine list featuring local wines. It's so popular that it has two sittings at weekends.

La Ribera

Restaurants

€€€ Hofmann, C de l'Argenteria 74-78, **T** 93 319 58 89. *Mon-Fri 1330-1515, 2100-2315. **M** Jaume I. Bus 17, 19, 40, 45. Map 6, H10, p255* Outstanding cordon bleu cuisine impeccably served in a series of charming, plant-filled dining rooms. The menu focuses on modern Mediterranean dishes: try the roast lamb and the mouth-watering *fondant de chocolat* which is served warm. There is a set lunch *menú* for around €30.

€€ La Flauta Magica, C Banys Vells 18, **T** 93 268 46 94. *Daily 2030-0000. **M** Jaume I. Bus 17, 19, 40, 45. Map 6, H11, p255* Friendly, stylish restaurant, serving organic meats and a good range of vegetarian dishes, with soft peach and violet walls and lots of dim lighting and candles.

€€ Salero, C del Rec 60, **T** 93 319 80 22. *Mon-Thu 0845-1730 and 2000-0100, Fri 0845-1730 and 2000-0300, Sat 2000-0300, Sun 1000-1700. **M** Jaume I. Bus 14, 39, 51. Map 2, G8, p249* An ultra-stylish, cool, white, New York-style restaurant in the heart of the Born district, serving creative Mediterranean-Japanese cuisine at surprisingly low prices. Breakfasts are good too.

€€ Senyor Parellada, C de l'Argenteria 37, **T** 93 310 50 94. *Mon-Sat 1300-1530, 2100-2330. **M** Jaume I. Bus 17, 19, 40 45. Map 6, G10, p255* Set in a magnificent 18th-century building, this is a stylish, buzzy restaurant. The menu concentrates on modern Catalan dishes using the freshest market produce; try the *papillotte* of French beans with mushrooms or the delicious sole cooked with almonds and pine nuts.

€€ Taira, C Comerç 7, **T** 93 319 24 97. *M Barceloneta. Bus 14, 39, 51. Tue-Sun 1300-1600 and 2100-2430. Map 2, D8, p248* A slick Japanese restaurant-bar-club with even slicker New York-style decor which has become extremely popular with the local fashionistas, so don't bother to turn up without a reservation at weekends.

€ Comme Bio I, Via Laietana 28, **T** 93 319 89 68. *Mon-Fri 0900-1600, 2000-2330, Sat 0900-1600, 2030-0000, Sun 2000-2300. M Jaume I. Bus 17, 19, 40 45. Map 6, E9, p255* Big vegetarian restaurant and shop with a buffet, a good lunchtime menu and all kinds of organic goodies. No smoking during the week. There's another branch in the Eixample at Gran Via 603, **T** 93 301 03 76.

Tapas bars and cafés

Cal Pep, Plaça Olles 8, **T** 93 310 79 61. *Tue-Sat 1300-1645, 2000-0000, Sun and Mon 2000-0000. M Barceloneta. Bus 14, 39, 51. Map 6, H12, p255* A classic: there's a smart, brick-lined restaurant at the back, but it's more entertaining to stand at the bar as charismatic Pep grills fish and steaks and holds court at the same time. The house cava is particularly refreshing.

Euskal Etxea, Plaçeta Montcada, **T** 93 310 21 85. *Bar Tue-Sat 0900-2330, Sun 1245-1530; restaurant Tue-Sat 1330-1530, 2100-2330. M Jaume I. Bus 17, 19, 40 45. Map 6, H12, p255* Where better to tuck into Basque *pintxos* than the Basque cultural centre. These typical tapas are made of pieces of French bread with an array of toppings, held together with a cocktail stick. Get a plate from the bar staff, help yourself and count up the cocktail sticks at the end.

Hivernacle, Parc de la Ciutadella, **T** 93 295 40 17. *Daily 1000-0100. **M** Arc de Triomf. Bus 14, 39, 51. Map 2, E8, p248*
A beautiful, relaxing café-bar set in an elegant iron and glass pavilion built for the 1888 Universal Exposition; lots of shady palms, a terrace, changing art exhibitions and weekly jazz concerts in summer.

S:Pic, C Ribera 10, **T** 93 310 15 95. *Mon 1300-1600, Tue-Thu 1900-0100, Fri and Sat 1900-0300. **M** Barceloneta. Bus 14, 39, 51. Map 2, F8, p248* A funky cellar bar lit with weird projections. Excellent, imaginative tapas (the chef worked with Ferran Adrià of El Bulli, arguably the most famous chef and restaurant in Spain) and a very fashionable, clubby crowd. It also serves dinners (moderate prices) and an excellent-value lunch *menú* for less than €10.

Tèxtil Café, C Montcada 12, **T** 93 268 25 98. *Tue-Sun 1000-2345. **M** Jaume I. Bus 17, 19, 40, 45. Map 6, G11, p255* Set in the graceful courtyard by the Textile Museum (see p50), this delightful café has a good range of snacks, including hummus, sandwiches, salads and pastries.

La Vinya del Senyor, Plaça Santa Maria 5, **T** 93 310 33 79. *Tue-Sun 1200-0100. **M** Jaume I. Bus 17, 19, 40, 45. Map 6, H10, p255* One of the finest selections of wines, cavas and sherries in the city, accompanied by excellent tapas (in minuscule portions). A summer terrace faces the beautiful church of Santa Maria del Mar.

El Xampanyet, C Montcada 22, **T** 93 319 70 03. *Tue-Sat 1200-1600, 1830-2330, Sun 1200-1600. **M** Jaume I. Bus 17, 19, 40 45.*

Map 6, G12, p255 A classic little bar with old barrels and colourful tiles, serving simple tapas like *bacalao* (salt cod, which is better than it sounds) and anchovies and tortilla washed down with a delicious house *xampanyet* – poor man's cava.

El Raval

Restaurants

€€€ **Ca L'Isidre**, C Flors 12, **T** 93 441 11 39. *Mon-Sat 1330-1600, 2030-2330. **M** Paral.lel. Bus 20, 36, 57, 64, 91, 120, 157. Map 2, E1, p248* This celebrated family-run restaurant proudly displays a photograph of the owners posing with King Juan Carlos, who is said to be a big fan of the classic Catalan cuisine on offer. Try the *cabrit*, goat marinaded and roasted slowly in a wooded oven, or the succulent loin of lamb.

€€€ **Casa Leopoldo**, C Sant Rafael 24, **T** 93 441 30 14. *Tue-Sat 1330-1600, 2130-2300, Mon 1330-1600. **M** Liceu. Bus 14, 38, 59, 91. Map 2, D2, p248* This family-run restaurant has been going since 1929 and not much has changed since – you'll still find solid wooden tables, dark beams and tile-covered walls. Hearty Catalan dishes using the freshest market produce are on offer, like an excellent *sopa de pesca* (fish soup) and perfectly grilled meat.

€€ **Mamacafé**, C Doctor Dou 10, **T** 93 301 29 40. *1300-0100, until 1700 on Mon. Food served 1300-1730, 2100-2330. Closed Aug. **M** Plaça de Catalunya. Bus 120. Map 6, A2, p254* Bright colours, bold design and great music have made the Mamacafé a very stylish hang out in the Raval. The menu offers an eclectic selection of dishes from around the world including several vegetarian options. There is a lunchtime *menú* for €8.

★ **Summer terraces**

Best

• Café de l'Acadèmia (Barri Gòtic), p139
• El Cangrejo Loco (Seaside), p155
• Els Pescadors (Seaside), p154
• Pla dels Àngels (El Raval), p148
• La Verónica (Barri Gòtic), p142

€€ **Silenus**, C Àngels 8, **T** 93 302 26 80. *Daily 1000-0100.*
M *Plaça de Catalunya. Bus 120. Map 6, A1, p254* A cool and arty
restaurant serving top-notch international and Catalan dishes in a
long narrow space with pale walls lined with comfy sofas and
dotted with changing art exhibitions and projections. There's a
good lunchtime *menú* for €10.20 and you can linger over a coffee
in the afternoons.

€ **Elisabets**, C Elisabets 2-4, **T** 93 317 58 26. *Mon-Thu and Sat
1300-1600, Fri 1300-1600, 2100-2330.* **M** *Plaça de Catalunya. Bus 14,
38, 59, 91. Map 2, B3, p248* Tasty Catalan dishes at low prices are
served up in this classic neighbourhood restaurant catering to
locals. The *menú del día* (€6.80) usually offers several choices and
is very good value.

€ **Imprévist**, C Ferlandina 34, **T** 93 342 58 59. *Tue-Sun
1230-2430.* **M** *Universitat. Bus 120. Map 2, C2, p248* This cool
café-bar, with funky industrial-style decor is relaxed and arty. It
serves good light dishes – salads, pasta and noodle dishes, falafel
platters – and sometimes holds poetry readings or performances.

€ **Pla dels Àngels**, C Ferlandina 23 (opposite MACBA),
T 93 329 40 47. *Daily 1300-1500, 2030-0030.* **M** *Universitat. Bus
120. Map 2, B2, p248* With bright, modern decor and dark blue
walls, this is a large, popular restaurant with a summer terrace,

Eating and drinking

which serves extremely well-priced dishes (salads, meats, pastas). Good service and excellent wine – try the fantastic Tinto Artesano, which is less than €5 and exceptionally good.

€ **Sésamo**, C Sant Antoni Abat, **T** 93 441 64 11. *Daily 1100-0100, closed Mon night and Tue.* **M** *Sant Antoni. Bus 20, 24, 64, 91. Map 2, C1, p248* A laid-back, tiny organic restaurant serving tasty vegetarian dishes with an Oriental twist. Service is friendly and prices are very low.

Tapas bars and cafés

Bar Bodega Fortuny, C Pintor Fortuny 31, **T** 93 317 98 92. *Tue-Sun 1000-0000.* **M** *Plaça de Catalunya. Bus 14, 38, 59, 91. Map 6, A1, p254* A colourful conversion changed this old-fashioned bodega into a popular hangout for arty locals. It opens up onto the street in summer and delicious snacks and light meals are always on offer.

Bar Kasparo, Plaça Vincent Martorell 4, **T** 93 302 20 72. *Winter 0900-1000, until 0000 in summer.* **M** *Plaça de Catalunya. Bus 14, 38, 59, 91. Map 2, B4, p248* A popular, Australian-run café-bar overlooking the playground in the square (which makes it a good place to bring kids). Tasty sandwiches and hot dishes; friendly and unhurried service.

Bar Ra Town, Plaça Gardunya 7, **T** 93 301 41 63. *Mon-Sat 0930-0230.* **M** *Liceu. Bus 14, 38, 59, 91. Map 6, C1, p254* Friendly, hip little bar-café just behind the Boquería market, offering tasty breakfasts out on the terrace and a wider night-time menu with Thai, Mexican and Mediterranean influences. There are also audiovisuals, DJs and a clubby feel Thursday to Sunday nights.

★ **Tapas**

𝐁𝐞𝐬𝐭
- Cal Pep (La Ribera), p145
- Bar Pinotxo (Las Ramblas), p138
- El Roble (Gràcia), p153
- La Vinateria del Call (Barri Gòtic), p143
- La Vinya del Senyor (La Ribera), p146

Quimet & Quimet, C Poeta Cabañas 25, **T** 93 442 31 42. *Tue-Sat 1200-1600, 1900-2230, Sun 1200-1600.* **M** *Paral.lel. Bus 20, 36, 57, 64, 91, 120, 157. Map 2, G1, p249* A small, traditional *bodega* usually packed with crowds; it's got one of the best selection of wines in the city and a range of excellent tapas to match.

Eixample

Restaurants

€€€ **Beltxenea**, C Mallorca 275, **T** 93 215 30 24. *Mon-Fri 1330-1530, 2100-2300, Sat 2100-2300.* **M** *Diagonal. Bus 20, 43, 44. Map 3, E6, p250* A grand restaurant overlooking an immaculately manicured garden which has a romantic terrace in summer. The cuisine is as magnificent as the surroundings, featuring Basque classics like *merluza koskera a la vasca*, a delicate dish of hake cheeks simmered with clams and parsley. A real treat.

€€€ **Casa Calvet**, C Casp 48, **T** 93 413 40 12. *Mon-Sat 1300-1530, 2030-2300.* **M** *Urquinaona. Bus 47, 62. Map 3, J5, p251* Gaudí designed the building, and it retains some beautiful Modernista touches inside, including exquisite stained-glass windows. Fresh, modern Catalan cuisine is on offer; try the smoked foie gras with mango sauce and the fabulous desserts.

€€€ L'Olivé, C Balmes 47, **T** 93 452 19 90. *Mon-Sat 1300-1600, 2030-2400, Sun 1300-1600* **M** *Hospital Clínic. Bus 7, 6, 17, 63, 67, 68. Map 3, J4, p251* A popular, lively restaurant, L'Olivé serves traditional Catalan dishes, using the freshest market produce. Try the *rap amb all cremat* (monkfish with roasted garlic, or the *calçots* when in season.

€€ Domèstic, C Diputació 215, **T** 93 453 16 61. *Tue-Sun 1830-0230 (kitchen until 0100), until 0300 Fri and Sat.* **M** *Universitat. All buses to Plaça Universitat. Map 3, K2, p251* Welcoming, hip bar and restaurant with a resident Brazilian DJ playing mellow sounds. An excellent, highly creative menu combines unusual ingredients to great effect and there is a fantastic red-painted bar area with sofas to sink into.

€€ Tragaluz, Passatge de la Concepció 5, **T** 93 487 06 21. *1330-1600, 2030-2430; until 0100 Thu, Fri and Sat.* **M** *Diagonal. Bus 7, 16, 17, 22, 24, 28. Map 3, G5, p251* In a pretty side street off the Passeig de Gràcia, this is a stylish, fashionable restaurant on two levels with a huge glass skylight (the eponymous *tragaluz*), which slides open in summer. The food is fresh, simple Mediterranean-style fare, with a range of low-calorie and vegetarian dishes also on offer. The downstairs bar has tapas and light snacks all day. They also run a slick Japanese restaurant across the street, El Japonés, **T** 93 487 25 92.

€ L'Hostal de Rita, C d'Aragó 279, **T** 93 487 23 76. *Daily 1300-1545, 2030-2330.* **M** *Passeig de Gràcia. Bus 7, 16, 17, 22, 24, 28. Map 3, I6, p251* Part of the chain which includes La Fonda (see p141) and Les Quinze Nits (see p138). They don't take bookings and there are always long queues. Simple Catalan favourites and stylish, understated decor draw big crowds.

Tapas bars and cafés

La Bodegueta, Rambla de Catalunya 100, **T** 93 215 48 94.
Mon-Sat 0800-0200, Sun 1830-0100. **M** *Passeig de Gràcia. Bus 7, 16, 17, 22, 24, 28.* *Map 3, G5, p251* A charming, old-fashioned little cellar bar lined with bottles, which serves a selection of excellent tapas and does a very good-value, fixed-price lunch.

Laie Llibreria Café, C Pau Claris 85, **T** 93 302 73 10. *Mon-Fri 0900-0100, Sat 1000-0100.* **M** *Urquinaona. Bus 39, 45.* *Map 3, L6, p251* Barcelona's original bookshop café has comfy armchairs and magazines to flick through. A range of tasty snacks and light meals includes a good-value *menú del dia*.

Bracafé, C Casp 2, **T** 93 302 30 82. *Daily 0700-2230.* **M** *Plaça de Catalunya. All buses to Plaça de Catalunya.* *Map 2, A6, p248* A busy café just around the corner from Plaça de Catalunya; it has tables outside in summer and a cosy little glassed-in area in winter.

Gràcia and Park Güell

Restaurants

€€€ Botafumeiro, C Gran de Gràcia 81, **T** 93 218 42 30. *Daily 1300-0100.* **M** *Fontana. Bus 22, 24, 28, 87.* *Map 3, C6, p250* An outstanding Galician seafood restaurant, with a stunning array of sea creatures on the menu; the excellent value *menu de degustación* is highly recommended. They also run the tavern next door which serves fresh oysters among the tapas.

€€€ Jaume de Provença, C Provença 88, **T** 93 430 00 29. *Tue-Sat 1330-1530, 2030-2300, Sun 1330-1530.* **M** *Entenç. Bus 41.* *Map 1, D4, p246* Decor verges on the austere but the food is emphatically the opposite: chef Jaume Bargués is renowned for his adventurous and imaginative Catalan cuisine – like the lobster tempura served with a poached egg and truffle sauce.

€€ **Bar-Restaurant del Teatre Lliure**, C Montseny 47, **T** 93 218 67 38. *Mon-Sat 1330-1530, 2030-2330, Sun 1330-1530. Closed two weeks in Aug.* **M** *Fontana. Bus 22, 24, 28, 87. Map 3, B7, p250* Attached to the prestigious Catalan theatre, this large, airy restaurant is very popular with locals and serves excellent, highly imaginative regional cuisine at very reasonable prices. Tables on the balcony overlook the narrow street.

€ **Flash Flash**, C Granada del Penedès 25, **T** 93 237 09 90. *Daily 1300-0130, bar daily 1100-0200. FGC Gràcia. Bus 16, 17, 22, 24, 28. Map 3, D3, p250* Classic 1970s black and white decor with white leatherette seating and black silhouettes on the walls. Best known for its excellent selection of tortillas, it also does great burgers and steaks and attracts a trendy uptown crowd.

Tapas bars and cafés

El Roble, C Lluis Antúnez, **T** 93 218 73 87. *Mon-Sat 0700-0100. **M** Diagonal. Bus 7, 16, 17, 22, 24, 26. Map 3, C5, p250* A roomy old-fashioned tapas bar which hasn't changed in decades. There's a rickety, yellowing old sign showing what's on offer, or you can go and inspect the dishes lined up along the counter. Long-aproned waiters dash about the place and it's a big favourite with locals.

Sol Solet, Plaça del Sol 21, **T** 93 217 44 40. *Mon and Tue 1900-0200, Wed and Thu 1500-0200, Fri , Sat and Sun 1200-0300. **M** Fontana. Bus 22, 24, 28, 87. Map 3, C7, p250* One of the prettiest bars in Gràcia, with marble-topped tables, old tiles and paddle fans, which looks out onto the square. An excellent range of unusual tapas are on offer, including several vegetarian options.

Seaside

Restaurants

€€€ **Antigua Casa Solé**, C Sant Carles 4, **T** 93 221 51 12.
Tue-Sat 1300-1600, 2000-2300. **M** *Barceloneta. Bus 36, 39, 45, 57, 59,
64, 157. Map 2, J7, p249* A pretty restaurant set in a 19th-century
building with breezy blue and white tiles and lots of flowers. The
local fish stew *sarsuela* was invented here and it's still a great place
to try traditional Catalan fish recipes.

€€€ **Els Pescadors**, Plaça Prim 1, **T** 93 225 20 18. *Daily
1300-1545, 2000-0000.* **M** *Poble Nou. Bus 41. Map 1, H11, p247*
Way off the beaten track, but with a fine reputation for its seafood
dishes, this charming whitewashed restaurant has a terrace
overlooking a magical square surrounded by tumbledown
buildings and shaded by two huge mulberry trees.

€€€ **Torre d'Alta Mar**, Passeig Joan de Borbó 88,
T 93 221 00 07. **M** *Barceloneta. Bus 17, 36, 39, 45, 57, 59, 64, 157.
Map 2, L5, p249* The latest of Barcelona's designer restaurants is also
one of the most unusual: in the cable car terminal it has 360-degree
views of the city and the Mediterranean. The slightly retro decor (Egg
chairs and spidery modern candelabras) has caused almost as much
of a stir as the much- vaunted cuisine: try the *suquet de pescadors*, a
delicious fish stew.

€€ **Agua**, Paseig Marítim 30, **T** 93 225 12 72. *Mon-Wed
1330-1600, 2030-0030; Thu-Sat 1330-1600, 2030-0100.*
M *Barceloneta. Bus 36, 45, 57, 59, 157. Map 5, E4, p253* A slick,
stylish restaurant overlooking the sea, Agua specializes in rice
dishes, often with an unusual twist (try the wild rice with greens
and ginger) but there are plenty of good meat and fish dishes.

€€ **El Cangrejo Loco**, Moll de Gregal 29, **T** 93 221 05 33. *Daily 1300-0100.* **M** *Ciutadella-Vila Olímpica. Bus 36, 45, 57, 59, 157. Map 5, F6, p253* The 'Crazy Crab' offers excellent, very reasonably priced paellas and other seafood dishes. The *menú de degustación* is a particular bargain. It's a big, bustling, cheerful place, on two levels with a terrace right by the shore, but it's always full and you may wait a while for service.

€€ **Set Portes**, Passeig de Isabel II 14, **T** 93 319 30 33. *Daily 1300-0100.* **M** *Barceloneta. Bus 14, 36, 57, 59, 64, 157. Map 2, G7, p249* A famous old restaurant, with frilly net curtains, a piano and aproned waiters, the 'Seven Doors' has been dishing up Catalan cuisine since 1836. It's now fairly touristy, but the food remains excellent, particularly the house speciality, *paella de peix*.

€ **La Taverna de Cel Ros**, Moll de Mestral 26, **T** 93 221 00 33. *Mon-Wed and Fri-Sun, 1300-1700, 2000-0000.* **M** *Ciutadella-Vila Olímpica. Bus 10, 45, 49, 57, 71, 92, 157. Map 5, F6, p253* An unpretentious place amidst of the bustle of the Port Olímpic, this is popular with sailors and port workers and has a good-value lunch.

Tapas bars and cafés

El Tío Che, 44 Rambla de Poble Nou, **T** 93 309 18 72. *Daily 1000-0100, until 0200 Fri and Sat.* **M** *Poble Nou. Bus 41. Map 1, H11, p247* One of the most famous *orxaterias* in the city, this old-fashioned café, in a lovely, faded Modernista mansion, is the perfect spot to try *orxata* (a creamy drink made with tiger nuts) or an ice-cold *granizado* (a crushed-ice drink).

Taverna Can Ramonet, C Maquinista 17, **T** 93 319 30 64. *1000-1600, 2000-0000, closed Aug.* **M** *Barceloneta. Bus 17, 36, 39, 45, 57, 59, 64, 157. Map 5, E1, p253* This is the oldest tavern in Barceloneta, set in a pretty, pink two-storey house covered in flowers. Wine from the barrel accompanied by tasty seafood tapas, or there's a smart (expensive) seafood restaurant at the back.

Xiringuito Escribà, Platja de Bogatell, **T** 93 221 07 29. *Summer Tue-Sun 1100-0100; winter Tue-Thu 1300-1600, Fri-Sun 1300-1600, 2100-2300.* **M** *Ciutadella-Vila Olímpica or Llacuna. Bus 40, 71, 92. Map 1, H11, p247* The celebrated Escribà confectioners serve delicious seafood tapas and main dishes followed by truly mouthwatering desserts. Book well in advance.

Montserrat

Bring a picnic or pick up supplies from the deli-bakery-shop. There is also a self-service cafeteria serving undistinguished but perfectly adequate food in the monastery complex.

Sitges

€€€ Maricel, Passeig de la Ribera 6, **T** 93 894 20 54, www.maricel.es *Closed Tue and 2nd 2 weeks in Nov.* Probably the best seafood restaurant in town; right on the beachfront with a pale, elegant dining room full of floral prints and oil paintings.

€€€ El Velero, Passeig de la Ribera 38, **T** 93 894 20 51. *Mon-Sat 1330-1500, 2030-2330, Sun 1330-1500.* Another classic seafood restaurant on the main drag, with a loyal, local clientele and an excellent tasting menu (*menú degustación*).

€ Pizzeria Cap de la Villa, Cap de la Villa 3, **T** 93 894 10 91. *Mon-Sat 1330-1500 and 2030-2330, Sun 1330-1500.* There's not much in the way of budget food in Sitges, but the pizzas here are pretty good and very reasonable.

★ **Veggie/veggie-friendly restaurants**

Best

- Juicy Jones (Barri Gòtic), p143
- La Flauta Magica (La Ribera), p144
- Living (Barri Gòtic), p140
- Mamacafé (El Raval), p147
- Sésamo (El Raval), p149

Tarragona

€€€ **Merlot**, C Caballers 6, **T** 977 22 06 52. *Closed Sun and Mon lunch.* Chic, fashionable restaurant in a Modernista townhouse, serving some of the finest contemporary Mediterranean and French cuisine in the region. The wine list is equally impressive.

€€ **Cal Martí**, C Sant Pere 12, **T** 977 21 23 84. *Closed Sun night, Mon and Sep.* One of the best of several seafood restaurants on this street in Tarragona's port: try the suquet, or the baked fish.

€€ **El Tiberí,** C Martí d'Ardenya 5, **T** 977 23 54 03. *Closed Sun and Wed nights and all day Mon and Tue.* Sturdy, Catalan buffet, with a wide range of dishes from stuffed pigs' feet to *fideuejat* (a fish broth with small noodles) and the fresh local salad, *escalivada*.

Girona

€€€ **Celler de Can Roca**, Ctra Taialà 40, **T** 972 22 21 57. *Closed Sun, Mon, 1st fortnight in July and Christmas.* You wouldn't think so from the outside, but this is one of the finest restaurants in the region and a great place for a treat. Brothers Joan and Josep dish up refined Catalan cuisine with a French twist (it's got two of those coveted stars). It's on the outskirts of the city, so get a taxi.

€€ **La Penyora**, C Nou del Teatre 3, **T** 972 21 89 48. *Daily 1330-1500, 2030-2330.* Relaxed, arty spot serving fresh, imaginative Catalan dishes. There are changing art exhibitions and a laid-back boho crowd.

€ **La Crêperie Bretonne**, C Cort Reial 14, **T** 972 21 81 20. *Tue-Sat 1300-1600, 2000-2230, Sun 1300-1600.* Good for veggies, this friendly, French-owned place is a big favourite for its delicious crêpes and huge salads. Budding artists can draw their impression of Girona on the paper tablecloths with the crayons provided.

Figueres

€€€ **Hotel Durán**, C Lasauca 5, **T** 972 50 12 50. *Daily 1245-1600, 2030-2300.* This is a classic in Figueras: an old-fashioned hotel with an exceptionally good restaurant specialising in regional cuisine.

€€ **El Mesón del Conde**, Plaça del Esglesia 4, **T** 972 77 03 06. *1300-1600 and 2100-0000.* Sit out on the huge terrace of this traditional Catalan restaurant and enjoy some fine fresh local seafood. It's very popular with local families.

€ **El Café del Barri Vell**, Plaça de las Patates, no **T**. *Daily 1100-2300.* A simple, laid-back vegetarian café on a pretty little square just behind the Dalí museum, which puts on poetry readings and concerts out on the terrace in summer.

With thousands of bars and clubs catering to every conceivable musical taste, you'll be spoilt for choice in Barcelona. This style-obsessed city has a staggering number of ultra-hip bars and clubs playing the latest dance music, but you can also enjoy a mellow *copa* on a candle-lit terrace, tango until dawn at an old-fashioned music hall, or sip an absinthe in a louche bar untouched by time. DJ culture dominates the music scene and Barcelona is a popular stop on the international circuit. To find out what's on and who's playing where, check out listings guide *Guia del Ocio*, the slick magazine *B-Guided* (available free in some bars, or at news kiosks) or pick up flyers at fashion or music shops (those on Carrer Avinyó in the Barri Gòtic and Carrer Tallers in the Raval are good starting points). Many regular Spanish-style bars function as cafés during the day and close around midnight. *Bares de copas* don't generally serve tapas or food and are open in the evenings. Clubs (*discotecas*) won't get going until at least midnight and usually stay open until dawn at weekends.

Las Ramblas and Plaça Reial

Bars

Boadas, C Tallers 1, **T** 93 318 88 26. *Mon-Thu 1200-0200, Fri and Sat 1200-0300. **M** Plaça de Catalunya. Bus 14, 38, 59, 91. Map 2, B4, p248* Elegant, classy art deco cocktail bar which began life in 1933; celebrity drinkers, including Miró, have left sketches and mementoes along the walls.

Clubs

Café Royale, C Nou de Zurbano 3, **T** 93 412 14 33. *Sun-Thu 1800-0230, Fri and Sat 1800-0300. **M** Liceu. Bus 14, 38, 59, 91. Map 6, G3, p254* A hip, sleek bar and club just off Plaça Reial, with big sofas and two dancefloors playing the best in soul, jazz and funk. It does great breakfasts but can get uncomfortably mobbed at weekends.

Jamboree, Plaça Reial 17, **T** 93 301 75 64, www.masimas.com *Tue-Sun 0000-0500. **M** Liceu. Bus 14, 38, 59, 91. Map 6, G3, p254* This jazz club (see p174) becomes a nightclub when the sets end: after about 0100, the crowds pour in to enjoy the R&B, soul and funk which plays until dawn.

Barri Gòtic

Bars

Malpaso, C Rauric 20, **T** 93 412 60 05. *Sun-Thu 2130-0230, Fri and Sat 2130-0300. **M** Liceu. Bus 14, 38, 59, 91. Map 6, F3, p254* Just down an alley behind Plaça Reial, this is a groovy, red-painted little bar with decks playing an eclectic range of music and a few punters dancing under the revolving disco ball.

Pilé 43, C N'Aglà 4, **T** 93 317 39 02. *Sun-Thu 1900-0200, Fri and Sat 1900-0300.* **M** *Liceu. Bus 14, 38, 59, 91. Map 6, G4, p254* A brightly lit, hyper-fashionable bar filled with retro furniture, lights and knick-knacks – everything you see and sit on is for sale.

Clubs

Dot Light Club, C Nou de Sant Francesc 7, **T** 93 302 70 26. *Sun-Thu 2330-0230, Fri and Sat 2300-0300.* **M** *Drassanes. Bus 14, 38, 59, 91. Map 6, H3, p254* One of the trendiest (and smallest) clubs around, Dot has a minuscule dance floor, with groovy lighting, cult films and wall projections. The varied line up of DJs provides the latest sounds from across the spectrum of dance music.

La Macarena DJ Zone, C Nou de Sant Francesc 5, no **T**. *Sun-Thu 1900-0430, Fri and Sat 1900-0500.* **M** *Liceu. Bus 14, 38, 59, 91. Map 6, H3, p254* Small, intimate club playing jazzy electronica, beloved by DJs from around the world. Buzzy, upbeat and very, very cool.

La Ribera

Bars

Gimlet, C Rec 24, **T** 93 310 10 27. *Daily 2000-0300.* **M** *Arc de Triomf. Bus 14, 39, 51. Map 6, H12, p255* Classic, stylish cocktail bar which draws the fashion crowd as well as plenty of celebrities (not that anyone would deign to notice).

Pitín Bar, Passeig del Born 34, **T** 93 319 50 87. *Daily 1800-0200.* **M** *Barceloneta. Bus 14, 39, 51. Map 6, H12, p255* Pitín has been going for years and years, unaffected by changes in fashion yet effortlessly managing to stay cool. It's a split-level bar with a tiny spiral staircase, decorated with all kinds of junk and lit with fairy lights.

Ribborn, C Antic de Sant Joan 3, **T** 93 310 71 48. *Wed-Sat 1900-0200, Fri and Sat 1900-0300, Sun 1800-0300. **M** Barceloneta. Bus 14, 39, 51. Map 6, H12, p255* A relaxed, thoroughly unpretentious bar with simple tapas and a small stage for live jazz, funk and blues.

Clubs

Astin, C Abaixadors 9, **T** 93 301 0090. *Thu-Sat 2200-0330. **M** Barceloneta/Jaume I. Bus 17, 19, 40, 45. Map 6, H10, p255* A small, chrome-filled, ultra-hip bar and club run by the Nitsa (see p166) crew, playing the very latest pop, house and breakbeat. Guest DJ sessions and concerts.

Magic, Passeig Picasso 40, **T** 93 310 72 67. *Thu-Sat 2300-0600. **M** Arc de Triomf. Bus 14, 39, 51. Map 2, F8, p248* Big, popular club with two dance floors serving up everything from classic Spanish rock and pop to the latest techno dance sounds. Regular live acts.

El Raval

Bars

Benidorm, C Joaquim Costa 39, **T** 93 317 80 52. *Mon-Thu, Sun 1900-0200, Fri and Sat 1900-0230. **M** Universitat. Bus 64, 91, 141, 120. Map 2, B2, p248* This a tiny, funky little space decked out with eccentric furnishings – a Baroque bench, 70s wallpaper – and has a miniature dance floor complete with disco ball.

El Café Que Pone Meubles Navarro, Carrer de la Riera Alta 4-6, **T** 607 18 90 96 (mobile). *Tue-Thu 1700-0100, ri and Sat 1700-0200. **M** Universitat. Bus 64, 91, 141, 120. Map 2, C2, p248* A New York-warehouse-style café-bar set in a converted furniture shop with a mellow retro air and a fashionable, arty crowd.

Bars and clubs

★ **Best**

Places to see and be seen

- Astin (La Ribera), p163
- Café Royale (Las Ramblas), p161
- Dot Light Club (Barri Gòtic), p162
- Lupino (El Raval), p165
- La Macarena DJ Zone (Barri Gòtic), p162

La Ruta dels Elefants, C Hospital 48, no **T**. *Daily 2000-0200.* *M Liceu. Bus 14, 38, 59, 91. Map 6, D1, p254* Very close to Plaça San Augustin, this is a popular, laid-back bar with African art all over the walls, an upbeat, friendly atmosphere and live music most nights – you never know what you might get, from old-fashioned cabaret to teenage rock or reggae.

Marsella, C Sant Pau 65, **T** 93 442 72 63. *Mon-Thu 2200-0230.* *M Liceu. Bus 14, 38, 59, 91. Map 2, E2, p248* The big, dusty, bottle-lined Marsella was started by a homesick Frenchman more than a century ago. The smell of absinthe hits you as soon as you walk in; get there early to grab a battered, marble-topped table under the lazy paddle fans and soak up the atmosphere.

Clubs

Bongo Lounge at La Paloma, C Tigre 27, **T** 93 317 79 94. *Thu 0100-0500. M Universitat. Bus 64, 91, 141, 120. Map 2, A2, p248* On Thursday nights, the ballroom dancers make way for clubbers at this old-fashioned, much-loved dance hall. The Bongo Lounge is one of the best nights out in the city, with resident DJs spinning funky Latin grooves. Check out the listings in the Guia del Ocia for other club nights at La Paloma.

Lupino, C Carme 33, **T** 93 412 36 97. *Daily 0900-0300.* **M** *Liceu. Bus 14, 38, 59, 61.* *Map 6, B2, p254* This new 'restaurant-lounge-cocktail club' is ultra-stylish in a fashionably minimalist way. The music is laid back and loungey and the Mediterranean menu is very decent. Mobbed by the fashion pack at weekends.

Eixample

Bars

La Fira, C Provença 171, **T** 617 77 65 89 (mobile). *Tue-Thu and Sun 2300-0300, Fri and Sat 2300-0500.* **M** *Hospital Clínic or FGC Provença. Bus 31, 37.* *Map 3, G2, p251* One of the most original bars in town, this cavernous 'bar-museum' is stuffed with old fairground memorabilia; sit in a Dodgem sipping a beer or find a swing at the bar. Raucous weekend parties.

La Pedrera de Nit, C Provença 261-265, **T** 93 484 59 00, tickets through Tel-Entrada **T** 902 101 212. *Jul-Aug, Fri and Sat 2100-0000.* **M** *Diagonal. Bus 7, 16, 17, 22, 24, 28.* *Map 3, G6, p251* Sip a cocktail and check out the live music and stunning views across the city from the undulating, magical rooftop of Gaudí's La Pedrera. A hundred tickets are sold in advance (€10) – bag one or be prepared for long queues.

Clubs

Row Club (at Nick Havanna), C Rosselló 208, **T** 93 215 65 91. *Bar Sun-Thu 2300-0400, Fri and Sat 2300-0500; club Thu nights only.* **M** *Diagonal. Bus 7, 16, 63, 67, 68.* *Map 3, F5, p250* This regular Thursday night club is hosted by the organizers of the Sónar festival (see p182) and the music runs from house and techno to the latest experimental sounds. A great night out.

Montjuïc

Bars

BCN Rouge, C Poeta Cabañas 21, **T** 93 442 49 85.
Daily 2300-0300. ***M*** *Poble Sec. Bus 20, 24, 57, 61, 64, 121, 157.*
Map 1, G5, p246 Ring for entry to this intimate and very slick
chill-out bar, with lots of big sofas and tables (everything is red,
of course). Bizarrely, it turns into a football bar on Sun nights.

Clubs

La Terrrazza Discothèque, Poble Espanyol, **T** 93 423 12 85.
May-Oct Thu-Sun and days before bank holidays 0000-0600.
M *Espanya, then bus 13, 23, 50, 61. Map 4, C1, p252* The biggest
summer party in the city, La Terrrazza is a hugely popular outdoor
venue, where you can chill out under the pine trees or prance on
the podiums to excellent dance music played by an impressive list
of guest DJs. Massive queues and a strict door policy. When the
temperatures drop, the party at Terrrazza comes indoors and calls
itself Discothèque.

Nitsa (Sala Apolo), C Nou de la Rambla 113, **T** 93 441 40 01,
www.nitsa.com *Fri and Sat 2430-0600.* ***M*** *Paral.lel. Bus 20, 24, 57,*
61, 64, 121, 157. Map 2, G1, p249 The club takes over when the
gigs have ended at the Sala Apolo, a converted ballroom; this big
weekend party is very popular so be prepared for massive queues.
The main dance floor features hard techno, breakbeat and house,
but the two smaller rooms off the upper gallery are mellower.

Gràcia and Park Güell

Bars

Café del Sol, Plaça del Sol 16, **T** 93 415 56 63. *Sun-Thu 1300-0200, Fri and Sat 1300-0230.* *M Fontana. Bus 22, 24, 28, 87.* *Map 3, C7, p250* This is a very mellow spot during the day, with creamy white walls showing changing art exhibitions. There's a good selection of tapas on Sunday mornings and a delightful terrace out on the square in summer. DJ sessions on Friday and Saturday nights.

Mond Bar, Plaça del Sol 29, **T** 93 457 38 77. *Daily 2100-0230.* *M Fontana. Bus 22, 24, 28, 87.* *Map 3, C7, p250* A small, slinky bar on the lively Plaça de Sol, with soft lighting, plush sofas, chilled-out house, lounge and trance and a friendly, laid-back crowd.

Seaside

Clubs

Razzmatazz/The Loft, C Almogàvers 122, **T** 93 320 82 00, www.salarazmatazz.com *Fri and Sat 0100-0500.* *M Bogatell. Bus 6, 40, 42, 141.* *Map 1, G9, p247* Razzmatazz is a popular party spot at weekends with three spaces catering to all musical tastes: pop, rock and techno in the Razz Club; and house, electronica and Djs in the trendy Loft.

Outskirts

Bars

Mirablau, Pza Dr Andreu s/n, **T** 93 418 58 79. *Daily 1100-0500. FGC Avinguda del Tibidabo then taxi uphill. Off map 1, p246* Plaça Dr Andreu is where the Tramvia Blau stops and the funicular climbs up Tibidabo; the Mirablau bar is a swanky, elegant spot with a terrace overlooking the whole city, perfect for a cocktail or tapas.

Clubs

Bikini, C Deu i Mata 105, (in L'Illa shopping centre), **T** 93 322 00 05, www.bikinibcn.com *Tue-Thu 0000-0430, Fri and Sat 0000-0530. M Les Corts. Bus 6, 7, 33, 34, 63, 66, 67. Map 1, C4, p246* The original legendary Bikini was bulldozed to make room for the L'Illa shopping centre but the club has been recreated among the shops and offers three different spaces, offering everything from live gigs (very big names) to Latin sounds and lounge.

Bars and clubs

In the arts, as in almost everything else, Barcelona is at the cutting edge. Challenging contemporary music, dance and theatre are plentiful and there are a number of excellent annual events, ranging from the hugely popular Sónar music festival to the Grec festival of performing arts (see Festivals and events, p179). A night at the beautiful Liceu opera house or a rousing performance by the Orfeo Catalá at the opulent Palau de la Música are unforgettable and surprisingly affordable experiences. Jazz is very strong in the city and Latin and African music is also big thanks to the large immigrant population. Although most bands in the Spanish charts are from the UK or the States, Catalan rock and pop hold their own in Barcelona: look out for bands like Sopa de Cabra or the hip hop group 7 Notas 7 Colores. Spanish cinema has enjoyed a high profile over the last decade or so thanks to the success of directors like Pedro Almodóvar and there are several arthouse cinemas where you can catch cult movies by celebrated directors. Prices, again, are low in comparison with London and New York.

The weekly listings guide *La Guia del Ocio* (www.guiadelocio.com, €1) is on sale at most news kiosks (in Spanish with an English-language spread at the back). *LaNetro* is a comprehensive listings freebie (www.lanetro.com, distributed in hotels and shops) but it's in Spanish only. The free English-language *Guide Out To Barcelona* is also distributed in shops and hotels with restaurant and bar listings. You'll also find entertainment supplements in Friday or Saturday editions of newspapers (*La Vanguardia*, *El Pais* or *El Mundo*). For information on theatre, classical music and opera, visit the helpful Centre d'Informació de la Virreina (see p30) and pick up free leaflets. For comprehensive, up-to-date information, look at the cultural agenda section of the city's website, www.bcn.es

Cinema

The Catalans have long been at the cutting-edge of avant garde cinema; the lushly named Fructuós Gelabert was its earliest exponent, back in the 1890s and almost all the major Spanish film companies were based in Barcelona during the early 20th century. Look out for works by Francesc Bertriu, Pere Portabella, Vicente Aranda and Ventura Pons. Monday is traditionally the cheapest night for cinema tickets. Check for VO (*version originale*) in cinema listings for non-dubbed English-language films. You can pre-book cinema tickets online at www.cinetickets.com Barcelona also has an IMAX cinema (see p209).

Filmoteca de la Generalitat de Catalunya, Cinema Aquitania, Avda Sarrià 31-33, Eixample, **T** 93 410 75 90. **M** *Hospital Clínic. Bus 54, 59, 66. Map 1, D5, p246* The Catalan government funds the Filmoteca, offering an overview of the history of cinema, with changing series of films devoted to themes, directors or countries.

Renoir-Les Corts, C Eugeni d´Ors 12, Les Corts, **T** 93 490 55 10, www.cinesrenoir.com **M** *Les Corts. Bus 15, 43, 59. Map 1, C3, p246*

A comfortable, well-equipped six-screen cinema which usually offers at least two films in English. It also offers the best facilities for disabled people.

Verdi, C Verdi 32 and **Verdi Park**, C Torrijos 49, **T** 93 328 79 00, www.cinemes-verdi.com *M Fontana. Bus 22, 24, 28, 87. Map 3, A8, p250* Two attractive cinemas in Gràcia showing international and Spanish art and independent films.

Comedy

The Spanish don't go in for stand-up comedy in the way that northern Europeans do. There are no dedicated comedy clubs in Barcelona, but you might catch a one-off comedy night geared towards the sizeable foreign student contingent at one of the English/Irish pubs. Check for details in the listings guides.

Dance

Barcelona's contemporary dance scene is the best in Spain, with dozens of innovative dance groups producing some of the most striking and exciting dance in Europe. Names to look out for include Cesc Gelabert, *Danat Dansa*, *Mudances* (founded by Angels Margarit) and *La Fura dels Baus*. Watch out for special events at some of the museums and cultural institutions like the CCCB (p60) and MACBA (p58) and try to catch **Dies de Dansa**, a three-day dance festival in mid-September, or the dance programme **Dansa + a prop**, which offers a range of dance performances in several venues every three months. There are always dance events in the summer Grec festival (see p182), which usually feature the best of local talent. Andalucían immigrants have kept the flamenco tradition alive and there's a Flamenco Festival in early May where it's often possible to see some great visiting performers. **El Mercat de les Flors**, **Teatre Nacional**, **Teatre Lliure** and the **Sala**

Booking tickets

Theatre, opera and concert tickets can be often be bought through one of the two savings banks, through their websites or over the phone. Some concert tickets can be bought through music shops (look out for details on posters) or at Fnac. The Centre d'Informació de la Virreina (see p30) also has a ticket sales service.

Fnac, El Triangle, Plaça de Catalunya 4, **T** 93 344 18 00. Best for pop and rock concerts.

Servi-Caixa, **T** 902-33 22 11, www.servicaixa.com This service is run by the biggest savings bank. Servi-Caixa machines are next to the ordinary ATMS at the banks; buy concert tickets using your credit card, or order by phone (some of their staff speak English) or over the internet.

Beckett regularly host dance events (details under Theatre, p177). The *tablaos* (flamenco shows) are touristy, but can be fun.

L'Espai de Dansa i Música, Travessera de Gràcia 63, Gràcia, **T** 93 414 31 33, www.cultura.gencat.es *M Diagonal. Bus 27, 30, 32. Map 3, C3, p250* One of the few venues in the city with a dedicated dance slot; contemporary dance and music.

El Tablao de Carmen, Poble Espanyol, Montjuïc, **T** 93 325 68 95. *M Espanya, then bus 9, 13, 30, 50, 55. Map 4, C1, p252* Set inside the 'Spanish village', this is a pricey flamenco joint geared towards coachloads of tourists, but features high-class acts and if you book in advance you won't have to pay the entrance fee into the Poble Espanyol.

Los Tarantos, Placa Reial 17, Barri Gòtic, **T** 93 318 30 67. *M Liceu. Bus 14, 38, 59, 91. Map 6, B4, p248* Popular, touristy *tablao*, but with the attraction of a late-night club and other performances.

Music

Contemporary

There's always plenty going on in Barcelona, from impromptu performances in shabby bars to huge concerts with all the big names. The Sónar festival of multimedia music and art is fantastic (see p182) and the BAM festival which runs at the same time as the Festa de la Mercè (see p184) is a great way to catch some alternative sounds. Barcelonan jazz is traditionally excellent while Andalucían immigrants and their children ensure that the flamenco scene retains its energy. Clubs like Jamboree and Luz de Gas offer a real mixed-bag of musical styles and are always worth checking out. There are plenty of venues covering everything else, from tiny, hip bars with the latest in *electrónica* to huge crowded *salas* with mainstream rock and pop. Pick up flyers at music shops to discover some of the lesser-known venues.

Bikini, C Deu i Mata 105, **T** 93 322 00 05. *M Les Corts. Bus 6, 7, 33, 34, 63, 66, 67. Map 1, C4, p246* See Bars and clubs, p168.

Harlem Jazz Club, C Comtessa de Sobradiel 8, **T** 93 310 07 55. *M Liceu. Bus 14, 38, 59, 91. Map 6, H6, p254* A dynamic jazz club, small but atmospheric, with very creative programming.

Jamboree, C Plaça Reial 17, **T** 93 301 75 64. *M Liceu. Bus 14, 38, 59, 91. Map 6, G3, p254* Hugely popular and always packed. The programme includes jazz, blues, funk and hip-hop and the Sunday night blues night is the best way to finish up the weekend. After performances, Jamboree becomes a late-night club (p161).

Jazz Sí Club, C Requesens 2, **T** 93 329 00 20. *M Sant Antoni. Bus 120. Map 2, B1, p248* Impromptu performances from students of

Musical youth

An aspect of Barcelona's lively outlook is its love of dynamic and interesting contemporary music.

the music school who run the place, as well as a diverse programme of live music each night, ranging from Cuban folk to soul and jazz to rock.

Luz de Gas, C Muntaner 246, **T** 93 209 77 11. *FGC Muntaner. Bus 58, 64. Map 1, B6, p246* A stunning turn-of-the-20th-century music hall, with a wide selection of live music: everything from soul, jazz and salsa to rock and pop.

Razzmatazz, C Almogàvers 122, **T** 93 320 82 00. *M Poble Nou. Bus 6, 40, 42, 141. Map 1, G9, p247* See Bars and clubs, p167.

Sala Apolo, C Nou de la Rambla 113, **T** 93 441 40 01. *M Paral.lel. Bus 20, 36, 57, 64, 91, 120, 157. Map 2, G1, p249* One of the best-known live music venues in the city, with a varied programme of concerts including pop and rock, reggae and world music.

Classical

The city's churches often offer concerts, particularly in the summer (details from the Centre d'Informació de la Virreina, p30). The church of Santa Maria del Mar is one of the loveliest, with perfect acoustics, but the cathedral of la Seu, the churches of Santa María del Pi, Santa Anna, Sant Felip Neri and the Monastery in Pedralbes all offer a sporadic programme of concerts. The Festival de Música Antigua (p181) is not to be missed, with early music in some of the city's most beautiful venues, like the Saló de Tinell in the Palau del Rei. Many of the museums also offer concerts: it's always worth checking out what's on at the CCCB (p60) and the Fundació Miró (p77) and there are concerts in the city parks and streets during the summer Festa de la Música (see p182).

Gran Teatre del Liceu, Las Ramblas 51-59, **T** 93 485 99 00, www.liceubarcelona.com *M Liceu. Bus 14, 38, 59, 91. Map 6, E2,* *p254* The (almost) faithful reincarnation of the celebrated opera house has become extremely popular, so getting hold of tickets can be difficult. There's a modern extension which offers recitals, talks, children's puppet shows and other events, usually related to the main programme (see also p36).

Palau de la Música Catalana, C Sant Francesc de Paula 2, **T** 93 295 72 00, www.palaumusica.org **M** *Urquinaona. Bus 17, 19, 40, 45. Map 6, A10, p255* The acoustics may be terrible, but the triumphant Modernista setting makes any performance worthwhile (see also p56).

Theatre

Barcelona's theatrical tradition is both accessible and highly innovative, with several experimental theatre groups demonstrating the city's flair, verve and innovation. The widespread use of multimedia, mime and choreography means that theatre in the city can easily cross any linguistic barriers. The latest project in the city's ambitious drive for redevelopment is the **Ciutat del Teatre**, which opened in 2001 and offers theatres, student spaces, a museum of theatre (see p80), the Institut del Teatre, part of the Teatre Lliure and the Mercat de las Flors theatre. The Bofill-designed Teatre Nacional de Catalunya has been another key player in drawing crowds to theatre since 1997. Pick up the free theatre guide *Teatre BCN* (Catalan only) from the Centre d'Informació de la Virreina (p30) or the tourist information offices.

Institut del Teatre, Plaça Margarida Xirgú, **T** 93 227 39 00, www.diba.es/iteatre **M** *Poble Sec. Bus 55, 57. Map 4, E5, p252* Student productions in Barcelona's theatre school, which has been given elegant new premises in the Ciutat del Teatre. The work is always interesting and very inexpensive.

Mercat de les Flors, C Lleida 59, **T** 93 426 18 75, www.bcn.es/icub/mflorsteatre *M Poble Sec. Bus 55, 57. Map 4, D4, p252* This beautifully converted flower market has become one of the main venues for the Grec festival (see p182) and puts on productions from some of the city's most innovative performers. Excellent contemporary dance as well as cutting-edge drama.

Sala Beckett, C Alegre de Dalt 55 bis, **T** 93 284 53 12, www.teatral.net/beckett *M Joanic. Bus 39, 55, 114. Map 1, C8, p247* Founded by the *Teatro Frontizero* group, which includes the eminent contemporary playwright José Sanchis Sinistierra. Interesting new theatre and contemporary dance.

Teatre Lliure, C Montseny 47, **T** 93 218 92 51, www.teatrelliure.com *Bus 22, 24, 28, 87. Map 3, B7, p250* One of the most prestigious theatres in Catalunya, Lliure has produced some of its leading actors and directors. It has a new outpost, the Espai Lliure, part of the city's Ciutat del Teatre complex in Montjuïc.

Teatre Nacional de Catalunya (TNC), Plaça de les Arts 1, Eixample, **T** 93 306 57 07, www.tnc.es *M Glòries. Bus 10, 62. Map 1, F9, p247* Inaugurated in 1997, this strikingly modern Ricardo Bofill-designed building is the flagship of the city council's efforts to smarten up the grim Glòries district. Performances range from high-quality drama to contemporary dance.

Festivals and events

Barcelona loves a party and festivals provide an excellent excuse. The city's biggest traditional festival is the exuberant Festa de la Mercè in September, with parades featuring the popular *gegants* (giants) and *capgrossos* (fatheads), *castellers* (human castles) and plenty of music and dancing. Smaller but just as colourful are the neighbourhood festivals, particularly those in Barceloneta and Gràcia. Barcelona also offers excellent cultural festivals, from the Grec festival of performing arts to the Sónar festival of music and multimedia which is one of the best parties on the Mediterranean coast. Classical music lovers can enjoy festivals dedicated to everything from flamenco to Baroque and the city sponsors free classical concerts in the parks throughout Barcelona during the summer. The helpful tourist office and websites can provide full information, or ring the city information line on **T** 010. Contact the Centre d'Informació de la Virreina (see p30) for information on cultural festivals and events.

January

Cap d'Any/Noche Vieja (1st) Street parties and carousing to bring in the New Year. Big club nights – with high prices.

Cavalcada des Reis (5th) The Three Kings parade through the city throwing sweets to the kids.

February/March

Carnestoltes/Carnaval Carnival is not as big as in other parts of Spain, but there's a great party atmosphere all the same. In Sitges it is a big and extravagantly colourful gay event.

April

Sant Jordi (23rd) Big festival of the patron saint of Catalunya. Lovers traditionally exchange gifts.

Holy Week: Setmana Santa Parades and religious processions take place across the city, centred around the Gothic cathedral.

Feria de Abril (late Apr/early May) Flamenco and carousing.

May

Dia del Treball (1st) Labour Day. Street marches and speeches.

Festa de Sant Ponç (11th) Pretty street market along Carrer Hospital to honour the patron saint of beekeepers and herbalists.

Festival de Flamenco and Festival de Música Antigua
Flamenco and early music concerts. **T** 93 476 86 00.

June

Corpus Christi (May/Jun – dates vary) See the *ou com balla* (egg dancing on a fountain) in the cathedral cloister.

Trobada Castellera The casteller groups from across the region build human castles in Plaça Sant Jaume.

Marató de l'Espectacle (early Jun) Non-stop alternative performances at the Mercat de les Flors. www.marato.com

Festa de la Música (21st) An imported French tradition, free concerts are held on the streets throughout the city. www.fusic.org

Festa de Sant Joan (23rd and 24th) An exuberant Catalan festival: fireworks, demons, cava and beach parties.

Dia per l'Alliberament Lesbià i Gia (28th) Gay pride (*Orgull*) parade though the city, with lots of action in the bars and clubs.

Sónar (Jun/Jul) Exciting multimedia and music; beachside raves and events across the city. www.sonar.es

Classics als Parcs (Jun/Jul) Classical concerts in the city's parks. www.bcn.es/parcsijardins

Festival del Grec (Jun/Jul) Classical music, jazz, rock, theatre, dance and cinema fill the city. www.bcn.es/grec

August

Festa Major de Gràcia (mid-late Aug) Each street in Gràcia vies to create the best decorations; huge outdoor parties.

Giants, dragons and castles in the air

After years of repression under Franco, Catalunya celebrates its festivals with exuberance, resuscitating centuries-old customs in an outpouring of pride and optimism. These are some of the most popular.

Correfoc 'Fire-running' goes back hundreds, if not thousands, of years. Parading drummers beat a pulse-quickening march through the streets, heralding the arrival of dragons (*dracs*), surrounded by leaping demons (*demonis*) setting off fireworks. Wear protective, cotton clothing if you want to join in.

Gegants and capgrossos The *gegants* (giants) first appeared at Catalan festivals in the middle ages. They are enormous figures made of wood and papier mâché who lumber along in the festival parades. The *capgrossos* (fatheads) are squat leering versions, who accompany the giants on the parades. Mischievous little figures, some modern ones bear the faces of celebrities and politicians.

Castellers The art of building human towers dates back to the 1700s and has undergone a major revival. The bottom layer with a central sturdy knot of people is known as the *pinya* (pine cone). Upon this, carefully, the layers are built up. A child (the *aixedor*) provides the support for an even smaller child (the *anxenata*) who scampers to the top and grins like a gargoyle, waving down to the crowd below.

Sardana The grave, stately circle dance of the Catalans is an ancient folkloric tradition which you can see outside the cathedral of La Seu . The *cobla* (band) strike up and a group of people, sometimes as few as four, will link hands and circle with slow sedate steps, interspersed with longer, rising ones. The circles get bigger and bigger as more and more people join in. True aficionados wear espadrilles that are tied with coloured ribbons.

September

Diada National de Catalunya (11th) Catalan National Day, celebrated with speeches and parades. There is always a ceremony at the Fossar de les Morares in La Ribera (see p52).

Dies de Dansa (mid-Sep) Three days of dance. www.marato.com

Festa de la Mercè (24th) A massive week-long celebration, with dragons, fatheads, human castles, fire-running and fireworks, all kinds of free events, a swimming race across the harbour, as well as concerts and the BAM alternative music festival.

Festa Major de la Barceloneta (late Sep) Barceloneta's neighbourhood festival. See also p88.

October

Tots Sants (Castanyada) (1st) All Saints Day; people visit family graves and eat traditional foods.

International Jazz Festival (Oct-Dec) Concerts by local and international jazz groups in venues across the city, including the Palau de la Música. www.the-project.net

December

Fira de Santa Llúcia (1st-22nd) Santa Llúcia marks the beginning of the festive season and the start of the Christmas market.

Nadal and Sant Esteve (25th-26th) Christmas and the Catalan equivalent of Boxing Day are low-key family affairs, with big family lunches. The main present giving doesn't happen until 6th Jan.

The designer shop Galleries Vinçon on the Passeig de Gràcia used to have the slogan 'I shop therefore I am' blazoned across its packaging. Barcelona has more retail outlets per capita than anywhere else in Europe, ranging from tiny old-fashioned shops which haven't changed in decades, to grand glitzy shopping malls where you can get everything you want under one roof. Best buys are leather goods, designer fashions and unusual household goods, local wines and deli items. The Barri Gòtic has most of the unusual one-off shops as well as branches of most of the fashion chains along Carrer Portaferrissa, while the Eixample (particularly the Passeig de Gràcia and the Diagonal) has big international fashion names and smart boutiques. The Raval has the fashionable vintage clothes stores and hip music outlets and the Ribera has lots of unusual fashion and interior design shops. Look for signs saying *rebaixes* (Catalan) or *rebajas* (Castilian). The January sales begin after the 8th of January and last for about six weeks. There are also summer sales in July and August.

Smaller shops tend to open from 0900 or 1000 until about 1330 and then reopen from around 1600 until 2000 or 2100. Large chain stores, department stores and shopping malls often stay open all day. Most shops, including supermarkets, close on Sundays.

Department stores

El Corte Inglés, Plaça de Catalunya 14, **T** 93 306 38 00, www.elcorteingles.com *Mon-Sat 1000-2200.* ***M** Plaça de Catalunya. All buses to Plaça de Catalunya. Map 2, A6, p248* This huge department store is part of a vast Spanish chain. There's a basement supermarket and delicatessen, plus fashion, leather goods, toiletries, electrical goods and souvenirs. There's a top floor café with fabulous views and look out for the *opportunidads* (bargains) on the 8th floor. There's another branch just down the road at Avda Portal de l'Àngel which has books, music and DVDs.

Bookshops, newspapers and magazines

The stalls along the Ramblas all have a good selection of foreign newspapers and magazines and occasionally novels in English.

Altaïr, C Gran Via 616, **T** 93 342 71 71. *Mon-Sat 1000-1400, 1630-2030.* ***M** Passeig de Gràcia. Bus 7, 50, 54, 56, 67, 68. Map 2, K5, p251* A huge travel bookshop, with an excellent selection of guidebooks and maps covering all corners of the world (including Catalunya), many in English.

Fnac, El Triangle, Plaça de Catalunya, **T** 93 344 18 00. *Mon-Sat 1000-2130.* ***M** Plaça de Catalunya. All buses to Plaça de Catalunya. Map 2, A4, p248* Enormous store with books, music, a concert ticket service and an international news-stand and café on the ground floor.

Design, decorative and household goods

BD Edicions de Disseny, C Mallorca 291, **T** 93 458 69 09. *Mon-Fri 1000-1330, 1600-2030, Sat 1000-1330, 1630-2030. M Verdaguer. Bus 43, 44. Map 3, H7, p251* Set in a stunning Modernista mansion, the BD group was founded in 1972 by the prestigious architect Òscar Tusquets among others. Exquisite, expensive furniture – both reproduction Modernista and contemporary designs – and other household goods.

Galeries Vinçon, Passeig de Gràcia 96, **T** 93 215 60 50, www.vincon.com *Mon-Sat 1000-1330, 1630-2030. M Diagonal. Bus 7, 16, 17, 22, 24, 28. Map 3, G6, p251* The most influential design emporium in the city, located right next to La Pedrera, with everything for the home from furniture and lighting to kitchenware and table accoutrements.

Ici et Là, Plaça Santa María del Mar 2, **T** 93 268 11 67, www.icietla.com *Mon 1630-2030, Tue-Sat 1030-2030. M Jaume I or Barceloneta. Bus 14, 39, 51. Map 6, H11, p255* Affordable, unusual creations for the home from around the world.

Fashion

Bad Habits, C València 261, **T** 93 487 22 59. *Mon-Sat 1030-1430, 1630-2030. M Passeig de Gràcia. Bus 20, 43, 44. Map 3, H6, p251* Strikingly original, androgynous designs from Mireya Ruiz.

Camper, C València 249, **T** 93 215 63 90. *Mon-Sat 1000-2100. M Passeig de Gràcia. Bus 20, 43, 44. Map 3, H5, p251* Trendy, comfortable shoes at a reasonable price. Several branches, including one in the El Triangle shopping mall on Plaça de Catalunya.

Fórum Ferlandina, C Ferlandina 31, **T** 93 441 18 80. *Tue-Fri 1030-1400 and 1700-2030, Sat 1100-1400.* **M** *Universitat. Bus 21, 44, 55. Map 2, B2, p248* Original jewellers, just around the corner from MACBA, with a range of unusual contemporary designs from gold to plastic.

Jean-Pierre Bua, Avda Diagonal 469, **T** 93 439 71 00. *Mon-Sat 1000-1400, 1630-2030* **M** *Diagonal. Bus 6, 7, 15, 27, 32, 33, 34. Map 3, D1, p250* The original and best-known designer fashion shop, with the latest from names like Marni, Miu Miu, Dolce & Gabbana and Balenciaga.

Mango, Passeig de Gràcia 65, **T** 92 419 10 40, www.mango.es *Mon-Sat 1000-2030.* **M** *Passeig de Gràcia. Bus 7, 16, 17, 22, 24, 28. Map 3, I6, p251* Catwalk knock-offs at affordable prices, with ranges for work, evening and casual wear, including shoes and accessories. Several branches.

Mies & Felj, C Riera Baixa 4-5, **T** 93 442 07 55. *Mon-Sat 1030-1400, 1700-2030.* **M** *Liceu or Sant Antoni. Bus 120. Map 2, C2, p248* Great second-hand jackets, dresses, hats, bags and T-shirts.

Tribu, C Avinyó 12, **T** 92 318 65 10. *Mon-Sat 1100-1430 and 1630-2030.* **M** *Jaume I. Bus 14, 38, 59, 91. Map 6, G5, p254* One of several slick fashion boutiques on this street. Trendy outlet for designers as well as their own label. Look out for guest DJ nights.

Zara, C Pelai 58, **T** 93 301 93 78. *Mon-Sat 1000-2100.* **M** *Plaça de Catalunya. Bus 9, 14, 16, 17, 24, 38, 4, 42, 55, 58, 59, 66, 91, 141. Map 2, B4, p248* Great fashion for men, women, teenagers, kids and babies at very low prices but not always of the best quality. There are several branches throughout the city.

Food and wine

Casa del Bacalao, C Comtal 8. *Mon-Sat 0900-1430 and 1700-1830* **M** *Urquinaona. Bus 17, 19, 40, 45. Map 2, B5, p248* This ancient, delightful little shop sells nothing but dried and salted cod. They will pack it specially if you want to take it home.

Escribà, Gran Via de les Cortes Catalanes 546, **T** 93 454 75 35/29. *Mon-Sat 0800-2100.* **M** *Urgell. Bus 9, 50, 56. Map 3, L1, p251* Chocolate heaven: it's worth coming just to see the incredible window displays. Wonderful cakes and pastries and beautifully packaged chocolates.

Queviures Murrià, C Roger de Llúria 85, **T** 93 215 57 89. *Mon-Sat 1000-1400, 1700-2030.* **M** *Passeig de Gràcia. Bus 39, 45, 57. Map 3, I7, p251* This old-fashioned grocery store was established in 1948 and is set in beautiful old Modernista premises. You'll find a range of farmhouse cheeses, excellent hams and a good selection of wines and cavas.

Markets

La Boquería (Mercat de Sant Josep), Las Ramblas 91. *Mon-Sat 0800-1700, a few stalls stay open later.* **M** *Liceu. Bus 14, 38, 59, 91. Map 6, C2, p254* Barcelona's best-loved food market with hundreds of stalls. Stalls at the front have tourist prices – be prepared to browse and price check.

Els Encants, Plaça de las Glòries Catalanas. *Mon, Wed, Fri and Sat 0900-1700.* **M** *Glòries. Bus 7, 56. Map 1, F10, p247* A sprawling flea market; get there early if you want a bargain and keep a close eye on your belongings. It's under threat – property developers want the land – but the locals have put up a struggle.

Shopping

Mercat de Sant Antoni, C Comte d'Urgell 1. *Mon-Thu and Sat 0700-1430, 1700-2030, Fri 0700-2030; Sun 1000-1400. **M** Sant Antoni. Bus 20, 37, 64. Map 1, F5, p246* Another wrought-iron Modernista market, the fresh produce is replaced by a second-hand book and coin market on Sundays.

Mercat Mon Raval, Rambla de Raval. *Sat and Sun 1000-2100. **M** Liceu or Paral.lel. Bus 120. Map 2, D/E1/2, p247* Bringing some welcome liveliness to the city's newest Rambla, this weekend market is a trendy mix of new and old clothes, sunglasses, food, jewellery and crafts. There is sometimes live music.

Plaça del Pi. *M Liceu. Bus 14, 38, 59, 91. Map 6, E4, p254* On the first Friday and Saturday of the month, there's a honey market, when you'll also find other things like cured hams and farmhouse cheeses for sale. There's an antiques market on Thursdays and art is for sale on weekends in the adjoining Plaça Josep Oriol.

Music

Discos Castelló, C Tallers 3,**T** 93 318 20 41, www.discoscastello.com *Daily 1000-1400 and 1730-2030. **M** Plaça de Catalunya. Bus 14, 38, 59, 91. Map 2, B4, p248* There are several branches of this music shop, including three along this small street; this particular branch specializes in classical music, with a wide range of contemporary music available at 7 and 79. For Spanish and international dance music, head to C Nou de la Rambla 15.

Etnomusic, C Bonsuccés 6, **T** 93 301 18 84, www.etnomusic.com *Mon-Sat 1100-1400, 1700- 2000. **M** Plaça de Catalunya. Bus 14, 38, 59, 91. Map 2, B4, p248* Well-known world music shop with very helpful staff.

Shopping malls

El Triangle, C Pelai 39. *Most shops Mon-Sat 1000-2200.* **M** *Plaça de Catalunya. All buses to Plaça de Catalunya. Map 2, A4, p248* This gleaming mall contains an enormous Fnac (books, music and concert tickets), Habitat, Sephora (perfumes and cosmetics), a Camper shoe store and several other smaller fashion shops.

L'Illa, Avda Diagonal 545-557, www.lilla.com *Most shops Mon-Sat 1000-2130.* **M** *Maria Cristina. Buses 6, 7, 33, 34, 63, 67, 68 and Tombus (special shopping bus). Map 1, C4, p246* The largest mall in the city, this has all the fashion chains along with a Fnac and several upmarket boutiques.

Unusual shops

Almacenes del Pilar, C Boquería 43, **T** 93 317 79 84, www.almacenesdelpilar.com *Mon-Sat 1000-1330 and 1700-2000.* **M** *Liceu. Bus 14, 38, 59, 91. Map 6, E4, p254* A beautiful selection of traditional fringed Spanish silk shawls and elaborate fans.

El Ingenio, C Rauric 6, **T** 93 317 93 38, www.el-ingenio.com *Mon-Fri 1000-1330, 1645-2000, Sat 1000-1400, 1715-2030.* **M** *Liceu. Bus 14, 18, 38, 59. Map 6, F3, p254* Everything you need for a fiesta – puppets, masks, carnival and fancy dress outfits. Founded in 1838, it specializes in making traditional papier mâché figures.

El Rei de la Màgia, C Princesa 11, **T** 93 319 39 20. **M** *Jaume I. Bus 17, 19, 40, 45. Map 6, F10, p255* An extraordinary shop devoted to magic and magicians, with walls papered with photographs of celebrated magicians.

Sports

Among the two top-selling daily papers in Spain are two devoted exclusively to football, *La Marca* and *AS*. And Barcelona's football team, the legendary Barça, is one of the most popular in the world. Walk along any street on the night of a big match and you'll see every head in every bar craning up at the inevitable TV. Football, as the cliché goes, is a Spanish religion, closely followed by basketball. Getting tickets to either is difficult but not impossible. The city's sports facilities are excellent, partly thanks to the 1992 Olympics and there are several good municipally run sports centres. The Parc del Collserola and the long beachfront from Barceloneta out to the new Forum complex are great areas for cycling, jogging and strolling, although the beachfront is crammed in summer. The natural park of Montserrat is good for hiking and even rock-climbing. There are excellent ski stations in the Catalan Pyrenees: the information centre at the Palau Robert can advise, or you can pick up a package (travel, ski pass and accommodation) from most travel agents.

Spectator sports

Basketball

Basketball is massively popular throughout Spain. Barcelona's two biggest teams are FC Barça and Club Joventut Badalona. The season runs from September to May.

Club Joventut Badalona, C Ponent 143-161, Badalona (on the outskirts of the city), **T** 93 460 20 40, www.penya.com *M Gorg. Tickets €15-20.*

FC Barcelona, Palau Blau Grana (next to Camp Nou stadium), Avda d'Aristides Maillol, **T** 93 496 36 75, www.fcbarcelona.com *M Collblanc. Bus 15, 52, 54, 56, 57, 75. Map 1, C2, p246 €5-25.*

Bullfighting

Plaza de Toros Monumental, 749 Gran Via de les Catalanes 749, **T** 93 245 58 02. *M Monumental. Bus 6, 7, 56, 62. Map 1, F9, p247* Bullfighting is not very popular in Barcelona, but bullfights (*corridas*) are still held during the summer, April to September. Tickets €15-90. Children under 14 are not admitted.

Football

The city has two first-division clubs: FC Barcelona and RCD Espanyol. Getting hold of tickets for many games at the Camp Nou stadium is next to impossible, but you stand a good chance of seeing Espanyol play. The season runs from late August to May.

FC Barcelona, Camp Nou, Avda d'Aristides Maillol, **T** 93 496 36 00, ticket hotline **T** 93 496 37 02, www.fcbarcelona.com *M Collblanc. Bus 15, 52, 54, 56, 57, 75. Map 1, C2, p246* There is an online ticket sales service or you can buy tickets directly from the stadium ticket office, available two days before a match. Tickets €20-90.

RCD Espanyol, Estadi Olimpic, Passeig Olimpic, 17-19, **T** 93 292 77 00, www.rcdespanyol.com *M Paral.lel then funicular, or M Plaça Espanya then shuttle bus (match days only). Map 4, G2, p252* Tickets for Barcelona's less famous team can be purchased near the Olympic Stadium entrance.

Grand Prix

Circuit de Catalunya, Montmeló (near Granollers), **T** 93 571 97 08, www.circuitcat.com The Spanish Grand Prix and the Catalunya Motorcycling Grand Prix are held here. Tickets can be ordered online or purchased at the circuit.

Tennis

Reial Club de Tennis Barcelona – 1899, C Bosch i Gimpera 5-13, **T** 93 203 78 52, www.rctb1899.es *Bus 63, 78. Map 1, B3, p246* The Barcelona Open, a prestigious ten-day international tournament, takes place at Barcelona's smartest tennis club during the last week of April. Tickets €23-70.

Participation sports

Gyms and fitness clubs

Centres de Fitness DiR. There are seven well-equipped (pools, saunas, weight rooms, etc) DiR fitness centres in the city which offer day and short-term membership; for information on the one closest to you, call **T** 901 30 40 30 or check out the website, www.dirfitness.es Bring your passport to sign up.

Golf

Club de Golf El Prat, El Prat de Llobregat, **T** 93 379 02 78. *Daily 0800-2200.* Out near the airport, in past years this club has been used for the Spanish Open (tickets €23-70). You must be a member of a federated club to play.

Club de Golf Sant Cugat, C de la Villa s/n, Sant Cugat del Vallès, **T** 93 674 39 58. *FGC from Plaça de Catalunya to Sant Cugat. Daily 0800-2200.* 18-hole course with a bar, restaurant and pool.

Jogging

Best places to jog include the boardwalk from Barceloneta to Mar Bella – run early before the crowds come. Parc de Collserola (see p92) is another great place for a run. The park information centre has maps. There are fantastic views along the Carretera de les Aigües at the top of Avinguda Tibidabo in the Collserola.

Sailing and watersports

Base Nàutica de la Mar Bella, Avda de Litoral (between the beaches of Bogatell and Mar Bella), **T** 93 221 04 32, www.basenautica.net *Winter daily 0930-1730; summer daily 0930-2100.* **M** *Poble Nou. Bus 41. Map 5, F9, p253* Windsurfing, snorkelling equipment and boat rentals, plus a wide range of courses. There's also the added bonus of DJ sessions in summer.

Centre Municipal de Vela, Moll de Gregal, Port Olímpic, **T** 93 221 14 99, www.vela-barcelona.com *Mon-Fri 0900-2100, Sat and Sun 0900-2000, office daily 1000-2000.* **M** *Ciutadella-Vila*

Olímpica. Bus 10, 45, 59, 71, 92. *Map 5, G7, p253* The municipal sailing school offers sailing courses for people of all levels of ability.

Swimming

Club de Natació Barceloneta/Banys de Sant Sebastià, Plaça del Mar 1, **T** 93 221 00 10, www.cnab.org *Jun-mid-Sep Mon-Sat 0700-2300, Sun 0800-2000; mid-Sep-Jun Mon-Sat 0700-2300, Sun 0800-1700.* **M** *Barceloneta. Bus 17, 36, 39, 45, 57, 59, 64, 157. Map 2, M5, p249* Very close to Barceloneta beach. Indoor and outdoor pools, gym, sauna, restaurant and café.

Piscina Bernat Picornell, Avda de l'Estadi 30-40, **T** 93 423 40 41, www.picornell.com *Indoor pool Mon-Fri 0700-0000, Sat 0700-2100, Sun 0730-1600 (until 2000 Jun-Sep); outdoor pool Mon-Sat 1000-2000 (until 2100 in summer), Sun and holidays 1000-1430 (0900-0800 in summer).* **M** *Paral.lel then funicular, or* **M** *Plaça Espanya then bus 61. Map 4, E1, p252* Magnificent pools used in 1992 Olympics. Indoor and outdoor pools, sauna and gym/weights room.

Tennis

Centre Municipal de Tennis Vall d'Hebron, Psg de la Vall d'Hebron 178-196, **T** 93 427 65 00. *Mon-Sat 0800-2300, Sun 0800-1900.* **M** *Montbau. Bus 20, 60, 73, 76, 173, 185. Off map 1, p247* This municipal sports centre has 18 clay courts, seven asphalt courts and two open-air pools.

Barcelona's vibrant gay scene is growing all the time and it's generally an easy place for gay and lesbian travellers to feel safe and comfortable. Just half an hour by train out of the city is the seaside town of Sitges (see p101), one of the most popular gay holiday spots in Europe. In Barcelona itself, most of the gay bars, restaurants and clubs are located in the Left Eixample (see p64), which is known as the *Gaixample* or *Eixample Rosa*. Spring and summer are the best times to come, but the Carnaval in mid-February is a blast. There are several helpful information centres (see below), which deal with cultural, health and other issues. If you are just looking to party, head straight for Zeus, Carrer Riera Alta 20, **T** 93 442 97 95, or Sestienda, Carrer Rauric 11, **T** 93 318 86 76, two gay sex shops which produce a free gay map to Barcelona and Sitges with everything you ever wanted to know clearly marked.

Bars and clubs

Arena Vip's, Gran Via de les Corts Catalanes 593, **T** 93 487 83 42. *Fri and Sat 0000-0500.* **M** *Universitat and Passeig de Gràcia. Bus 7, 50, 54, 56, 67, 68. Map 3, K4, p251* There are four Arena clubs in Barcelona, all popular with a good cross-section.

Bahia, C Sèneca 12, no **T**. *Daily 1000-0300.* **M** *Fontana. Bus 22, 24, 28, 87. Map 3, E5, p250* Gothic-style, friendly lesbian bar with good music.

Café Bar Aire (Sala Diana), C València 236, **T** 93 451 58 12, Eixample. *Mon-Sat 2300-0200, Sun 1800-2200.* **M** *Passeig de Gràcia. Bus 7, 16, 17, 63, 67, 68. Map 3, H4, p251* Airy, friendly lesbian bar with a pool table and a scattering of tables. After midnight, the dance floor begins to fill up, as the crowds get down to 80s sounds and Spanish pop under the huge disco ball.

G Café, C Muntaner 24, Eixample. *Mon-Fri 1600-0230, Sat and Sun 1600-0300.* **M** *Universitat and Urgell. All buses to Plaça Universitat. Map 3, K2, p251* Friendly café-bar with Gaudíesque decor and changing art exhibitions. There's a big terrace which is perfect for people-watching/cruising in summer.

Martin's, Passeig de Gràcia 130, **T** 93 218 71 67. *Daily 0000-0500.* **M** *Passeig de Gràcia. Bus 7, 16, 17, 22, 24, 28. Map 3, F6, p250* This three-floor club is a classic on Barcelona's gay scene and is back in fashion for its popular theme nights.

Salvation, Ronda de Sant Pere 19-21, **T** 93 318 06 86. *Fri-Sun 0000-0500.* **M** *Urquinaona. Bus 14, 39, 40, 41, 42, 55, 141. Map 2, A7, p248* One of the most fashionable spots on the gay circuit, with two dance floors, DJs, go go dancers and a beautiful crowd.

Gay and lesbian

Bookshops

Antinous, C Josep Anselm Clave 6, **T** 93 301 90 70. *Mon-Fri 1100-1400, 1700-2100, Sat 1200-1400, 1700-2100.* **M** *Drassanes. Bus 14, 38, 59, 91. Map 2, H4, p249* Books, magazines, a charming café and lots of information on gay activities. You can pick up the useful free gay nightlife map of Barcelona and Sitges here.

Complices, C Cervantes 2, **T** 93 412 72 83. *Mon-Fri 1030-2030, Sat 1200-2030.* **M** *Liceu. Bus 14, 38, 59, 91. Map 6, G6, p254* Books and magazines in English and Spanish as well as T-shirts and gifts.

Festivals

Carnaval in Sitges is one of the biggest gay events in Spain, with parades featuring flamboyant floats and a serious party schedule across the town. Book accommodation well in advance.

Hotels

D Central Town Rooms & Apartments, Ronda San Pau 51, 5º, **T** 93 442 70 57, www.centraltown.com **M** *Sant Antoni. Bus 20, 24, 64, 91. Map 2, B8, p248* A gay-run guesthouse on the edge of the hip, bohemian Raval with simple rooms and apartments.

D Hostal Que Tal, C Mallorca 290, **T** 93 459 23 66. **M** *Passeig de Gràcia. Bus 43, 44. Map 3, H7, p251* Spotless, friendly and cheerful, this is a very popular spot in the Eixample, so book well in advance. Double rooms come with and without bathrooms.

E Hotel California, C Rauric 14, **T** 93 317 77 66, **F** 93 317 54 74, www.seker.es/hotel_california **M** *Liceu. Bus 14, 38, 59, 91. Map 6, E4, p254* Affordable and central; functional rooms but friendly.

Magazines and newspapers

You'll find gay info in the *Guia del Ocio* and other listings magazines under 'El Ambiente'. There are listings and articles in *Shangay* and *Shanguide*, freely available in most gay bars and clubs.

Organizations

Casal Lambda, C Verdaguer i Callís 10, **T** 93 319 55 50 (lines open Mon-Sat 1700-2100), www.lambdaweb.org *M Urquinaona. Bus 17, 19, 40, 45. Map 6, A10, p255* Dealing with political, social and cultural issues affecting the gay community, Casal Lambda has a library and documentation centre and hosts all kinds of activities.

Coordinadora Gai-Lesbiana, C Finlàndia 45, **T** 93 298 00 29, www.cogailes.org *M Plaça de Sants. Bus 30, 56, 57, 153, 157. Map 1, E2, p246* An umbrella organization which encompasses a broad range of social, political and cultural groups, works with the city council on gay issues and produces a free magazine.

Restaurants

Castro, C Casanova 85 , **T** 933236784, Eixample. *Sun-Fri 1300-1600, 0900-1330, Sat 0900-1300. M Hospital Clínic. Bus 14, 59. Map 3, I1, p251* Very camp, with innovative Mediterranean and international dishes.

La Diva, C Diputació 172, **T** 93 454 63 98. *Mon-Fri 1300-1530, 2100-0000, Sun 2100-0000. M Urgell. Bus 14, 20, 37, 59. Map 3, K1, p251* A flamboyant gay cabaret restaurant with delicious Mediterranean cuisine and spectacular drag shows.

Gay and lesbian

Ovlas, C Portaferrissa 25, **T** 93 412 38 36. *Mon-Sat 0930-2030.*
M Liceu. Bus 14, 38, 59, 91. Map 6, B5, p254 Italian food in over
the top surroundings. Very popular, so book ahead.

La Singular, C Francisco Giner 50, Gràcia, **T** 93 237 50 98. *Mon-Fri
1300-1600, 2000-0000, Sat 2000-0100. M Diagonal. Bus 22, 24, 28,
87. Map 3, D6, p250* Run by women, serving good pasta, seafood
and tapas.

Saunas

Sauna Casanova, C Casanova 57, **T** 93 323 78 60,
www.grupopases.com *24-hours. M Universitat. All buses to Plaça
Universitat. Map 3, K1, p251* One of the most popular saunas in
Barcelona, with a good location in the heart of the Gaixample.

Sauna Thermas, C Diputació 46, **T** 93 325 93 46,
www.grupopases.com *24-hours. M Universitat. Bus 14, 20, 37,
59. Map 1, E4, p246* This is the biggest sauna complex in Spain,
with a range of facilities including gym, TV room, restaurant and
Sala X.

Websites

www.gaybarcelona.net and www.guiagay.com (both in Castilian
Spanish) are useful portals offering a range of information.
www.gaywired.com and www.gay.com have useful links and
are in English. www.gayinspain.com (in Castilian and English)
has everything from bars and accommodation to saunas and
shops. Barcelona and Sitges are regularly featured in the online
gay and lesbian travel magazine, www.qtmagazine.com.

Barcelona is a great place to visit with children, with fairy-tale buildings, beaches and plenty of child-friendly activities from sailing ships to mountain-top funfairs. The Spanish love children and you'll find yours are treated indulgently wherever you go – however badly they behave. Most museums offer reduced admission for children between four and 12 and free admission to children under four. Public transport is also free for children under four. You'll find everything you might need (nappies, formula milk etc) in the local supermarkets and pharmacies, but bear in mind that almost everything is closed on Sundays. Festivals usually offer fireworks, flamethrowers and parades that kids love (although they can sometimes be scary for very young children), see Festivals and events p179. The two biggest listings guides – the *Guia del Ocio* and the free *LaNetro* guide both have a section devoted to children's activities (look under *Niños*), with theatre, cinema, exhibitions and other events.

Activities

Most children will enjoy Barcelona's cable cars and funiculars. The **Telefèric de Montjuïc** is especially exciting (see p79).

Golondrinas (see p29). Old-fashioned double-decker sightseeing boats do tours around the port.

Childcare facilities

There are a few babysitting services, if you want to take the night off and most of the larger hotels can arrange babysitting if you give them sufficient notice. The tourist information office has a full list, or you could call one of the agencies listed below.

Baby Home, C Diputació 188, **T** 93 453 85 29.
Cangur Serveis, C Aragó 50, **T** 93 488 26 01.
Happy Parc, C dels Comptes de Bell Lloc 74-78, **T** 93 490 08 35.
This is a drop-off daycare centre with indoor play facilities.
Servinens, Travessera de Gràcia 117, **T** 93 218 23 87.

Eating

Eating out with children is no problem in Barcelona. Children are treated like small adults and it's not unusual to see them out in restaurants with their parents late at night, or playing outside a café while their families chat away. Perversely, this also means that few restaurants have child-specific facilities – high chairs are rare and you'll probably have to ask for a small portion rather than be given a child's menu. Tapas bars are a good place to get a taste of local food and still get them to bed before 2200.

Kids

Bosc de les Fades, Passatge de la Banca 7, **T** 93 317 26 49. *Mon-Thu 1030-0100, Fri 1030-0300, Sat 1100-0300, Sun 1100-0100.* **M** *Drassanes. Bus 14, 38, 59, 91. Map 2, H3, p249* This pretty café is part of the wax museum (no admission necessary to café) and has a delightfully kitsch fairy forest peopled with wax figures. A good place to stop for a cold drink just off the Ramblas.

Parks and beaches

Barcelona has six beaches stretching from Barceloneta out past the Port Olímpic. There are dozens of snack bars, ice-cream vendors and cafés close by. There are outdoor showers but no changing facilities, unless you use a restaurant bathroom. The beaches get jam-packed at weekends. The city council organizes children's sports and activities on the beaches between March and May, culminating in the **Festa de la Platja** in May. The tourist office can supply all the details (p30).

Park Güell (p82). Gaudí's dreamy park is always a kids' favourite.

Parc de Collserola (see p92). Wonderful natural park with hiking trails, horse-riding and picnic spots.

Shopping

Imaginarium, Rambla de Catalunya 31, **T** 93 487 67 54. *Mon-Fri 1000-2030, Sat 1000-2100.* **M** *Plaça de Catalunya. All buses to Plaça de Catalunya. Map 3, K5, p251* A branch of the Spanish toy shop chain, with a range of toys for kids of all ages and a play area.

Jacardi, Rambla de Catalunya 79, Barcelona, **T** 93 487 58 40. *Mon-Sat 1000-1400, 1600-2000.* **M** *Passeig de Gràcia. Bus 7, 16, 17, 22, 24, 28. Map 3, I5, p251* Colourful, durable and fashionable clothes for kids.

Kinder Trenes Eléctricos, C Corsega 415, **T** 93 457 20 81. *Mon 1700-2100, Tue-Sat 1100-1500, 1700-2100.* **M** *Verdaguer. Bus 20, 45, 57. Map 1, D9, p247* An astonishing shop, entirely dedicated to model trains, from old-fashioned steam to the most modern and sophisticated speed-merchants.

Mullor Infants, Rambla de Catalunya 102, **T** 93 215 12 02. *Mon-Sat 1000-1400 and 1615-2015.* **M** *Diagonal. Bus 7, 16, 17, 22, 24, 28. Map 3, H5, p251* Beautiful, handmade, traditional clothes for newborn babies, from knitted booties to pretty smocked dresses.

Sights

L'Aquàrium (p86). Sharks, penguins and jellyfish with an interactive centre for very young children.

IMAX, Moll d'Espanya-Port Vell, **T** 902 400 222. *Daily 1200-0030, consult film listings (*cartelera*) in listings magazines for shows and times. €7 single session, €10 double.* **M** *Barceloneta. Bus 14, 17, 19, 36, 39, 40, 45, 57, 59, 64 and 157. Map 2, I5/6, p249* Everything from alien adventures to dinosaurs in enormous 3-D and surround sound, but in Catalan and Castilian only.

Museu de la Ciència (p94). Science museum with a special section for the under-fives.

Museu de la Xocolata (p52). Chocolate museum with tastings and interactive exhibits.

Museu FC Barcelona President Nuñez (p90). A mecca for football fans of all ages.

La Pedrera (p66), **CCCB** (p60), **Fundació Miró** (p77), **MNAC** (p75) and **MACBA** (p58) all offer family entertainment – puppet

Kids

shows and concerts – at weekends during the summer. Check the tourist office (p30) for details.

Las Ramblas (p33). Puppet shows, mime artists and buskers on the city's most famous street.

Tibidabo Parc d'Attraciones (p94). Funfair on top of the mountain. Get there by the old-fashioned Tramvia Blau and the Tibidabo funicular.

Theme parks out of town

Catalunya en Miniatura, Torrelles de Llobregat, **T** 936890960, www.catalunyaenminiatura.com   *Apr-Jun and Sep daily 1000-1900; Jul-Aug daily 1000-2000; Oct daily 1000-1800, Nov-Mar Tue-Sun 1000-1800. Adults €9, children under 12 €6.50, under-4s free.* One of the largest model villages in Europe, with 170 monuments of Catalunya; a mini-train does the rounds and there are clown shows on Sundays.

Isla Fantasia, Vilassar del Dalt, **T** 937514553, www.islafantasia.com   *End Jun-mid-Sept daily 1000-1900. Adults €11, children aged 2-11 €8.   24 km from Barcelona, trains from Plaça de Catalunya.*   One of the largest waterparks in Europe.

Universal Mediterranea/Port Aventura, Salou, **T** 977 77 90 90 (reservations from the UK **T** 0800 96 65 40), www.portaventura.es   *Mar-Oct daily 1000-2000, late Jun-mid-Sep daily 1000-0000. Jul-mid-Sep 1 day adult €34, €27 children 5- 12. Low season €32 adults, €17 children. 75 mins by train from Passeig de Gràcia or Sants.*   Massive theme park with plenty of scary rides, a virtual underwater Sea Odyssey and a huge new waterpark called the **Costa Caribe** (separate admission available).

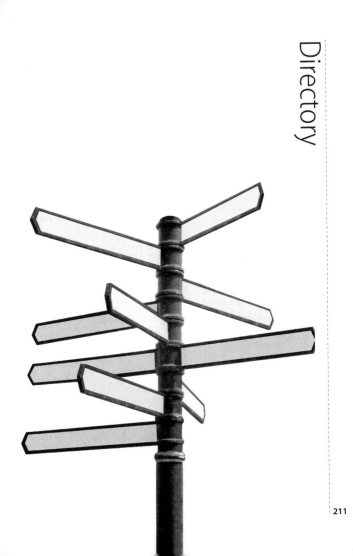

Airline offices

Air France T 93 379 74 63, www.airfrance.com **British Airways T** 902 111 333, www.british-airways.com **Delta T** 901 116 946, www.delta-air.com **easyJet T** 902 299 992, www.easyjet.com **Iberia T** 902 400 500, www.iberia.com **Ryanair T** 972 47 36 50, www.ryanair.com (For **T** numbers in the UK, see box, p22).

Banks and ATMs

You'll find banks and ATMs everywhere in Barcelona, particularly on Plaça de Catalunya and along the Ramblas. They are usually open Mon-Fri 0830-1400 and some of the larger branches are open Sat 0830-1300 (although not generally in Aug).

Bicycle hire

Biciclot, Passeig Marítim 33, **T** 93 221 97 78 (p28). **Un Cotxe Menys**, C Esparteria 3, **T** 93 268 21 05, (p28).

Car hire

Offices of the major car hire companies can be found at the airport and at Barcelona-Sants train station. The best deals are almost always available online and you should find out if the airline you fly with offers special car hire deals. Vanguard are a local car hire firm who also rent out motorbikes and scooters. **Avis**, **T** 902 135 531, www.avis.com **Europcar**, **T** 93 491 48 22, www.europcar.com **National**, **T** 902 100 101, www.national.com, www.atesa.es **Vanguard**, **T** 93 439 38 80, C Villadomat 297, www.vanguardrent.com

Consulates (see under Embassies)

Credit card lines

If your cards are lost or stolen, call: **American Express T** 902 475 637; **Diners Club T** 91 701 59 00; **Mastercard T** 900 99 1 231; **Visa T** 900 991 124.

Cultural institutions

British Council, C Amigó 83, **T** 93 241 97 00, www.britishcouncil.es English lessons, library and noticeboard full of accommodation ads. **Institut Français**, C Moià 8, **T** 93 209 59 11. French lessons, library and cultural events. **North American Institute**, Via Augusta 123, **T** 93 240 51 10. Useful reference library.

Dentists

Dentistry is not covered by the UK's E111 agreement and treatment can be very expensive. The following have English-speaking staff. **ADE Central Clinic**, C Bruc 146, **T** 93 457 31 62. Also has a 24-hour emergency service. **Clínica Dental Barcelona**, Passeig de Gràcia 97, **T** 93 487 83 29. Emergencies daily 0900-0000, 24-hour emergency service in Aug.

Disabled

Barcelona is making a concerted effort to improve its services for disabled travellers, but it's still not great. Most of the newer and bigger museums have wheelchair access, as do many of the more expensive hotels. The sightseeing **Bus Turístic** and the **Aerobús** service from the airport are equipped for wheelchairs, as are about half of public buses. Taxis are required by law to transport wheelchairs and guide dogs free of charge, although in practice cars are too small and drivers usually unhelpful. The Taxi Amic service, **T** 93 420 80 88, can provide mini-vans but there is high demand. Few metro and FGC train stations have lifts. The city's bureau for the disabled has detailed information on building access to museums, restaurants, monuments and other venues: **Institut Municipal de Persones amb Disminució**, C Llacuna 161, **T** 932918400. *M* Glories, bus 56, 60, 92.

Doctors

EU-residents are entitled to make use of Spanish state healthcare if they are in possession of an E111 form (available from major post offices, health centres and Social Security offices in the UK). But this can be a complicated process and private holiday insurance is recommended. The following private clinics offer a range of services. The US and UK consulates keep up-to-date lists of English-speaking doctors. **Clínica Corachán**, C Bugas 19, **T** 93 254 58 00, emergency **T** 93 254 58 07, www.corachan.com **Policlínica Barcelona**, C Guillem Tell 4, **T** 93 416 16 16.

Electricity
The current in Spain is 220V 50hz. North American appliances will require a special transformer and UK plugs will need a 2-pin adaptor, easily available from department stores.

Embassies and consulates
There's a full list of embassies and consulates in the phone book under *Consolats/Consulados*. **Australia**: Gran Via Carles III 98, **T** 93 330 94 96, www.spain.embassy.gov.au **M** *Maria Cristina*. **Canada**: Plaça de Catalunya 9-10, **T** 93 412 72 36, www.canada-es.org **M** *Plaça de Catalunya*. **Ireland**: Gran Via Carles III 94, **T** 93 451 90 21. **M** *Maria Cristina*. **New Zealand**: Travessera de Gràcia 64, **T** 93 209 03 99, www.nzemb.org *FGC Gràcia*. **UK**: Avda Diagonal 477, **T** 93 366 62 00, www.ukinspain.com **M** *Hospital Clínic*. **USA**: Passeig Reina Elisenda 23, **T** 93 280 22 27, www.embusa.es *FGC Reina Elisenda*.

Emergency numbers
There is a single number for all the emergency services (ambulance, fire and police): 112.

Hospitals
Centre d'Urgències Perecamps, Avda Drassanes 13-15, **T** 93 441 06 00. **M** *Drassanes or Paral.lel*. This clinic deals with less serious emergencies and injuries. **Hospital Clínic i Provincial**, C Villarroel 170, **T** 93 227 54 00. **M** *Hospital Clínic*. **Hospital de la**

Santa Creu i Sant Pau, Avda Sant Antoni Maria Claret 167,
T 93 291 91 01. ***M*** *Hospital de Sant Pau.*

Internet/email

BCNET Internet gallery Café, C Barra de Ferro 3, **T** 93 268 15 07.
Daily 1000-0100. ***M*** *Jaume I/Barceloneta. Bus 14, 17, 19, 36, 39, 40,
45, 51. Map 6, F11, p255* Relaxed little internet café in a cool brick-
vaulted space, down a side street close to the Picasso Museum. It's
very friendly and has its own decks playing soothing music, as well
as regularly changing art exhibitions on the walls. Rates start at
€1.50 for 30 minutes.

EasyEverything, Ronda Universitat 35. *Both branches 24
hours.* ***M*** *Plaça de Catalunya, all buses to Plaça de Catalunya.
Map 3, L4, p251* The monster of the internet cafés, there are 300
terminals in the Ronda Universitat branch and 450 at the branch
on Las Ramblas. Prices depend on demand, but €1 will get you
about 30 minutes at peak times (lunchtime and early evening) and
up to two hours early in the morning. Also Las Ramblas 41 ***M***
Liceu, bus 14, 38, 51, 59.

Idea, Plaça Comercial 2, **T** 93 268 87 87, www.ideaborn.com
Mon-Thu 0830-0000, Fri 0830-0300, Sat 1000-0300, Sun 1000-2300.
M *Jaume I. Bus 14, 17, 19, 39, 40, 45, 51, 59. Map 2, F8, p248*
Delightful bookshop, café and internet centre in La Ribera, with
comfy chairs, reading areas, books for sale or loan, magazines to
flick through with your coffee. Prices start at €1 for 30 minutes.

Language schools

American British College, Guillem Tell 27, **T** 93 415 57 57,
www.ambricol.es ***M*** *Fontana. Bus 22, 24, 28, 87. Map 1, C7, p247*
A large language school with a good reputation, offering Spanish
courses for all levels. It can also arrange accommodation.

Consorci per a la Normalització Lingüística, C Mallorca 272, **T** 93 272 31 00, www.cpnl.org **M** *Verdaguer. Bus 43, 44. Map 3, H7, p251* Catalan language courses for all levels from the official Generalitat organization.

Don Quijote, Gran Via 629, **T** 923 277 200, www.donquijote.org /english/barcelona.asp **M** *Tetuan, bus 7, 50, 54, 56, 62. Map 3, K7, p251* A large branch of the well regarded language school, with a wide variety of courses. It can arrange accommodation, including home stays.

Left luggage
There are left luggage lockers at the airport and at Barcelona-Sants train station. Prices are €4.50 for 24 hours in a medium-sized locker.

Libraries
Biblioteca Nacional de Cataluya, Antic Hospital de la Creu, C Hospital 56, **T** 93 317 07 78. **M** *Liceu. Bus 14, 38, 59.* Readers' cards are required for the Catalan national library, but 1-day research passes are available with ID.

Lost property
There is a lost property office in the Ajuntament (City Hall) on Plaça Sant Jaume. For information call **T** 93 401 31 61, or the city information line **T** 010. If you lose something on the metro or bus, call the TMB on **T** 93 318 70 74, or visit the main information office in Plaça Universitat metro station to fill out a claim form. Unclaimed goods are sent to the lost property office in the Ajuntament.

Media
As in most of Spain, regional papers are much more popular than the national press and Spanish taste runs more to tabloids than broadsheets. *La Vanguardia* is a traditionally conservative newspaper, which has got livelier over the years and has an

excellent local listings section on Fridays. The Catalan-language newspaper *Avui* has a pro-Generalitat bias and the tabloid-style *El Periódico* appears in Spanish and Catalan. The left-leaning national broadsheet *El País* has a section devoted to Catalunya and produces a good entertainment and arts supplement.

Spanish television can sometimes seem to consist almost entirely of game shows and ads. Most films are dubbed – look out for the *VO* sign in TV listings for original version films. There are hundreds of radio stations, mainly in Catalan and particularly on the FM band. The BBC World Service can be found on shortwave at 15485, 12095, 9410 and 6195 KHz, depending on the time of day.

Pharmacies (late night)
Farmàcia Alvarez, Passeig de Gràcia 26, **T** 93 302 11 24. *M Passeig de Gràcia*   **Farmàcia Clapés**, Las Ramblas 98, **T** 93 301 28 43. *M Liceu.*

Police
There is one number for all the emergency services (ambulance, fire and police): 112.

The most central *comisarías* (police stations) are at C Nou de la Rambla 76-80, **T** 93 290 48 49, and C Bosch 4-8, **T** 93 290 30 87. If you have to report a crime, go immediately to the **Turisme Atenció** station on the Ramblas (Las Ramblas 43, **T** 93 301 90 60 or **T** 93 344 13 00, daily 24 hours), a special police service for assisting tourists, with multilingual staff.

Post offices (Correos)
Postboxes, marked Correos y Telégrafos, are yellow. Most tobacconists (*estancos*, marked with a brown and yellow symbol) sell stamps. You can send or receive faxes from any post office.

Main post office: Plaça d'Anton López (at the port end of Via Laietana), **T** 93 412 41 66, www.correos.es *Mon-Sat 0830-2130, Sun 0900-1400.   Map 2, G6, p249*

Street life
Take a break from the heat of summer in the city.

Public holidays

On public holidays, many bars and restaurants close down, as do most shops. The transport system runs restricted services.

1 Jan – *Cap d'Any* (New Year's Day); **6 Jan** – *Día des Reis* (Three Kings); **Mar/Apr** – *Divendres Sant* (Good Friday); **Mar/Apr** – *Pasqua Florida* (Easter Monday); **1 May** – *Festa del Treball* (Labour Day); **May/Jun** – *Dillluns de Pasqua Granada* (Whit Monday); **24 June** – *Sant Joan* (St John's Day); **15 Aug** – *L'Assumpció* (Assumption); **11 Sep** – *Diada Nacional de Catalunya* (Catalan National Day); **24 Sep** – *La Mercè* (Our Lady of Mercy); **12 Oct** – *Día de la Hispanitat* (Columbus Day); **1 Nov** – *Tots Sants* (All Saints' Day); **6 Dec** – *Día de la Constitució* (Constitution Day); **8 Dec** – *La Imaculada* (Immaculate Conception); **25 Dec** – *Nadal* (Christmas Day); **26 Dec** – *Sant Esteve* (St Stephen's Day).

Religious services

International Church of Barcelona, C Comte de Urgell 133, **T** 93 451 75 79, www.icbspain.org   Services in English Sun 1100.
Israeli Community Synagogue (Orthodox), C Avenir 24, **T** 93 200 61 48.   **Jewish Community Atid of Catalonia** (Reformed), C Castaner 27, **T** 93 417 37 04, www.atid.info
Santa María Reina (Roman Catholic), Carretera de Esplugues 103, **T** 93 203 55 39.   Services in English.   **St George's Church** (Anglican/Evangelical), C Horacio 38, **T** 93 417 88 67.   Services in English Sun 1100.

Student organizations

Consell Nacional de la Joventut de Catalunya (CNJC), Plaça Cardona 1-2, **T** 93 368 30 80, www.cnjc.net   The National Youth Council of Catalunya organizes conferences, seminars, study groups and exchanges and ensures that issues affecting young people are raised with the Spanish and Catalan governments.

Taxi firms

See p27.

Telephone

Public payphones will accept coins and pre-paid telephone cards (available from tobacconists). Phone centres (*locutorios*) are the cheapest way of calling abroad: there's one in Plaça de Catalunya RENFE station and several around the Rambla de Raval.

Time

Local time is 1 hr ahead of GMT/UTC. Clocks go forward 1 hr on the last Sun in Mar and back one hour on the last Sun in Oct (as in the rest of the EU).

Toilets

Public toilets are rare, but it's usually fine to pop into a café or bar. There are toilets in the train stations and in department stores like El Corte Inglés on Plaça de Catalunya.

Transport enquiries

FGC (Catalan railways), **T** 93 205 15 15, www.fgc.catalunya.net **RENFE** (local, regional and national trains), **T** 902 240 202, www.renfe.es   **TMB** (metro and bus), **T** 93 443 08 59, www.tmb.net

Travel agents

There are expensive but reliable travel agents in most branches of the department store **El Corte Inglés**. **Atlanta Viajes**, C Calvet 55, **T** 93 200 70 88. An upmarket travel agency. **Rosa dels Vents**, Avda Madrid 95, **T** 93 409 20 71. Specializes in youth travel.

A sprint through history

Prehistory	The first known settlers in the Barcelona area are the Laetani.
8th century BC	Greek and Phoenician traders begin to settle along the coast and eventually establish an important permanent trading post at Empúries.
15 BC	The Roman colony of Barcino is established, but it is a backwater in comparison with Tarragona and Empúries which both have better ports.
5th century AD	The Visigoths declare Barcelona capital of one of their kingdoms.
AD 711	A Muslim Berber army from North Africa crosses the Straits of Gibraltar. They briefly occupy Barcelona before being expelled by the Franks from north of the Pyrenees.
c. 700-800	The Visigothic empire crumbles as the Berbers march steadily northwards. Christian armies gather in the north of Spain and the *Reconquista* (Reconquest) is launched.
c. 850-898	The reign of Guifré el Pilos (Wilfred the Hairy). He unites the earldoms of the area becoming known as Catalunya under the House of Barcelona, a dynasty which was to last 500 years.
12th-14th centuries	A Golden Age: the city prospers as the Catalan empire begins to expand. It eventually encompasses the Balearic islands, Sicily, Sardinia and Corsica. A network of very profitable trade routes are established around the Mediterranean and the newly rich merchants build palaces and invest in the arts.

1243	Anti-Jewish feeling intensifies. By decree of Jaume I, Jews are forced to remain within the ghetto (known as El Call) and identify themselves with capes and hats.
1391	Thousands of Jews are massacred in bloody pogroms across Spain; hundreds are killed in Barcelona alone.
1469	Marriage of Isabella I of Castile and Ferdinand II of Aragon; the joining of their kingdoms by marriage is traditionally considered to mark the birth of modern-day Spain. The balance of power shifts from Catalunya to Castile and Barcelona is sidelined as Madrid emerges as the new political centre of Spain.
1492	The Jews are expelled from Spain. Columbus 'discovers' the Americas.
17th and 18th centuries	Europe is ravaged by war and Barcelona keeps picking the losing side and is severely punished in consequence. Revolt against the repressive Castilian regime is followed by siege and vicious reprisal in 1640 and again in 1714; despite defeat, the Catalans named their national anthem after the heroic protestors of the 1640 rising, *Els Segadors* (the Reapers) and 11 September, the day the city fell to the Castilian armies in 1714, is now celebrated as Catalunya's National Day.
19th century	Barcelona begins to prosper once again thanks to the opening up of trade routes with the Americas. The cotton trade flourishes and the city grows

rapidly. This is also the age of the *Renaixença*, a profound cultural revival which celebrates the Catalan language and all areas of the arts, particularly architecture. The Modernistas, particularly Gaudí, create a magical cityscape in the new extension (Eixample in Catalan), built after the old city walls are torn down in 1854.

1888   Universal Exhibition of 1888. This is held to bring Barcelona to the world's attention and the city is transformed for the event (a forerunner of the Olympics nearly a century later).

1898   Defeat in the Spanish-American war means the loss of Spain's last remaining colonies and the trade routes. Barcelona's factory workers, crammed into slums and working in unspeakably miserable conditions, become increasingly politicized.

1909   Tensions erupt on the streets of Barcelona in 1909 in the Setmana Tragica – a week of carnage and destruction which leaves 116 people dead and 80 buildings torched.

1923   Primo de Rivera suspends the constitution and declares himself Dictator. He resigns, exhausted, seven years later.

1929   The International Exhibition is held in a series of specially built pavilions on Montjuïc.

1931-36 Spanish Civil War. Barcelona is in the front line, a period memorably described by George Orwell in *Homage to Catalonia*. The Nationalists, led by General Franco, eventually win and Franco's dictatorship begins.

1936-75	Under Franco's repressive regime, the city suffers through the 'years of hunger' during the 1940s and 50s, but the surge of tourism in the 1960s and 70s ushers in a new period of prosperity. There is a huge influx of migrants from other parts of Spain looking for work.
1975	Franco dies. The citizens of Barcelona celebrate wildly, popping every bottle of cava in the city. To everyone's surprise, Franco's protegé King Juan Carlos II begins a determined programme to reinstate democracy in Spain.
1980	The Catalan government (Generalitat) is reinstated under Jordi Pujol. Catalunya is granted a statute of autonomy.
1992	Barcelona hosts the Olympics. The city undertakes massive restoration and rebuilding projects which transform the cityscape. This event puts Barcelona on the international map once and for all.
2002	The city celebrates the Year of Gaudí, a festival of the work of its most famous son.
2003	Pasqual Maragall succeeds Jordi Pujol as President of the Generalitat.
2004	Universal Forum of Cultures is held in a specially built complex on a huge swathe of reclaimed land in Poble Nou.

Art and architecture

until 5th century AD
Prehistoric and Roman
Very little prehistoric art has survived in Catalunya. The Romans brought sophisticated construction techniques, enabling them to build aqueducts, city walls, arches, vaults and columns. The most striking examples of their skills (and those of the Greeks who preceded them) are to be found in the Greco-Roman town of Empúries on the Costa Brava. Many of the treasures found during excavation are now in the Museu de Arqueologia (p79) and some fine surviving examples still *in situ* can be seen in Tarragona (p104). You can visit the remnants of the Roman colony of Barcino as part of the Museu d'Història de la Ciutat (p111) and see part of a sepulchral way in Plaça Via de Madrid (p47).

6th-8th centuries
Visigothic
The Visigoths left little evidence of their occupation of Catalunya, but what there is (mainly jewellery kept in the Museu d'Arqueologia in Barcelona) shows a refined and skilled workmanship.

8th-14th centuries
Arabic
The arrival of the Berber-Arabs in the 8th century led to a fusion of local, Christian and Islamic styles, especially in architecture. But their power base was in the south of Spain and they only occupied Barcelona briefly at the end of the 10th century, leaving no enduring reminders of their presence.

11th-13th centuries
Romanesque
An extraordinary collection of Romanesque architecture can be found in the Vall de Boí (in the

Catalan Pyrenees), which was declared a World Heritage Site in 2000. The valley contains a clutch of churches built between the 11th and 13th centuries, with characteristic bell towers, barrel-vaulted naves, rounded arches, fantastic sculptures and above all, spellbinding murals. Particularly in the stylization of the hands and faces, they bear a remarkable resemblance to the Romanesque/Byzantine murals in Constantinople and Ravenna and were probably executed by peripatetic artists who travelled across Europe hiring out their skills. Many of these paintings have been transferred to the Museu Nacional d'Art de Catalunya (MNAC), which contains the largest Romanesque collection in the world. The 12th-century church and cloister of Sant Pau del Camp, built as part of a larger monastery and the 9th-century church of Sants Just i Pastor are both beautiful surviving examples of Romanesque architecture in the city centre.

13th-15th centuries

Gothic

As Barcelona became rich on the profits of expanding Mediterranean trade routes, it began a spate of massive ecclesiastic and civic construction. Catalan Gothic is simple: the number of columns are kept to a minimum and decorative elements are reserved for windows, arches and portals. Fine examples include the Gothic cathedral (p39), the church of Santa María del Mar (p51), the Casa de la Ciutat (Ajuntament, p43), the Palau de la Generalitat (p43), the magnificent shipyards (p63) and the string of palaces along Carrer Montcada (p48). Catalan painting from this period displays the influence of the Sienese School, French Gothic and, later on, Flemish naturalism. The best example of the new 'international' style from the 14th century is the work of Ferrer Bassa, who painted the Giotto-esque mural in the Monestir de Pedralbes. In the 15th century, the work of three major artists – Bernat Martorell, Luis Dalmau, Jaume Huguet, all admirably represented in MNAC, p75 – shows the increasing influence of Flemish naturalism.

16th-18th centuries

Renaissance and Baroque

The Golden Age of Castilian Spain was known as the *decadencia* for the people of Catalunya which became a cultural and artistic backwater. The Baroque churches of Betlem on the Ramblas and the Basilica de la Mercè (Plaça Mercè 1) are among the only survivors of this period.

19th century

Renaixença to Modernisme

By the 1850s, the great rediscovery and celebration of Catalunya's cultural identity known as the Renaixença (Renaissance) was beginning. Architecture, literature, painting, sculpture, furniture, crafts and the design of everyday objects were galvanized by the new spirit of cultural and political optimism. This movement across the arts came to be known as Modernisme and was partly influenced by the international art nouveau and Jugenstil movements. When the city walls were torn down in 1854, Ildefons Cerdà's airy grid-shaped extension (*Eixample* in Catalan) was constructed, giving the most influential architects of the day the chance to display their astonishing originality and virtuosity. Three names stand out: Antoni Gaudí i Cornet, Lluis Domènech i Montaner and Josep Puig i Cadafalch. You can choose your favourite in the Mansana de la Discòrdia (p64), where mansions by each of the celebrated trio display their very different styles. The list of Modernista monuments in Barcelona is breathtakingly long, but highlights include Gaudí's Casa Batlló, La Pedrera, Palau Güell, Park Güell and the Sagrada Família cathedral; Montaner's Palau de la Música Catalana and the Hospital de la Sant Creu i Sant Pau; and Puig i Cadafalch's Casa Amattler and the Casa de les Punxes. You can get more information from the information centre in the Casa Amatller (see p65).

20th century	**Rationalism to Surrealism**

By the second decade of the 20th century, artistic opinion was swinging away from the excesses and individualism of Modernisme towards the rationalism and order of Noucentisme. The architecture of this new style was largely pompous and uninspired, particularly the heavily neoclassical new pavilions and palaces built on Montjuïc for the International Exhibition of 1929. Painting and sculpture did better: three of the greatest artists of the 20th century are associated with the city. Picasso spent his early years in Barcelona (where he famously immortalized local prostitutes in the celebrated painting *Les Demoiselles d'Avignon*). The city's poor and dispossessed feature in the works of his Blue Period, amply represented in the Museu Picasso (p50). Salvador Dalí (1904-89) was the most surreal of the Surrealists and his museum in Figueres (p114) provides a theatrical backdrop for his fantastical creations. Joan Miró (1893-1983) was initially influenced by the Surrealists, but gradually created a highly individual symbolic language that was entirely his own. The excellent Fundació Miró (p77) contains a fine collection of his paintings, sculpture and ceramics. Antoni Tàpies, possibly the best known living Spanish artist, first made his name with his ripped, daubed, multi-layered 'Material Paintings' in the 1950s and 60s and the Fundació Tàpies (p71) contains the world's largest collection of his works.

Into the 21st century

Contemporary art

Franco's death in 1975 breathed life into Barcelona's lethargic artistic scene, which was marked by a lighthearted playfulness which reflected the new optimism. The best known artist of this generation was Javier Mariscal, whose designed everything from bars (most notoriously the over-the-top bar in the entrance to the Poble Espanyol) to the cuddly mascot 'Cobi' for the 1992 Olympics. The city's growing reputation for cutting edge design was cemented by the 1992 Olympics, which utterly transformed the cityscape. Architecturally, the new work was often disappointing, particularly the Vila Olímpica, although the stadium on Montjuïc is a fine exception. The city's most daring architectural project yet is the complex constructed on reclaimed land for the Universal Forum of Cultures 2004 in Diagonal Mar.

Books

Fiction

Catalá, Victor, *Solitude* (Readers International, 1992). A novel which shocked the public when it first appeared with its candid account of a woman in love.

Genet, Jean, *The Thief's Journal* (Faber, 1973). Famous autobiographical account of life during the heyday of the Barri Xinés in the early part of the 20th century.

Marsé, Juan, *The Fallen* (Quartet Books, 1994). Grim tale of the struggle for survival in Barcelona after the Civil War.

Mendoza, Eduardo, *City of Marvels* (Collins, 1999). A wonderful, richly detailed novel set around the time of the 1888 Universal Exhibition.

Montalbán, Manuel Vázquez, *Offside*, *Olympic Death* and *South Seas*. (Harvill Press). Brilliant series describing the adventures of the gourmet detective Pepe Carvalho, set in Barcelona.

Nuñez, Raul, *Lonely Hearts Club* (Serpent's Tail, 1988). Amusing, quirky novel full of bizarre characters about a strange love affair in Barcelona.

Orwell, George, *Homage to Catalonia* (Penguin, 2003; originally published 1938). The classic account of the Civil War; perceptive and personal.

Non-fiction

Andrews, Colman, *Catalan Cuisine: Europe's Last Great Culinary Secret* (Grub Street, 1998). Plenty of interesting details and delicious recipes.

Burns, Jimmy, *Barça: A People's Passion* (Trafalgar Square, 2000). Fascinating history of possibly the most popular football club in the world.

Carr, Raymond, *Modern Spain 1875-1980* and *The Spanish Tragedy; the Civil War in Perspective* (OUP, 1982). Excellent, well-written accounts of recent Spanish history.

Hooper, John, *The New Spaniards* (Penguin, 1995). An updated version of his excellent portrait of Spain post-Franco, *Spaniards: A Portrait of the New Spain*.

Hughes, Robert, *Barcelona* (Harvill Press, 2001). A highly personal, entertaining history of the city by the outspoken art critic.

Leiz, Juliet Pomés, and **Feriche**, Ricardo, *Barcelona Design Guide* (Gustavo Gili, 2003). Everything you ever wanted to know about design in Barcelona, including a list of designer bars and shops.

Tóibín, Colm, *Homage to Barcelona* (Simon & Schuster, 1991). Affectionate, wry account of life in the city in the 1970s and 80s by a well-known Irish journalist.

van Hensbergen, Gijs, *Catalonia's Son* (Harper Collins, 2001). One of the most illuminating biographies to appear on the city's most famous architect, Gaudí.

Language

Barcelona is a bilingual city; Catalan is the dominant language of street signs, opening hours, menus and other areas crucial to visitors, although standard Spanish (or Castilian, as it is more properly called) is spoken by pretty much everyone. English is not as widely spoken as some travellers presume and any efforts to get by in Catalan (or even Castilian) are much appreciated.

Catalan/Català
Catalan is a Romance language and not too difficult to read if you have any grasp of French, Italian or Spanish. Understanding spoken Catalan – a mixture of short, choppy sounds and syrupy whispering sounds – is not so easy, until you get the hang of the pronunciation. Accents indicate stress rather than changing the sound of the letter.

Catalan pronunciation (basic guidelines)
Vowels: In Catalan there are five vowels but eight sounds, depending on whether they are stressed or unstressed (open or closed).

a (stressed) a short 'ah' as in 'father'; (unstressed) like the final syllable of sug*ar*

e (stressed) as in 'sell'; (unstressed) a weak sound like the 'e' in 'open'

i like 'ee' in 'seen'; the sound is longer when stressed

o (stressed) short 'o' of 'pot'; (unstressed) like 'zoo'

u like the 'u' in hue

Consonants (other letters are pronounced similarly to English)

b pronounced 'p' at the end of a word, unless preceded by an 'm' when it's silent

c hard like 'cat' before 'a', 'o', 'u'; soft like 'sit' before 'i' and 'e'

ç pronounced 'ss'

233

d pronounced 't' at the end of a word, 'th' in the middle of the word

g hard before 'a', 'o', 'u'; before 'i' or 'e', pronounced as the 's' in 'measure'

h silent at the beginning of a word

j like the 's' in 'pleasure', or the 'j' in 'joke'

ll like the 'lli' in 'million'

l.l peculiar to Catalunya, this sound is slightly longer than 'll'

ny sounds like the Castellano 'ñ' as in Catalunya

r/rr rolled; silent at the end of a word

s/ss is soft like 'sit' at the beginning and end of words

v pronounced as a 'b' in Barcelona, sometimes as a 'v' elsewhere

x usually soft 'sh' as in 'shop'; when followed by an 'x' (tx) it sounds like the 'tch' in 'catch'

Greetings and basic expressions
(English *Castilian* Catalan)

Hello *hola (diga on phone)* hola

goodbye *adios* adéu

please *por favor* si us plau

thank you (very much) *(muchas) gracias* (moltes) gràcies

How are you? *Cómo está?/Que tal?* Com està?/Que tal?

Fine, thank you *Muy bien, gracias* Molt bé, gràcies

My name is… *Me llamo…* Em dic…

Do you speak English? *¿Habla inglès?* Parla anglés?

I don't speak Spanish/Catalan *No hablo Castellano/Catalàn* No parlo Castellà/Català

I don't understand *No entiendo* No l'entenc

Speak more slowly, please *Hable más despacio, por favor* Pot parlar més poc a poc, si us plau?

How do you say that in Catalan? *¿Me lo puede decir en Catalan?* Com es diu aix ò en Català?

Getting around

Where is… ? *¿Dónde está…?* On és…?

I'm lost *Me he perdido* M'he perdut

airport *aeropuerto* aeroport

arrivals *Llegadas* Arribades

departures *Salidas* Sortides

entrance *entrada* entrada

exit *salida* sortida

What time does it leave (arrive)? *¿Sale (llega) a qué hora?*
  A quina hora surt (arriba)?

From where does it leave? *¿De dónde sale?* D'on surt?

I'd like a (return) ticket to… *Quisiera un billete (de ida y vuelta) para…*
  Voldria un bittlet (d'anada i tornada) a…

here/there *aquí/allí* aquí/allà

near/far *cerca/lejos* a prop/lluny

left *izquierda* esquerra

right *derecha* dreta

Accommodation

Do you have a room *¿Tiene una habitación?* Té alguna habitació?

…for one person? *…para una persona?* …per a una persona?

…with twin beds *…con dos camas* …amb dos llits

…with double bed *…con una cama matrimonial* …amb llit per
  dues persones

…with shower/bath *…con ducha/baño* …amb dutxa/bany

…for one night *…para una noche* …per una nit

Is breakfast included? *Incluido el desayuno?* Inclòs l'esmorzar?

How much is it for one night? *¿Cuál es el precio por una noche?*
  Quin és el preu per una nit?

Sightseeing and shopping

I would like… *Quisiera…* Vull…

Where is…? *¿Dónde está…?* On és…?

How much is it? ¿*Cuánto cuesta/vale?* Quant és/val?
I like/I don't like *Me gusta/No me gusta* m'agrada/no m'agrada
open/closed *abierto/cerrado* obert/tancat
change/exchange *cambio* canvi
free (no charge) *gratuito* gratuit
free (unoccupied) *libre* lliure
museum *museo* museu
market *mercado* mercat
post office *correos* correus
toilet/toilets *servicios/aseos* lavabos/els serveis
men *señores/hombres/caballeros* homes
women *señoras/damas* dones

Eating out
breakfast *desayuno* esmorzar
lunch *almuerzo* dinar
dinner *cena* sopar
snack *merendar* berenar
a table for two *una mesa para dos persones*
  una taula per a dues persones
menu *carta (de platos)* carta (de plats)
fixed price menu *menú del día* menú del dia
bill/check *la cuenta* el compte
enjoy your meal ¡*Buen provecho!* Bon profit!

Food glossary
(**Catalan** *Castilian* **English**)

Pescados/Peix *Peix* Fish
anxoves *anchoas* anchovies
bacallà *bacalao* salt cod
gambes *gambas* prawns
llagosta *langosta* lobster
llenguado *lenguado* sole

llobarro *lubina* sea bass
mariscos *mariscos* shellfish
musclos *mejillones* mussels
pop *pulpo* octopus
sarsuela *zarzuela* fish stew
seitons *boquerones* fresh anchovies
tonyina *atún* tuna

Carn i aviram *Carnes y aves* Meat and fowl

ànec *pato* duck
be/xai/corder *cordero* lamb
botifarró *morcilla* blood sausage
bou *buey* beef
pernil serrà *jamón serrano* cured ham
llom *lomo* pork loin
mandonguilles *albóndigas* meatballs
pernil de York/pernil dolç *jamón de York* baked ham
porc *cerdo* pork
xoriço *chorizo* spiced sausage
Note: *potajes, cocidos, guisados (guisats), estofados (estofats), fabadas* and *cazuelas* are various kinds of stew and casseroles.

Verdures i llegums *Verduras y legumbres* Vegetables

albergínies *berenjena* aubergine (eggplant)
all *ajo* garlic
ceba *cebolla* onion
enciam *lechuga* lettuce
espinacs *espinacas* spinach
llenties *lentejas* lentils
mongetes (tendres) *judías (verdes)* beans (French)
olives *aceitunas* olives
pastanagas *zanahorias* carrots
patates (fregides/saltejades) *patatas (fritas/salteadas)*

potatoes (fried/sautéed)
pèsols *guisantes* peas
tomàquets *tomates* tomatoes
xampinyons *champiñones* button mushrooms

Dolços *Postres* Desserts
arròs amb llet *arroz con leche* rice pudding
crema cremada/catalana *crema catalana* crème caramel
formatges *queso* cheese
galetes *galletas* biscuits (cookies)
gelats *helados* ice creams
iogurt *yogurt* yogurt
pastís/tarta *pastel/torta* pie/tart
pastissos *pasteles* pastries
pijama *pajama* flan with ice cream
turró *turron* almond nougat

Miscellaneous
aigua mineral/amb gas/sense *agua mineral/con gas/sin gas*
  water (mineral/sparkling/still)
amanida *ensalada* salad
arròs *arroz* rice
cervesa *cerveza* beer
llet *leche* milk
oli/vinagre *aceite/vinagre* oil/vinegar
ous *huevos* eggs
pa/mantega *pan/mantequilla* bread/butter
sal/pebre *sal/pimienta* salt/pepper
suc *zumo* juice
sucre *azucar* sugar
truita *tortilla* omelette
vi (negre, blanc) *vino (tinto, blanco)* wine (red, white)

Index

Credits

Footprint credits

Text editor: Julius Honnor
Map editor: Sarah Sorensen

Publisher: Patrick Dawson
Series created by Rachel Fielding
In-house cartography: Claire Benison,
Kevin Feeney, Robert Lunn
Proofreading: Sarah Chatwin
Catalan proofreading: Jonathan Jefferies

Design: Mytton Williams
Maps: Footprint. The Barcelona metro
map is printed with the permission of the
Barcelona Transport Authority (TMB).

Photography credits

Front cover: Alamy
(chimneys on La Pedrera)
Inside: Alys Tomlinson
(p1 Park Güell, p5 Fundació Miró,
p31 Sagrada Família, p97 moped)
Generic images: John Matchett
Back cover: Alys Tomlinson (Casa Batlló)

Print

Manufactured in Italy by LegoPrint
Pulp from sustainable forests

Footprint feedback

We try as hard as we can to make
each Footprint guide as up to date
as possible but, of course, things
always change. If you want to let us
know about your experiences – good
bad or ugly – the don't delay, go to
www.footprintbooks.com and send
in your comments

Publishing information

Footprint Barcelona
2nd edition
Text and maps © Footprint Handbooks
Ltd May 2004

ISBN 1 904 777 04 X
CIP DATA: a catalogue record for this
book is available from the British Library

Published by Footprint
6 Riverside Court
Lower Bristol Road
Bath, BA2 3DZ, UK
T +44 (0)1225 469141
F +44 (0)1225 469461
discover@footprintbooks.com
www.footprintbooks.com

Distributed in the USA by
Publishers Group West

Complete title list

Latin America & Caribbean
Argentina
Barbados (P)
Bolivia
Brazil
Caribbean Islands
Central America & Mexico
Chile
Colombia
Costa Rica
Cuba
Cusco & the Inca Trail
Dominican Republic
Ecuador & Galápagos
Guatemala
Havana (P)
Mexico
Nicaragua
Peru
Rio de Janeiro
South American Handbook
Venezuela

North America
New York (P)
Vancouver (P)
Western Canada

Middle East
Israel
Jordan
Syria & Lebanon

Africa
Cape Town (P)
East Africa
Egypt
Libya
Marrakech (P)
Marrakech &
  the High Atlas
Morocco
Namibia
South Africa
Tunisia
Uganda

Asia
Bali
Bangkok & the Beaches
Cambodia
Goa
Hong Kong (P)
India
Indian Himalaya
Indonesia
Laos
Malaysia
Myanmar (Burma)
Nepal
Pakistan
Rajasthan & Gujarat
Singapore
South India
Sri Lanka
Sumatra
Thailand
Tibet
Vietnam

Australasia
Australia
New Zealand
Sydney (P)
West Coast Australia

Europe
Andalucía
Barcelona
Barcelona (P)
Berlin (P)
Bilbao (P)
Bologna (P)
Cardiff (P)
Copenhagen (P)
Croatia
Dublin (P)
Edinburgh (P)
England
Glasgow (P)
Ireland
London
London (P)
Madrid (P)
Naples (P)
Northern Spain
Paris (P)
Reykjavik (P)
Scotland
Scotland Highlands &
  Islands
Seville (P)
Spain
Tallinn (P)
Turin (P)
Turkey
Valencia (P)
Verona (P)

(P) denotes pocket
Handbook

For a different view…
choose a Footprint

Over 100 Footprint travel guides
Covering more than 150 of the world's most exciting
countries and cities in Latin America, the Caribbean, Africa, Indian
sub-continent, Australasia, North America, Southeast Asia, the
Middle East and Europe.

Discover so much more…
The finest writers. In-depth knowledge. Entertaining and accessible.
Critical restaurant and hotels reviews. Lively descriptions of all the
attractions. Get away from the crowds.

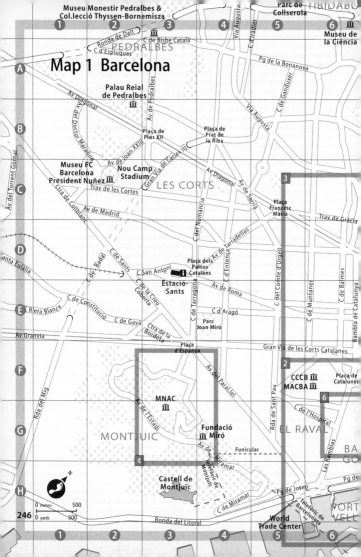

Map 1 Barcelona

Museu Monestir Pedralbes &
Col.lecció Thyssen-Bornemisza

Parc de Collserola

Museu de la Ciència

PEDRALBES

Ronda de Dalt

C de Bisbe Català

C d'Espluques

Pg de la Bonanova

Palau Reial de Pedralbes

Av Diagonal

Av de Pedralbes

Via Augusta

C de Ganduxer

Av del Doctor Marañón

Plaça de Pius XII

Plaça de Prat de la Riba

Via Augusta

Av de Joan XXIII

Av de Carles III

Museu FC Barcelona President Nuñez

Nou Camp Stadium

LES CORTS

Av de Serra

Av Diagonal

Plaça Francesc Macià

Gran Via de Carles III

Trav de les Cortes

Ctra de Collblanc

Av de Madrid

C de Numància

Trav de Gràcia

Av del Torrent Gornal

Santa Eulàlia

C de Sants

C de Badal

Plaça dels Països Catalans

Av de Tarradellas

d'Entença

C del Comte d'Urgell

C de Muntaner

C de Balmes

Estació Sants

Av de Roma

Rambla de Catalunya

Riera Blanca

C de Constitució

C de la Creu Coberta

C de Gavà

Ctra de la Bordeta

C de Tarragona

C d'Aragó

Parc Joan Miró

Av Granvia

Plaça d'Espanya

Gran Via de les Corts Catalanes

Plaça de Catalunya

Rda del Mig

Av del Paral·lel

Rda de Sant Pau

CCCB
MACBA

EL RAVAL

MNAC

Av de l'Estadi

MONTJUIC

Fundació Miró

Av de Miramar

Funicular

Rda de l'Hospital

Las Ramblas

BA
GO

Castell de Montjuïc

C de Miramar

Telefèric de Montjuïc

Pg de Josep

Telefèric de Barceloneta

Pg de

PORT VELL

N

0 metres 500
0 yards 500

World Trade Center

Ronda del Litoral

246

Map 2 Barcelona centre south

C de Vilarroel
Ronda de Sant Antoni
C de Casp
C Aus.. Marc
C de Ballen
Pg de Picasso
C de Girona
C de Girona
Taxis
C de Sant Pere mes Alt
Plaça de Sant Pere
SANT PERE
Plaça de Sant Agustí Vell
C del Comerç
C de la Fusina
C de Casp
C del Bruc
Ronda de Sant Pere
Taxis
C de Trafalgar
C de Sant Pere mes Baix
C Sant Pere mes Baix
C de la Princesa
Museu de Xocolata
C de Roger de...
Urquinaona
Plaça Urquinaona
Palau de la Música Catalana
C Sant Pere mes Alt
Museu d'Història de la Ciutat
Jaume I
C de Montcada
Santa Maria del Mar
Museu Picasso
C de Comtal
Via Laietana
El Corte Inglés
Santa Ana
Av Catedral
Museu Frederic Marès
CIUTAT VELLA
Jaume I
Plaça Catalunya
Fontanella
Santa Ana
Av del Portal de l'Àngel
Catedral de la Seu
Palau de la Generalitat
Plaça Sant Jaume
Ajuntament
BARRI GÒTIC
Catalunya
C de Palau
El Triangle Shopping Mall
Rambla de les Canaletes
C de Santa Ana
C Portaferrissa
C Boqueria
C de Ferran
Plaça Reial
Universitat
Ronda de la Universitat
C dels Tallers
C d'Elisabets
Les Rambles
C Pintor Fortuny
La Boqueria
C de la Unió
Gran Teatre del Liceu
Liceu
Palau Güell
C de l'Arc del Teatre
Centre de Cultura Contemporània de Barcelona (CCCB)
Museu d'Art Contemporani de Barcelona (MACBA)
Plaça dels Àngels
C del Carme
C de les Ramblas
C Nou de la Rambla
C del Tigre
C de la Lluna Alta
C del Peu de la Creu
C des Àngel
C de la Creu
C d'en Roig
C del Doctor Dou
C de l'Hospital
Antic Hospital de la Santa Creu
Junta de Comerç
Nou de Sant Francesc
C Guàrdia
C de l'Est
C de Sepúl...
C de Sant Vicens
C de la Riera Alta
C Riera Baixa
EL RAVAL
C de Sant Pau
Rambla de Raval
C Marques de Barbera
C Sant Pau del Camp
C de la Riereta
C de l'Aurora
C de St Rafael
C de les Tàpies
C de la Cera
C de les Carretes
C de la Reina Amàlia
C Nou de la Rambla
Paral·lel
Funicular Castle
Av del Paral·lel
C de St Antoni Abat

A B C D E F
1 2 3 4 5 6 7 8

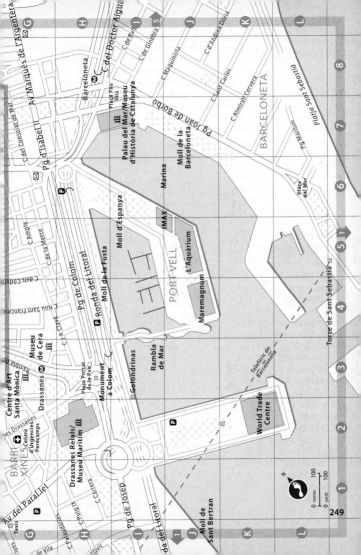

BARRI
XINES

Centre d'Art
Santa Mònica

Museu
de Cera

Centre
d'Urgèncias
Perecamps

les Drassanes

Drassanes Reials /
Museu Marítim

Drassanes

Monument
a Colom

Plaça Portal
de la Pau

Golondrinas

Rambla
de Mar

Av. del Paral·lel

Taxis

C. Carrera

C. de Josep

C. de Puig Xic

C. de Paludàlles

C. de Vila

C. del Litoral

Moll de
Sant Bertran

World Trade
Centre

Teleferic de
Barceloneta

Torre de Sant Sebastià

Pg. de Colom

Pg. de Ronda del Litoral

Moll de la Fusta

Moll d'Espanya

PORT VELL

Maremagnum

L'Aquàrium

IMAX

Marina

Moll de la
Barceloneta

Palau del Mar/Museu
d'Història de Catalunya

Plaça Pau
Vila

Pg. de Joan de Borbó

BARCELONETA

Plaça
del Mar

Platja Sant Sebastià

Pg. Marítim

C. d'Andreu Dòria

C. Almirall Cervera

C. Sant Carles

C. Maquinista

C. de Ginebra

C. de Bal

Barceloneta

Pg. d'Isabel II

del Consolat de Mar

C. del Doctor Aiguader

Av. Marquès de l'Argentera

C. de la Mercè

C. de la Merce

C. Ample

C. Nou Sant Francesc

C. dels Còdols

Rambla

N

0 metres 100
0 yards 100

249

G H I J K L

1 2 3 4 5 6 7 8

Av de Provença
Casa de
les Punxes
Verdaguer
Av. Diagonal
C de Girona

H
I
1
C de València
C de Bailén
C de Bruc
Taxis
C d'Aragó
C de Girona
Girona
L
C de Casp
C d'Ausias Marc

Casa
Thomas
C de Mallorca
M
C d'Aragó
Girona
K
C de la Diputació
C del Bruc
Taxis
P
de Girona
C de Casp
8

C de Roger de Llúria
EIXAMPLE

C de Provença
La Pedrera
C de Provença
C de la Concepció
Museu Egipci
de Barcelona
Fundació
Francisco Godia
Pau Claris
Gran Via de les Corts Catalanes
Roger de Llúria
C de
P
7
Urquinaona
6

Passeig de Gràcia
P de Domingo
Fundació
Antoni Tàpies
Casa Batlló
Casa Amatller
Casa Lleó i Morera
Passeig de
Gràcia
Mansana de
la Discordia
P

Rambla de Catalunya
P de Mercader
P

Catalunya
Plaça de
5

Provença
M
C d'Enric Granados
Taxis
P
Gran Via de les Corts Catalanes
Ronda de la Universitat
Universitat
C de Pelai
4
3

C d'Aribau
C de Mallorca
C de València
C del Consell de Cent
Universitat
Plaça de la
Universitat
P
2

C d'Aragó
C de Roma
P de Valet Serra
C de Casanova
C de la Diputació
Universitat
C de Sepúlveda
N
0 metres 100
0 yards 100
1

C de Provença
C de Villarroel
G
Av. de Roma
H
C d'Aragó
J
Av. de Villarroel
C de Villarroel
Urgell
K
1
Floridablanca

251

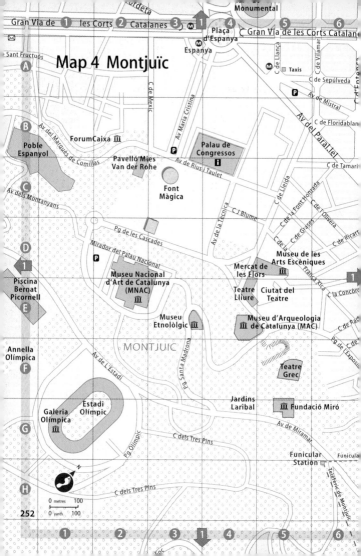

Map 4 Montjuïc

Monumental

Gran Via de les Corts Catalanes

Plaça d'Espanya

Gran Via de les Corts Catalanes

Espanya

Sant Fructuós

C de Mèxic

C de Llança

Taxis

C de Sepúlveda

C de Vilamarí

C de Floridablanca

Av de Mistral

Av del Paral·lel

Av del Marquès de Comillas

ForumCaixa

Poble Espanyol

Pavelló Mies Van der Rohe

Palau de Congressos

C de Tamarit

Av dels Montanyans

Av de Maria Cristina

Av de Rius i Taulet

Font Màgica

C de Lleida

C de la Font Honrada

C de Grases

C de Oliveras

C de Ricart

Pg de les Cascades

Av de la Tècnica

C J Blume

Mirador del Palau Nacional

Museu de les Arts Escèniques

Piscina Bernat Picornell

Museu Nacional d'Art de Catalunya (MNAC)

Mercat de les Flors

Franca Xica

C la Concòrdia

Teatre Lliure

Ciutat del Teatre

C de Rac

Museu Etnològic

Museu d'Arqueologia de Catalunya (MAC)

Pg de l'Exposi

MONTJUÏC

Annella Olímpica

Av de l'Estadi

Pg Santa Madrona

Teatre Grec

Estadi Olímpic

Jardins Laribal

Fundació Miró

Galería Olímpica

Av de Miramar

Pg Olímpic

C dels Tres Pins

Funicular Station

Funicular

C dels Tres Pins

Telefèric de Montjuïc

N

0 metres 100
0 yards 100

252

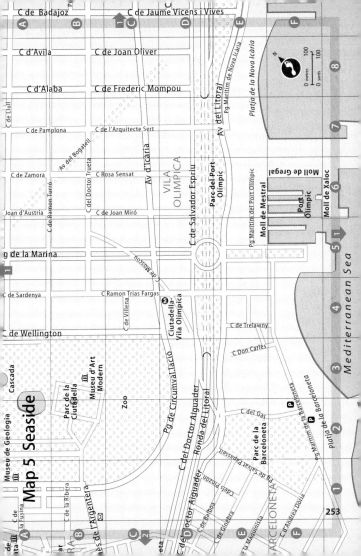

Map 5 Seaside

C de Badajoz
C de Jaume Vicens i Vives
C d'Avila
C de Joan Oliver
C d'Alaba
C de Frederic Mompou
C de Llull
C de Pamplona
C de l'Arquitecte Sert
Av del Bogatell
C de Zamora
C Rosa Sensat
C del Doctor Trueta
C de Ramon Turró
Joan d'Austria
C de Joan Miró
Av d'Icària
C de Sardenya
C Ramon Trías Fargas
g de la Marina
C de Mossèn
C de Villena
C de Wellington
C de Trelawny

VILA OLÍMPICA
C de Salvador Espriu
Parc del Port Olímpic
Av del Litoral
Pg Marítim de Nova Icària
Platja de la Nova Icària
Moll de Gregal
Port Olímpic
Moll de Mestral
Pg Marítim del Port Olímpic
Moll de Xaloc

Mediterranean Sea

Ciutadella-Vila Olímpica
C Don Carles

Cascada
Museu de Geologia
Parc de la Ciutadella
Museu d'Art Modern
Zoo
Pg de Circumval·lació
C del Doctor Aiguader
Ronda del Litoral
C del Gas
Parc de la Barceloneta
Pg de Salvat Papasseit
C dels Pinzón
C del Doctor Aiguader
C de Balboa
C de Ginebra
La Maquinista
Pg Marítim de la Barceloneta
Platja de la Barceloneta
C d'Andrea Dòria
BARCELONETA

de la Fusina
C de la Ribera
Pg de l'Argentera

0 meters 100
0 yards 100

253

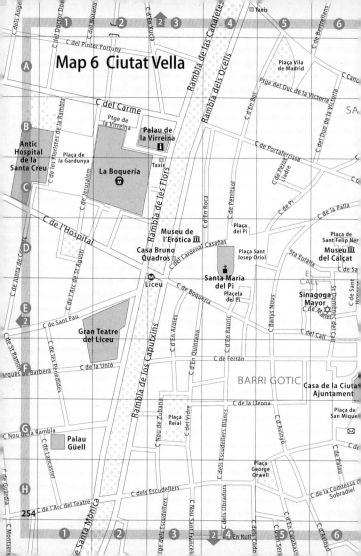

Map 6 Ciutat Vella

C dels Àngel

C del Doctor Dou

C de Notaria

C del Pintor Fortuny

☐ Taxis

C de Bertrellans

A

C del Carme

Plaça Vila de Madrid

Rambla de les Canalates

Rambla dels Ocells

Ptge del Duc de la Victoria

SA

B

Ptge de la Virreina

Palau de la Virreina ℹ

Plaça de la Gardunya

C de Portaferrissa

C del Duc de la Victoria

C d'En Bol

Antic Hospital de la Santa Creu

La Boqueria Ⓜ

C de les Floristes de la Rambla

Taxis

C de Pi

C de la Palla

C

C de Jerusalem

C de Petritxol

Plaça de Sant Felip Neri

D

C de l'Hospital

Museu de l'Eròtica 🏛

Plaça del Pi

C d'En Roca

Museu del Calçat 🏛

C de la Junta de Comerç

C de l'Arc de St Agustí

C d'En Xuclà

Rambla de les Flors

Casa Bruno Quadros

C del Cardenal Casañas

Plaça Sant Josep Oriol

Sta Eulalia

C de Sa

E CALL

E

Ⓜ **Liceu**

Santa María del Pi ✝

Plaçeta del Pi

Banys Nous

Sinagoga Mayor ✡

C d'En Malet

C de St Ramon

C de Sant Pau

C de Boqueria

C del Call

F

Gran Teatre del Liceu

C de les Penedides

C de la Unió

C d'En Aroles

C d'En Quintana

C d'En Rauric

C de Ferràn

BARRI GOTIC

G

C Nou de la Rambla

Palau Güell

Plaça Reial

C del Vidre

C de la Lleona

Casa de la Ciutat Ajuntament

Plaça de San Miquel

C d'Avinyó

C de les Penedides

C d'En Zubano

C dels Escudellers Blancs

C d'En

rques de Barbera

Rambla de los Caputxins

H

C de l'Arc del Teatre

Plaça George Orwell

C de la Comtessa de Sobradiel

C de Guàrdia

254

C de l'Arc del Teatre

C dels Escudellers

C Nou Sant Frances

En Rull

Codo

C d'En Crabass

C d'Avinyó

Montser

e Santa Mónica

C dels Escudellers

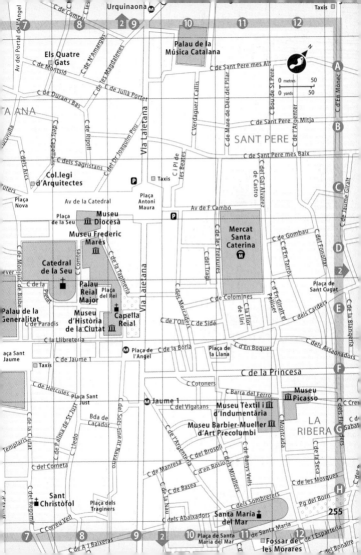

Map 7 Around Barcelona

256